THE DEMAND AND SUPPLY
OF SCIENTIFIC PERSONNEL

NATIONAL BUREAU OF ECONOMIC RESEARCH

NUMBER 62, GENERAL SERIES

The Demand and Supply
of Scientific Personnel

DAVID M. BLANK

GEORGE J. STIGLER

NATIONAL BUREAU OF ECONOMIC RESEARCH, INC.

NEW YORK

1957

NATIONAL BUREAU OF ECONOMIC RESEARCH
1957

Relation of the Directors
to the Work and Publications
of the National Bureau of Economic Research

1. The object of the National Bureau of Economic Research is to ascertain and to present to the public important economic facts and their interpretation in a scientific and impartial manner. The Board of Directors is charged with the responsibility of ensuring that the work of the National Bureau is carried on in strict conformity with this object.

2. To this end the Board of Directors shall appoint one or more Directors of Research.

3. The Director or Directors of Research shall submit to the members of the Board, or to its Executive Committee, for their formal adoption, all specific proposals concerning researches to be instituted.

4. No report shall be published until the Director or Directors of Research shall have submitted to the Board a summary drawing attention to the character of the data and their utilization in the report, the nature and treatment of the problems involved, the main conclusions and such other information as in their opinion would serve to determine the suitability of the report for publication in accordance with the principles of the National Bureau.

5. A copy of any manuscript proposed for publication shall also be submitted to each member of the Board. For each manuscript to be so submitted a special committee shall be appointed by the President, or at his designation by the Executive Director, consisting of three Directors selected as nearly as may be one from each general division of the Board. The names of the special manuscript committee shall be stated to each Director when the summary and report described in paragraph (4) are sent to him. It shall be the duty of each member of the committee to read the manuscript. If each member of the special committee signifies his approval within thirty days, the manuscript may be published. If each member of the special committee has not signified his approval within thirty days of the transmittal of the report and manuscript, the Director of Research shall then notify each member of the Board, requesting approval or disapproval of publication, and thirty additional days shall be granted for this purpose. The manuscript shall then not be published unless at least a majority of the entire Board and a two-thirds majority of those members of the Board who shall have voted on the proposal within the time fixed for the receipt of votes on the publication proposed shall have approved.

6. No manuscript may be published, though approved by each member of the special committee, until forty-five days have elapsed from the transmittal of the summary and report. The interval is allowed for the receipt of any memorandum of dissent or reservation, together with a brief statement of his reasons, that any member may wish to express; and such memorandum of dissent or reservation shall be published with the manuscript if he so desires. Publication does not, however, imply that each member of the Board has read the manuscript, or that either members of the Board in general, or of the special committee, have passed upon its validity in every detail.

7. A copy of this resolution shall, unless otherwise determined by the Board, be printed in each copy of every National Bureau book.

(Resolution adopted October 25, 1926 and revised February 6, 1933
and February 24, 1941)

PREFACE

THE present monograph is primarily a study of the methods by which one can explain movements in the supply and demand for scientific personnel. Rather than discuss the problem in abstract terms, however, we have deemed it more fruitful to apply the methods under examination to the recent situation in the technological professions in the United States, that is, up to 1955. We wish to forewarn the reader that these applications have been handicapped by limitations of data on salaries and fringe benefits, types of activities of engineers, sources of non-graduate engineers, and several other aspects of the problem. One of our chief products is a considerable list of further data collection and research which will be necessary to progress in the understanding of the rapidly growing professions under review.

The study was conducted under a grant by the National Science Foundation. The Foundation did not participate in the formulation or execution of the study, however, and the grant should not be interpreted as carrying any judgment on the methods or substantive findings.

We wish to express our gratitude to Dr. H. S. Conrad of the U.S. Office of Education, Harold Goldstein of the Bureau of Labor Statistics, and Thomas J. Mills of the National Science Foundation for invaluable assistance. We have profited from the suggestions of Solomon Fabricant, Daniel Holland, Albert Rees, and Leo Wolman. Jack Farkas assisted us throughout the investigation and Vera Eliasberg participated in the earlier stages.

DAVID M. BLANK
GEORGE J. STIGLER

CONTENTS

CONTENTS

Appendix

TABLES

TABLES

Age and Years of Schooling:

CHARTS

THE DEMAND AND SUPPLY

OF SCIENTIFIC PERSONNEL

CHAPTER I

A GENERAL VIEW OF THE
TECHNOLOGICAL PROFESSIONS

THE technological professions may be defined broadly as the professions whose subject matter is natural science and its applications. Much the largest of these is engineering, and much the second largest consists of the chemists. The rest—such as physicists, mathematicians, biologists, and geologists (but excluding the medical professions)—are even collectively slightly smaller in number than the chemists.

Our central purpose in this study is to investigate the methods by which one can explain—or predict, for explanation and prediction are equivalent—the supply and demand for technological and professional workers. But methods cannot be examined apart from the materials on which the methods are to be used—the world and the scholar are both so complex that it is easy to overlook real difficulties or to invent spurious ones. We shall examine techniques in the light of experience, and we begin with a broad survey of the technological professions. We trace first their growth, and in the process examine the boundaries of these groups; thereafter we summarize the growth of organized research—a development of considerable importance for our study.

1. *The Growth of the Technological Professions*

Two hundred years ago many of the technological professions did not exist, and none was large enough to be worthy of discussion as an element in an economy's labor force. The most famous and best established was mathematics, but one may conjecture that even the queen of the sciences was served full time by only a hundred or so men in the entire world. This is not to depreciate the progress of the sciences at the time, or to imply that a Newton can be replaced by 10,000 mediocre men. But the practitioners of the sciences did not constitute professions—they were small collections of gifted men.

Historians of engineering instruction differ as to when this largest of our technological professions began to be taught systematically and formally, rather than by the traditional methods of apprenticeship. Some set the beginnings in 1766, with the technical mining

3

school at Freiberg; some set the beginnings in 1775, with the French Ecole des Ponts et Chaussées; and some set the date in 1794, when the great Ecole Polytechnique was founded.[1] But it is not disputed that the nineteenth century saw the international development of instruction in applied sciences on a large scale, nor that the pure scientists first began in that century to be slightly more than infinitesimal in number. The heroic age of the industrial revolution was presided over by the untutored entrepreneur, not the engineer or scientist.

Growth took place at an enormous rate in all branches of higher education in the nineteenth century, and nowhere more rapidly than in the United States. West Point and Rensselaer Polytechnic Institute were the only engineering schools before 1847; in the decade of the 1870's alone some 68 colleges of agricultural and mechanical arts were established. It has been estimated that 866 engineers were graduated in the United States before 1870, 2,259 in the next decade, and on average the number doubled in each of the next three decades.[2] But by this time we may turn to comprehensive data in the population censuses.

The record of the chemists and the engineers in the population census begins in 1870 (Table 1). It is apparent from what we have just said of the number of engineering graduates that the vast majority were not graduates of engineering schools in the period before the first World War. Since there is no clean line that divides skilled workers from academically trained technicians, the early figures are especially subject to qualification—in particular the decline in the number of engineers from 1870 to 1880 may well represent only a lifting of the census standards for an engineer. In fact there appears to have been a steady tendency up to the present time to raise the qualifications for an engineer in the census (we discuss this below). If one could define an engineer or chemist precisely for the entire period, which one cannot do because the level of competence was steadily rising, there is little doubt that a growth even more rapid than that displayed in Table 1 would be found.

Even with the downward bias, however, the growth has been

[1] See W. E. Wickenden, *A Comparative Study of Engineering Education in the United States and in Europe*, Society for the Promotion of Engineering Education, 1929; Thomas T. Read, "The Beginnings of Engineering Education," *Journal of Engineering Education*, December 1939, pp. 348–353.

[2] C. R. Mann, *A Study of Engineering Education*, The Carnegie Foundation for the Advancement of Teaching, 1918.

immense, and retardation has been relatively slight in recent decades for the engineers. Over the eight decades the number of chemists and engineers grew 17 times as fast as the labor force. It is not unusual for a new occupation to grow at a very rapid rate, but it is unusual for the rate of growth to be sustained at so high a level when the numbers involved approach 1 per cent of the entire labor force.

TABLE 1

The Growth of Engineering and Chemical Professions, 1870–1950

			PERCENTAGE GROWTH IN DECADE	
	CHEMISTS	ENGINEERS	*Chemists*	*Engineers*
1870	774	7,094		
1880	1,969	7,061	154.4	—0.5
1890	4,503	28,239	128.7	299.9
1900	8,847	43,239	96.5	53.1
1910	16,273	88,755	83.9	105.3
1920	32,941	136,121	102.4	53.4
1930 a	47,538	227,590	44.3	67.2
1940	60,005	277,872	26.2	22.1
1940 b	56,825	291,465		
1950 b	75,747 c	534,424 c	33.3	83.4

a Average of figures comparable to earlier and later years with respect to occupational classification.

b Chemists excluding metallurgists; engineers including metallurgists but excluding surveyors (who were 16,444 in 1940 and 26,229 in 1950). These data are based on the 1950 census in which definitions of chemists and engineers are slightly different from those used in the 1940 census. For details, see Appendix B.

c Plus about 6,300 professors and instructors of chemistry and about 8,300 professors and instructors in engineering who were not classified in the published census materials as chemists or engineers (special experimental tabulation for the National Science Foundation).

Source: Alba M. Edwards, *Comparative Occupation Statistics for the United States, 1870 to 1940,* Bureau of the Census, 1943, pp. 49, 111; *Census of Population, 1940,* Series P-14, No. 13; *Census of Population, 1950,* Vol. II, Part 1, Tables 124, 125.

The beginning of instruction in the natural sciences naturally varies widely among disciplines. Mathematics, for example, has been a traditional subject of university instruction and research for centuries; chemistry began to be taught in universities about the same time as engineering; and some disciplines like statistics entered the curriculum only after the Civil War. We have already noted that none of these disciplines was of appreciable size in terms of personnel, and this is especially true in the United States, where in-

5

terest in pure science lagged considerably behind that of France and Germany in the nineteenth century.

It is not surprising, therefore, that information on the number of persons trained in pure science is very limited: the occupational census, for example, distinguishes this group for the first time in 1950. Some notion of the growth of their numbers, however, may be derived from the estimates of the number of baccalaureate degrees conferred, which have been prepared by the Commission on Human Resources (see Table 2). These estimates are based chiefly upon the departmental composition of the faculties of a small sample of schools, and probably have a large margin of error, but their general pattern is plausible.

TABLE 2

Bachelor's and First Professional Degrees in Natural Sciences since 1901
(in thousands)

	Chemistry	Physical Science	Earth Science	Biological Science	Total	Percentage Growth per Decade
1901–1905	5.5	5.5	1.7	7.2	19.9	
1906–1910	7.5	7.1	2.5	7.4	24.5	
1911–1915	9.7	8.6	3.4	7.9	29.6	48.7
1916–1920	10.4	8.6	3.6	7.5	30.1	
1921–1925	14.7	13.2	5.2	12.5	45.5	53.7
1926–1930	18.8	20.1	7.0	21.8	67.7	
1931–1935	19.5	20.7	7.1	24.1	71.4	56.9
1936–1940	25.3	23.4	8.5	28.8	86.1	
1941–1945	25.5	22.5	8.3	28.9	85.2	19.3
1946–1950	39.5	36.3	11.1	63.3	150.1	
1951–1955	33.2	36.9	14.0	69.0	153.1	79.7

Source: Dael Wolfle, *America's Resources of Specialized Talent*, Harper, 1954, Table B-2; *Earned Degrees Conferred by Higher Educational Institutions*, Office of Education, Circulars 418 and 461, December 1954 and 1955.

The increase in number has been about sevenfold in each of the natural sciences except biology, and about ninefold in this field, between 1901–1905 and 1946–1950. Large as these increases have been, however, they are less than the increase in the total number of bachelor's and first professional degrees; in the former period the natural sciences were 13.3 per cent of the total, and in the recent period 10.7 per cent of the total.

Nor do these holders of degrees in natural science constitute an occupation in the same sense that engineers do. Only one-fifth, it has been estimated, were active in natural sciences as a professional calling in 1953,[3] a quarter more were in health fields, and another quarter were still students (for advanced degrees) or outside of the labor force.

Moreover, the level of full professional preparation in these fields is commonly set at the level of the Ph.D., not the bachelor's degree. In some disciplines and lines of employment the goal is seldom reached: for example, only a small fraction of statisticians (classified as mathematicians) in industry or government have a doctorate; and only 20.8 per cent of the chemists surveyed by the Bureau of Labor Statistics in 1954 had doctor's degrees, although another 24.1 per cent had master's degrees.[4] On the other hand, most of the mathematicians and physicists of professorial rank—and universities have been the chief line of employment for these scientists—possess the Ph.D.

TABLE 3

Doctoral Degrees in Natural Sciences and Engineering since 1901

	Chemistry	Physical Science	Earth Science	Biological Sciences	Other	Engi-neering	Total
1901–1905							636
1906–1910							841
1911–1915	360	260	120	350		10	1,100
1916–1920	420	280	130	390		20	1,240
1921–1925	760	440	200	680		60	2,140
1926–1930	1,470	770	350	1,280		150	4,020
1931–1935	2,400	1,130	420	2,130		340	6,420
1936–1940	2,560	1,300	430	2,810		320	7,410
1941–1945	2,890	1,010	340	2,710		230	7,170
1946–1950	3,190	1,790	540	2,470	80	1,180	9,240
1951–1955	5,098	3,716	997	4,921	74	2,763	17,569

Source: Before 1911: D. E. Scates, B. C. Murdoch, and A. V. Yeomans, *The Production of Doctorates in the Sciences, 1936–1948,* American Council on Education, 1951, p. 25; 1911–1950: Dael Wolfle, *America's Resources of Specialized Talent,* Harper, 1954, p. 300; 1951–1955: *Earned Degrees Conferred by Higher Educational Institutions,* Office of Education, Circulars 418 and 461, December 1954 and 1955.

The growth of the number of doctorates in natural science has been even more rapid than that of first degrees (see Table 3). Again, however, the growth has not outstripped that of all doctorates: the

[3] Based upon a small sample of graduates in 1930, 1940, and 1951 (see Dael Wolfle, *America's Resources of Specialized Talent,* Harper, 1954, p. 302).

[4] *Factors Affecting Earnings in Chemistry and Chemical Engineering,* Bureau of Labor Statistics, Bull. 881, 1946, p. 5.

natural scientists formed 44.2 per cent of the total in 1901–1905 and 38.3 per cent in 1946–1950.[5]

The 1950 census reports that aside from the chemists—whose numbers have already been given in Table 1—the natural scientists numbered about 72,000, distributed as follows:

Physical sciences		37,812
Mathematics	7,259	
Physics	11,120	
Statistics	19,433	
Earth sciences		11,810
Biological sciences		18,547
Other		3,945

Since the total number of living doctorates in these fields was only about 25,000, and not all of these were professionally active, it is apparent that at most one scientist in three had the degree and that ·the average academic preparation was probably closer to a master's degree.

2. What is an Engineer?

A scientist or an engineer is a person with extensive knowledge of some area of technological science—knowledge which is at least somewhat formal and abstract, if we are to separate him from workers with purely empirical knowledge. How extensive this knowledge need be is obviously a matter of arbitrary decision, and if the decision is not to be absurd as well as arbitrary, it will vary with time and perhaps in space. The requirement of formal training, however, is essential: so long as one can acquire the necessary training wholly by experience, it is apparent that no sharp line can be drawn between professional and nonprofessional workers.

The problem of definition is acute especially in the case of engineers, for this profession is only a little over half way through the long transition from training through experience to training through formal education. The varying definitions of an engineer have been a source of major differences of opinion concerning the number of professional workers and their prospective number. Thus, the Bureau of Labor Statistics and the professional engineering societies estimate that the number of engineers in 1950 was about

[5] If the doctorates in engineering are added, the percentage is remarkably stable (at about 45 per cent) throughout the entire period.

400,000; [6] and the census reports 540,000. Before we turn to the differences in definition of an engineer, it will be instructive to examine the census data more closely.

The census data on engineers and chemists for 1940 and 1950 provide important clues on the sources and characteristics of new engineers. If we compare the number of engineers and chemists of (say) age 30 in 1940 with the number of age 40 in 1950, we would expect the latter number to be smaller if all new entrants came from graduating classes of engineering schools. Some engineers would have died during the decade (and in older age groups some

TABLE 4

Comparison of Numbers of Male Engineers and Chemists of Given Age in 1940 and 1950

Age Group in 1940	Number in 1940	Deaths and Retirements 1940 to 1950 [a]	Predicted Number 1950	Actual Number in 1950	Predicted Number as Per Cent of Actual Number
25–34	86,685	4,265	82,420	160,487	51.4
35–44	94,009	10,830	83,179	108,862	76.4
45–54	63,648	17,497	46,131	58,550	78.8
55–64	29,010	20,176	8,834	15,892 [b]	55.6
Total	273,352	52,768	220,584	343,791	64.1

[a] Estimated from *Tables of Working Life*, Bureau of Labor Statistics, Bull. 1001, 1950.

[b] 65 and over.

Source: *Census of Population, 1940*, Vol. III, *The Labor Force*, Part 1, Table 65, p. 98. *Census of Population, 1950*, Vol. II, Part 1, Table 127, p. 273.

would have retired), and some would have left engineering work. Of course some who had left engineering work before 1940 might return to this occupation during the decade—and no doubt a number did because of the increased employment opportunities. But as a rule this "re-entry" would be relatively small for an academically trained professional worker, simply because more could usually be earned even under depressed conditions in the field for which he was trained than in any other field. Such expectations are fully confirmed for a field like medicine, but not for engineers and chemists (Table 4).

We find, instead, at every age group for which a comparison can

[6] See *Effect of Defense Program on Employment Outlook in Engineering*, Bureau of Labor Statistics, Supplement to Bull. 968, 1951, p. 2; also Wolfle, *op. cit.*, pp. 95–96. We discuss the reconciliation of the 1950 census figures with those given for 1940 in Appendix E.

be made, that the expected number of 1940 survivors was only one-half to four-fifths of the actual number in 1950.[7] And this calculation makes no allowance for those who were engineers in 1940 but transferred to other occupations during the decade. Since relatively few of the men over 25 in 1940 would have acquired engineering degrees during the decade, we may infer that most of the new recruits were trained on the job rather than academically. These recruits were relatively most numerous in the younger age groups, but it is impressive that even in the age groups 55 to 65 (in 1950), at least one-fifth were new recruits. We may demonstrate our conclusion in another way. In the decade 1940–1950, the net increase in engineers was about 243,000 and the gross increase, about 333,000. The number of new graduates of engineering schools, however, was only 192,100, or 57.7 per cent of the gross increase. (We discuss the recruitment of new engineers in some detail in Chapter IV.)

In 1940, about 61 per cent of the engineers and chemists had attended college for 4 or more years,[8] and the percentage was almost the same in each of the major branches of specialization (see Table 5). We may estimate the total number of living graduates of engineering schools who were in the labor force in 1940 to be 226,000, and we find that they amounted to about 78 per cent of the number of engineers.[9] It appears, therefore, that a considerable number of engineering graduates leave the profession. Thus, if we may compare the 156,000 engineers with 4 or more years of college in 1940 (Table 5) with the 226,000 living graduates, we may say that three-tenths of the college-trained engineers had left the profession.[10]

The census definition of an engineer is less exacting than that of the professional engineering societies, but there is no evidence that

[7] Since the last 1950 group is 65 and over, rather than 65 to 75, it is a trifle too large for strict comparability, and the percentage of expected to actual numbers (55.6) is a trifle too small.

[8] Since the census does not distinguish types of college training, we cannot tell how many of these college-trained engineers studied in other fields. But we do know that about 15 per cent of those who were graduated by colleges in 1951 and entered engineering employment had specialized in nonengineering fields while in college (for details, see Chapter IV).

[9] We use Wolfle's series on graduates (*op. cit.*, pp. 294–295), and deduct deaths and retirements on the basis of *Tables of Working Life,* Bureau of Labor Statistics, Bull. 1001, 1950.

[10] Wolfle estimates the total number of persons living in 1953 with degrees in engineering to be 529,000; he estimates the number of college graduates employed in engineering in 1953 at 361,000 (Wolfle, *op. cit.*, p. 96).

it has become easier to qualify as an engineer in the successive censuses.[11] On the contrary, some categories which were once included have disappeared from the current enumerations, e.g., boat and steam shovel engineers (1910), foremen in radio stations (1920), mine experts (1920), factory experts, automobile factory (1930). One cannot doubt that the average level of skill of the engineers and chemists counted as such by the census has risen steadily.

TABLE 5

Educational Background of Employed Male Engineers and Chemists and Experienced Male Engineers and Chemists Seeking Work, 1940

	Total Number [a]	Number with 4 or More Years of College	Per Cent with 4 or More Years of College
Chemists, Metallurgists	55,420	32,620	58.9
Civil Engineers	85,920	51,000	59.4
Electrical Engineers	55,000	33,540	61.0
Mechanical Engineers	82,580	49,120	59.5
Other Technical Engineers	30,920	22,100	71.5
Total	309,840	188,380	60.8

[a] Excluding 1,260 who did not report their education.
Source: *Census of Population, 1940, The Labor Force, Occupational Characteristics*, pp. 59, 61.

The professional engineering societies vary somewhat in their requirements for membership, but currently they have either accepted in substance or are approaching the standards proposed by the Committee on Professional Recognition: [12]

1. Member

   Graduate of an approved engineering curriculum plus at least four years of "increasingly important engineering ex-

[11] There is a single exception to this generalization. In 1940 the Bureau of the Census did not count as an engineer anyone under 35 years of age who lacked four years of college training. In 1950, education information was collected only on a 20 per cent sample basis, and the census did not apply this criterion. Accordingly, the 1950 census volumes present data on the number of engineers in 1940 on a definitional basis comparable to 1950, i.e. including those engineers under 35 with less than four years of college. About 20,500 engineers were added to the original 1940 census total by this adjustment (letter from David L. Kaplan, Chief, Occupation and Industry Statistics Section, Population and Housing Division, Bureau of the Census, December 30, 1954). In general we use the 1950 census estimate of the number of engineers in 1940 throughout this study. For further details, see Appendixes B and E.
[12] *Seventeenth Annual Report,* Engineers Council for Professional Development, Sept. 30, 1949

11

perience," *or* at least ten years of increasingly important
engineering experience.
2. Associate Member

Graduate of an approved engineering curriculum, *or* at least
six years of experience of suitable character.

These requirements are sufficiently higher than those required for
census enumeration to permit a large difference in numbers.

One can use either the census definition or the stricter professional society definition so long as he is consistent, and for some
purposes no doubt the latter definition is superior. For the study of
supply and demand conditions, however, there are several reasons
for preferring the census definition. Most data, including the reports from employers, will be based upon a definition close to the
census practice, and it is therefore possible to bring much more
empirical material to bear on the problem. Moreover, the definitions
of the professional societies imply that a considerable number of
nonengineers do not differ appreciably from engineers: for example, the able graduate of a leading engineering school with three
years of experience is no doubt a better engineer than the mediocre
graduate of a second class school who has five years' experience,
yet the former would be ineligible for full membership in a society.
The proportion of society members to all engineers in an industry
would presumably be subject to varying influences which would
further complicate our analysis.

The difficulties in defining a scientist are less in one direction:
only the merest handful of people enter this group except through
formal instruction at a college level. There still remains the am-
biguity as to the level of academic preparation. We noticed above
that only one-third of the scientists reported in the 1950 census
could have possessed a doctor's degree. We shall argue for setting
a high level of education—the doctorate—because at lower levels
there is so much interdisciplinary mobility as to make it unneces-
sary to examine supply or demand for any one field.

3. *The Growth of Organized Research*

One modern development has left its imprint on many aspects
of the technological professions: it is the growth of organized research. The explanation of employment in research of the technological professions is of special interest and difficulty, we shall
find, because of two characteristics. The first is that research is not

closely geared to current activity, whether governmental or business or academic: the army or the chemical company or the university can exist for a time even if research is abolished. The second characteristic is that the federal government plays a dominant role in the determination of the level and directions of this research.

Before we set forth the general facts on the growth of separately organized research, we must enter a warning against reading the statistics too literally. Research is now fashionable in a way it never was before, and it is now easier to get funds for research, in competition with other activities, than it ever was in the past. There is therefore a strong temptation to bring under this heading activities which were once, and not always improperly, classified as some form of nonresearch activity. The growth of organized research has been so vast that it cannot possibly be treated as a statistical illusion, but one should be at least moderately skeptical of some of the details of this growth.

Presumably after a long but gradual rise, expenditures on research in the United States reached an estimated $166 million in 1930, of which federal funds accounted for about $25 million, universities and other nonprofit institutions accounted for about the same amount, and industry accounted for about $116 million.[13] By 1941, total expenditures on research had risen to $900 million of which the government contributed about four-tenths, industry almost six-tenths and nonprofit institutions only several per cent (Tables 6 and 7). By this time the current practice of governmental financing of a considerable portion of research carried on by nongovernmental institutions had appeared on a large scale. Thus the government actually spent only $200 million on its own research activities, while granting $170 million for research carried on elsewhere; industry spent $660 million on research, of which $510 million came from its own funds; and nonprofit institutions spent $40 million on research, of which only $20 million came from their own funds.

Total expenditures on research rose rapidly through World War II, stabilized for several years thereafter, and rose again after the outbreak of the Korean War, reaching a level of $3,750 million in 1952. The government's share in support rose during World

[13] *Science and Public Policy*, President's Scientific Research Board, 1947, Vol. I, Table I; *The Organization of Applied Research in Europe, the United States, and Canada*, Organization for European Economic Cooperation, 1954, Vol. III, pp. 15–17

TABLE 6

Source of Research and Development Funds, 1941–1952
(in millions of dollars)

	TOTAL	FUNDS RAISED BY			PERCENTAGE DISTRIBUTION		
		Govern-ment	Indus-try	Nonprofit Institu-tions	Govern-ment	Indus-try	Nonprofit Institu-tions
1941	$900	$370	$510	$20	41	57	2
1942	1,070	490	560	20	46	52	2
1943	1,210	780	410	20	64	34	2
1944	1,380	940	420	20	68	30	2
1945	1,520	1,070	430	20	70	28	2
1946	1,780	910	840	30	51	47	2
1947	2,260	1,160	1,050	50	51	47	2
1948	2,610	1,390	1,150	70	53	44	3
1949	2,610	1,550	990	70	59	38	3
1950	2,870	1,610	1,180	80	56	41	3
1951	3,360	1,980	1,300	80	59	39	2
1952	3,750	2,240	1,430	80	60	38	2

Source: *The Growth of Scientific Research and Development,* Dept. of Defense, 1953, p. 10.

TABLE 7

Performance of Research and Development, Measured by
Expenditures, 1941–1952
(in millions of dollars)

	TOTAL	PERFORMANCE BY			PERCENTAGE DISTRIBUTION		
		Govern-ment	Indus-try	Nonprofit Institu-tions	Govern-ment	Indus-try	Nonprofit Institu-tions
1941	$900	$200	$600	$40	22	73	5
1942	1,070	240	780	50	22	73	5
1943	1,210	300	850	60	25	70	5
1944	1,380	390	910	80	28	66	6
1945	1,520	430	990	100	28	65	7
1946	1,780	470	1,190	120	26	67	7
1947	2,260	520	1,570	170	23	69	8
1948	2,610	570	1,820	220	22	70	8
1949	2,610	550	1,790	270	21	69	10
1950	2,870	570	1,980	320	20	69	11
1951	3,360	700	2,300	360	21	68	11
1952	3,750	800	2,530	420	21	68	11

Source: *The Growth of Scientific Research and Development,* Dept. of Defense, 1953, p. 11.

War II to 70 per cent in 1945, dropped after the war to 51 per cent and then rose again in recent years; the government's share of research performance has continued to decline slightly since the early postwar years. Industry's share of both expenditures and performance moved inversely to the government's share over this period.[14] Nonprofit institutions have accounted for a rising share of actual expenditures, reaching 11 per cent in the early 1950's, but have contributed only about 2 or 3 per cent of total funds over the entire period.

TABLE 8

Number and Percentage Distribution of Research Engineers
and Scientists, 1941–1952

| | | NUMBER (in thousands) | | | PERCENTAGE DISTRIBUTION | | |
	TOTAL	Govern- ment	Indus- try	Nonprofit Institu- tions	Govern- ment	Indus- try	Nonprofit Institu- tions
1941	87	17	62	8	20	71	9
1942	90	18	64	8	20	71	9
1943	97	21	67	9	22	69	9
1944	111	27	72	12	24	65	11
1945	119	29	76	14	24	64	12
1946	122	28	80	14	23	66	12
1947	125	25	84	16	20	67	13
1948	133	25	90	18	19	68	14
1949	144	26	94	24	18	65	17
1950	151	25	100	26	17	66	17
1951	158	28	104	26	18	66	17
1952	180	33	118	29	18	66	16

Source: *The Growth of Scientific Research and Development*, Dept. of Defense, 1953, p. 12.

The estimated number of research scientists and engineers roughly doubled between 1941 and the early 1950's, rising from almost 90,000 to 180,000 in 1952 (Table 8). (The much smaller rise in personnel than in dollar expenditures reminds us that a considerable part of

[14] The aircraft and electrical machinery industries receive the bulk of federal grants for research and development. According to BLS estimates, the aircraft industry engaged in $350 million of government-financed research in 1951, and the electrical machinery industry $250 million. About $50 million of research in the professional and scientific instruments industry was similarly paid for by the federal government. The remaining $200 million of federally financed industrial research was carried on by the remaining manufacturing and nonmanufacturing industries. *Scientific Research and Development in American Industry*, Bureau of Labor Statistics, Bull. 1148, 1953, p. 22.

the expenditure increase was due to rising prices.) There were an estimated 151,000 research scientists and engineers in 1950; professional research personnel thus represented between a fifth and a fourth of all engineers and natural scientists in that year. About two-thirds of the research scientists and engineers worked for industry in the early 1950's, and about one-sixth each for the government and nonprofit institutions.

TABLE 9

Federal Government Expenditures for Research and Development
(in millions of dollars)

Fiscal Year	Expenditures for Conduct of Research and Development	Expenditures for Increase in Research and Development Plant	Total
1948	803	62	865
1949	981	116	1,097
1950	994	150	1,143
1951	1,126	216	1,342
1952	1,571	268	1,839
1953	1,846	262	2,108
1954	1,845	250	2,095
1955 [a]	1,829	242	2,071
1956 [a]	1,966	251	2,218

[a] Estimated.
Source: Raymond H. Ewell, "Estimated Volume of Research and Development Expenditures by Federal Government in 1955," *Papers of the Fourth Conference on Scientific Manpower*, National Science Foundation, December 1954, p. 24.

Other data on federal expenditures for the support of research carried on both within and without the government are available for more recent years and are presented in Table 9. These data overlap in time those discussed above and differ somewhat in coverage. The data in Tables 6 and 7 were prepared by the Department of Defense and include estimates of research and development costs included in procurement contracts,[15] as well as compensation for uniformed personnel assigned to research installations. Currently, government estimates of federal expenditures on research and development are prepared by the National Science Foundation and the latter's definitions exclude procurement costs and uniformed personnel compensation, but include capital ex-

[15] Such research and development costs have been estimated at about a half billion dollars in recent years.

16

penditures for research. In terms of the National Science Foundation definitions, federal expenditures rose about $700 million between fiscal years 1950 and 1952, of which almost $600 million was for current research operations, and almost $300 million more in fiscal 1953, all of which was for current operations. Federal expenditures stabilized at slightly more than $2.0 billion in 1954 and 1955, and increased again in 1956 to about $2.2 billion.[16]

The bulk of federal research funds (72 per cent in fiscal 1955) are spent by the Department of Defense. The agency with the next largest research budget is the Atomic Energy Commission, which accounted for 13 per cent of the total in 1955. The remaining 15 per cent of federal research funds are scattered widely over other government agencies.[17]

Of an estimated 60,000 engineers, physical scientists and mathematicians employed by the federal government in 1954, about 28,-000 were engaged in research activities.[18] Engineers were almost one-half of the research personnel and about two-thirds of all federally employed technological professional workers. The second largest group in government employment were the 5,400 physicists, of whom almost nine-tenths were in research. The third largest group consisted of 4,900 chemists (of whom three-quarters were in research).

Employment in organized industrial research, i.e., that portion of industrial research carried on in separately organized private research laboratories, grew from less than 10,000 in 1920 to 70,000 in 1940 and to 165,000 in 1950, according to surveys by the National Research Council.[19] Total professional personnel in such laboratories

[16] Of the total federal obligations for research in 1955, the physical sciences accounted for about 86 per cent, the biological sciences, about 4 per cent, the medical sciences, 5 per cent, the agricultural sciences about 2 per cent and the social sciences about 2 per cent. *Federal Funds for Science,* National Science Foundation, *III. Federal Research and Development Budget, Fiscal Years 1953, 1954, and 1955,* not dated, p. 7.

[17] *Ibid.,* p. 21.

[18] Raymond H. Ewell, "Estimated Volume of Research and Development Expenditures by Federal Government in 1955," in *Papers of the Fourth Conference on Scientific Manpower,* National Science Foundation, December 1954, p. 27. These totals do not include all research scientists who were federally employed; for example, they exclude those in the life sciences, as well as those physical scientists and engineers who were holding jobs whose civil service titles did not clearly indicate that they should be included.

[19] *Research—A National Resource,* National Resources Planning Board, 1940, Vol. II, pp. 174–176; *Research in Development Personnel in Industrial Laboratories, 1950,* Office of Education, 1952, p. 9. A portion of this apparent growth represents fuller coverage.

rose from 37,000 in 1940 to 71,000 in 1950. The major occupations represented in 1950 were engineers (including metallurgists) who accounted for 54.2 per cent of all professional laboratory personnel, chemists, 32.8 per cent, and physicists, 4.2 per cent. The only important changes since 1940 in the relative importance of the several scientific disciplines were the growth of engineers (who represented 46.6 per cent of the laboratory professionals in 1940) and the decline of chemists (who accounted for 42.9 per cent of all professions in 1940).

TABLE 10

Industrial Research Activities, 1952–1955

	PERFORMANCE OF RESEARCH (in millions)	SUPPORT OF INDUSTRIAL RESEARCH		Number of Industrial Research Scientists and Engineers
		Government (in millions)	Industry (in millions)	
1952 a	$2,030	$600	$1,430	95,000
1953	2,450	850	1,600	114,000
1954	2,580	850	1,730	120,000
1955	2,700	850	1,850	126,000

a On the earlier Department of Defense definitions, performance of research by industry and government support of such research were about $500 million higher, and the number of research scientists and engineers was 33,000 higher.

Source: A. L. Lyman, "Estimated Volume of Research and Development Expenditures by Industry in 1955," *Papers of the Fourth Conference on Scientific Manpower*, National Science Foundation, December 1954, pp. 32–34.

Estimates of the total number of research scientists and engineers in industrial employment since 1952 are presented in Table 10.[20] The volume of industrial research expenditures continued to rise in this period and the number of research scientists and engineers increased by 6,000 per year between 1953 and 1955.[21]

[20] A. L. Lyman, "Estimated Volume of Research and Development Expenditures by Industry in 1955," in *ibid.* The expenditure estimates were derived by means of a survey of a sample of large companies in those industries which account for the bulk of private research expenditures. Percentage changes since 1952 for each industry were weighted by the proportion of industrial research expenditures accounted for by each industry in 1952. The personnel figures were derived by assuming that the same volume of research expenditures per scientist was incurred in 1953–1955 as in 1952 under the Department of Defense definitions.

[21] Since these data are based upon National Science Foundation definitions, they exclude research carried on and personnel employed under procurement contracts.

CHAPTER II

DEMAND AND SUPPLY:
METHODS OF ANALYSIS

TO THE economist—and he is the one person who has a professional obligation to use these concepts carefully—demand and supply are schedules or functions. Each denotes a whole array of
quantities—quantities which will be offered, in the case of supply;
quantities which will be asked for, in the case of demand—varying
with certain governing factors such as prices, incomes, consumer
tastes, industrial techniques.

If these determining factors or variables of the supply and demand
functions are allowed to vary (that is, if the market is free), they
will move in such directions as will equate the quantity supplied
and the quantity demanded. If, for example, the number of engineers that employers seek to hire is in excess of the number
available, the salaries of engineers will rise. The higher salaries
will invariably reduce the number demanded, and sooner or later
increase the number seeking employment. In free markets, therefore, the actual number of engineers employed in a given past year
represents both the number demanded and the number supplied.

The foregoing sketch of the apparatus of supply and demand
analysis is of course immensely simplified, but the simplifications
are not important to the substance of the apparatus. For example,
engineers have varying amounts of experience, and the demand for
engineers with little experience might increase more rapidly than
that for engineers with much experience, as happened after 1950.
With an elaboration of the apparatus, we could readily deal with
this additional dimension of supply and demand. Or again, the
supply of engineers may have to be analyzed into the supplies of
engineers with different kinds of specialization, but again the underlying apparatus of supply and demand can readily be adapted.

If the historical figures on the number of engineers represent
both the number supplied and the number demanded, how can
one disassociate the two schedules and analyze separately their
determinants? The various answers that economists give to this
question are much easier to understand if we first restate the
question in graphical terms.

19

Let us represent the demand schedule for engineers in any year by D, and the supply schedule by S, and use subscripts to denote the year. We assume that the numbers supplied and demanded depend only, or at least proximately, upon the salary level; this assumption is made only to simplify the exposition. Then in (say) 1950, D_{50} and S_{50} will be equated to fix a number of engineers, Q_{50}, and a salary rate, W_{50}; we illustrate this situation in Figure 1. Corresponding schedules hold in each year (such as 1951 and 1952 in the figure) and the number of engineers and average salaries are known for each year. Normally the demand and supply schedules

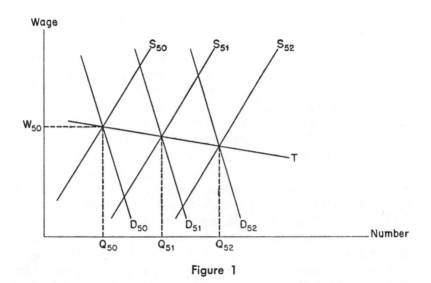

Figure 1

or curves will shift to the right each year, for in a growing economy on average a larger number will be sought and available in each succeeding year. In periods such as depressions or war, however, either the demand or the supply can rapidly shift a considerable distance in either direction.

We may now restate our question: how can one estimate the supply and demand curves when one knows only the historically recorded series of intersection points of the two curves? It is evident from the example in Figure 1, in which the intersection points trace out a curve (T) which represents neither supply nor demand, that in general one cannot estimate these curves, at least not without additional information.[1]

If we wish to predict the number of engineers in the future, it may not be necessary to do more than extrapolate the observed trend of numbers (curve T in Figure 1). Our example has been drawn so as to represent the general facts concerning engineers in the United States since 1890: demand has grown quite rapidly but supply has grown even more rapidly so salaries have drifted downward relative to those for the entire working population.[2] There are, however, two good reasons for not attempting a simple extrapolation of past relationships—one statistical, and one economic.

The statistical objection to extrapolation is that our data cover so short a period—only about 25 years in the case of salaries—and our historical observations are so few—only 7 on the number of engineers—that any prediction would command little confidence. Most of our information, in fact, pertains to two decades, one dominated by a great depression, the other dominated by a great war; so we are not inclined to press the representativeness of the data.

The economic objection to simple extrapolation is that the conditions of supply and demand may change—that is, the curves of supply and demand may change in shape, or the rate at which they shift through time may change. And unless one knows the demand and supply curves, he cannot make precise adjustments in his predictions even for known future changes in demand and supply conditions.

We shall not attempt to estimate the demand and supply curves directly; there are too few observations to allow experimentation with the known techniques in this area.[3] Instead we shall employ

[1] If one of the curves is much more stable than the other, then the intersection points will tend to fall along the more stable curve. The demand for agricultural produce is much more stable than the supply—at least in the case of those products whose supply is greatly influenced by variations in weather—so in this situation it has been possible to estimate demand curves.

[2] Our illustrative figure is somewhat more realistic if the horizontal axis is taken to represent the logarithm of the number of engineers.

[3] These techniques—aside from that for agricultural products referred to in footnote one of this chapter—all amount to relating the shifts of the supply and demand functions to other variables. For example, one might assume that the demand curve for engineers shifts to the right each decade by an amount that depends upon the growth of particular industries, and that the supply

what might be termed a quasi-analytical approach. In the case of demand, which is our special interest, we shall explore a variety of factors which general observation suggests are possible determinants of the level of employment of engineers. For example, we shall examine the influence of the industrial composition of the labor force upon the employment of engineers. If the differences among industries in the employment of engineers are large and stable—and we shall show that they are—then we are disentangling one of the forces which governs shifts in the demand curve for engineers.

This sort of approach is admittedly incomplete: it does not allow one to reach a single, comprehensive, explanatory system which accounts for all shifts in supply and demand, and accounts for them only once. But it serves the purposes of marshalling more or less systematically a considerable body of relevant empirical information and of formulating with some explicitness the areas of ignorance and the types of information necessary to remove them.

The economist's apparatus of supply and demand analysis, of which a portion has been summarized above, lends itself to an examination of the often claimed shortage of engineers and other technological professions, and we undertake this next. Thereafter we briefly summarize two common methods of making predictions of future demands for scientific personnel. We seek to judge their usefulness, and to learn from their deficiencies.

We shall not enter into a corresponding investigation of previous predictions of the future supply of engineers. All the predictions we have seen consist simply of finding the recent ratio of engineering students in colleges to some part of the population of college age (say, men in colleges) and applying the ratio, with or without a trend component, to predicted numbers in the underlying population group. A more comprehensive study of supply is made in Chapter IV.

1. *Has There Been a Shortage? A Survey of Earnings*

In recent years there has been much discussion of a shortage of engineers and natural scientists, and a variety of proposals have been made to alleviate a shortage that has been alleged to exist or to be imminent. We are not concerned in this study with public policy toward the technological professions, but we are deeply

---

curve shifts to the right each decade by an amount that depends upon the difference between the earnings of engineers and other workers.

interested in the economic questions implicit in an allegation of a shortage.

The word "shortage" is seldom defined precisely in these discussions, but it appears to be used in a variety of senses. In one sense, there is a shortage of members of a particular profession if the actual number is less than the number dictated by some social criterion or goal. For example, one might use the criterion that we should have enough engineers to conduct a major war in a particular manner, or that we should have ten per cent more engineers than a hostile power is believed to have. Such a criterion could be important and fully developed, but normally it is left undefined in the literature. Since there is no consensus on any such criterion, and since we cannot construct one, we shall not discuss this type of shortage.[4]

A second meaning of shortage is that the quantity of the labor services in question that is demanded is greater than the quantity supplied *at the prevailing wage*. In such a circumstance the wage normally rises, causing the quantity demanded to shrink and the quantity supplied to expand. The shortage vanishes as soon as the market can adjust to the excess demand. But if wages are regulated, and are not allowed to respond to the excess demand, the shortage will persist. Such a condition ruled in many labor markets, probably including engineering, during World War II, but there have been no general controls over engineering salaries since that time.[5]

The third meaning of shortage, and the one that is most natural

[4] With social criteria such as these, one may also have an oversupply; the most common example of a charge of oversupply is implicit in the complaint that members of a given profession do not have the thoroughness of training or the level of native ability that the speaker believes they once had or should now have. The master of political arithmetic, William Petty, dealt with the problem this way:

"As for Physicians, it is not hard by help of the observations which have been lately made upon the Bills of Mortality, to know how many are sick in *London* by the number of them that dye, and by the proportions of the City to find out the same for the Countrey; and by both, by the advice of the learned Colledge of that Faculty to calculate how many Physicians are requisite for the whole Nation; and consequently, how many Students in that art to permit and encourage; and lastly, having calculated these numbers, to adopt a proportion of Chyrurgeons, Apothecaries, and Nurses to them, and so by the whole to cut off and extinguish that infinite swarm of vain pretenders unto, and abusers of the God-like Faculty, which of all Secular Employments our Saviour himself after he began to preach engaged himself upon." *A Treatise of Taxes and Contributions*, 1662 (C. H. Hull edition of *Works*, Cambridge University Press, 1899, Vol. I, p. 27).

[5] The possible control of wages by a portion of the employers is discussed below. A related concept of shortage is noticed at the beginning of Chapter IV.

23

in an economy with a free labor market, is that a shortage exists when the number of workers available (the supply) increases less rapidly than the number demanded *at the salaries paid in the recent past*. Then salaries will rise, and activities which once were performed by (say) engineers must now be performed by a class of workers who are less well trained and less expensive. Such a shortage is not necessarily objectionable from a social viewpoint, but this is a separate question. In any event this is a well-defined and significant meaning of the word "shortage" and we propose to investigate now whether such a shortage has existed for engineers in recent decades. To this end we begin with a study of trends in earnings.

We begin with a comparison of engineering salaries with earnings or salaries in selected fields since 1929—the earliest year for which tolerably reliable engineering data are available (Table 11). Ratios of engineering salaries to earnings of three groups of independent professional practitioners—doctors, dentists, and lawyers —rose during the thirties but declined sharply after 1939. By 1951 the salary-income ratio for engineers compared with physicians was 40 per cent below its level in 1929; for engineers and dentists, 16 per cent below; for engineers and lawyers, 3 per cent below.[6] The decline was substantially greater when measured against a 1939 base. Salaries of engineers and full-time average earnings of manufacturing wage and salary employees and all wage and salary employees fluctuated in about the same manner between 1929 and 1939 but after 1939 wage earners increased their earnings more sharply than did engineers. From 1950 through 1954, the ratio of engineering salaries to earnings of wage and salary employees was about a third lower than in 1929.

The relationship between median engineering salaries and average salaries of college teachers varied considerably from the movements described above. Engineering salaries declined about 20 per cent relative to college teachers' salaries between 1929 and 1932, but then rose steadily to 1946 when the level of salaries of engineers relative to those of college teachers was 20 per cent higher than in 1929. Between 1946 and 1953 this ratio declined to about its 1929 level.

[6] A ratio computed on the basis of average engineering salaries, rather than medians, would probably have shown a larger decline in relative engineering salaries. Data from the 1940 and 1950 censuses show a larger percentage rise in median engineering salaries between 1939 and 1949 than in average salaries. Herman P. Miller, *Income of the American People,* John Wiley, 1955, Tables C-2 and C-4.

METHODS OF ANALYSIS

The pronounced downward drift of earnings in all professions (except medicine) relative to earnings of the working population as a whole is well-known, and it is apparent that the engineers have fully shared in this relative decline. This downward drift is known only for the period since 1929, but one may plausibly conjecture that it began much earlier because the main force working in this direction—the rapid expansion in the number of trained professional workers—also began much earlier.

TABLE 11

Index of Ratio of Median Engineering Salary to Average Wage and Salary or Net Income
of Selected Occupations, Benchmark Dates, 1929–1954
(1929 = 100.0)

	Ratio to Earnings per Full-Time Wage and Salary Employee	Ratio to Earnings per Full-Time Manufacturing Wage Earner	Ratio to Net Income of Lawyers [a]	Ratio to Net Income of Physicians [a]	Ratio to Net Income of Dentists [a]	Ratio to Salaries of College Teachers
1929	100.0	100.0	100.0	100.0	100.0	100.0
1932	102.0	109.1	108.3	133.7	139.9	79.9
1934	93.6	97.3	95.4	112.4	129.8	n.a.
1939	106.4	108.5	120.8	118.3	132.1	101.4
1943 [b]	83.2	76.0	107.6	72.2	86.3	116.3
1946	80.9	83.1	108.0	69.4	90.7	119.6
1949	69.9	70.8	98.5	63.1	84.7	102.4
1950	67.6	67.6	95.9	61.3	83.1	101.5
1951	66.2	65.4	95.6	59.5	83.5	97.8 [c]
1952	68.1	66.8	101.9			99.4
1953	67.9	66.1	102.2			96.3 [d]
1954	67.9	66.6	96.0			

[a] Limited to those in independent practice.

[b] Engineering salaries including payments for overtime.

[c] College teachers' salaries interpolated.

[d] Extrapolated by expenditures on resident instruction, land-grant colleges.

Source: *Engineering salaries:* Various surveys conducted by the Bureau of Labor Statistics and the Engineers Joint Council. 1929–1953 interpolated on the basis of the movement of salaries of research scientists and engineers, reported by the Los Alamos Scientific Laboratory in their annual national surveys of professional scientific salaries, and by average starting salaries of engineers, reported by Frank J. Endicott in various issues of the *Journal of College Placement*. For details, see Appendix A. Data for 1954 from the Los Alamos study.

Earnings of all wage and salary employees and manufacturing wage and salary employees: National Income Supplement, 1954, 1955, Survey of Current Business, Dept. of Commerce.

Net incomes of lawyers and physicians and salaries of college teachers: George J. Stigler, *Trends in Employment in the Service Industries,* Princeton University Press for National Bureau of Economic Research, 1956, p. 34; *Survey of Current Business,* December 1956, p. 27.

Net incomes of dentists: 1929–1946: *Survey of Current Business,* January 1950, p. 9; 1949–1951: *Survey of Current Business,* July 1952, p. 6.

For the period 1939–1949 we can compare increases in engineering salaries with the increases in wages or salaries for selected occupations within the professional and technical worker group. These data, drawn from census materials and covering a somewhat different universe than do the series in Table 11, indicate a smaller income rise for engineers than for male employees in five out of six other professional or technical occupations (Table 12). Only college teachers received smaller salary increases than the three main engineering branches, while chemists, clergymen, designers and draftsmen, and pharmacists had substantially larger increases. Public and private school teachers experienced larger percentage salary increases than two of the three engineering branches.

TABLE 12

Percentage Increase in Average Wage or Salary Income, Full-Time Male Wage or Salary Workers in Selected Professional and Technical Occupations, 1939–1949

Engineers, civil	65.1
Engineers, electrical	56.5
Engineers, mechanical	56.8
Chemists	80.5
Clergymen	72.4
College presidents, professors and instructors (n.e.c.)	32.3
Designers and draftsmen	82.5
Pharmacists	120.0
Teachers (n.e.c.)	62.6

n.e.c. = not elsewhere classified.
Source: Herman P. Miller, *Income of the American People*, John Wiley, 1955; Appendix Tables C-2 and C-4.

Since the close of World War II, it is possible to trace out annual changes in salaries of engineers. We report the annual percentage increases in starting salaries for graduating engineers and in salaries at the starting level and at the 9–11 years' experience level for research scientists and engineers (Table 13).[7] The broad outlines

[7] There is a minor timing difference in the two sets of data in Table 13. The Endicott data on starting salaries for engineers are collected in November and December of the preceding year and refer to current and prospective hiring plans of employers. The Los Alamos data are collected in the summer of the current year and relate to current salary scales for employees of research organizations. Thus the percentage changes in starting engineering salaries between 1949 and 1950 are based on data gathered in November–December 1948 and November–December 1949, while the corresponding change in salaries for researchers is based on data gathered in the summer of 1949 and the summer of 1950.

of salary experience for these various groups are clear. After some declines in 1949 and early 1950, salaries for young engineers and scientists rose substantially under the impact of the Korean defense program.[8] The largest increases took place in 1952, when apparently the full impact of the research and development programs of the federal government was felt (see below). Smaller percentage in-

TABLE 13

Annual Percentage Changes in Salaries of Engineers and Scientists at Selected Experience Levels, 1947–1956

	Average Starting Salaries of Graduate Engineers	Average Salaries of Research Scientists and Engineers with Bachelor's Degree		
		New Graduates	Graduates With 1 Year's Experience	Graduates With 9 to 11 Years' Experience
1947–1948	2.5			
1948–1949	4.4	−3.2	−0.3	1.6
1949–1950	−0.4	1.8	1.7	2.9
1950–1951	3.8	6.9	5.0	7.0
1951–1952	13.0	11.3	12.7	8.6
1952–1953	6.6	6.7	6.7	4.1
1953–1954	6.2	3.7	5.5	2.4
1954–1955	4.6	7.2	5.0	11.2
1955–1956	9.1			

Source: *Graduate Engineers*—Frank S. Endicott, "Trends in the Employment of College and University Graduates in Business and Industry," *Journal of College Placement*, May 1952, p. 44; March 1953, p. 56; March 1954, p. 60; March 1955, p. 41; *Management Record*, National Industrial Conference Board, January 1956. Based on surveys of hiring plans of several hundred large and medium-sized companies. *Research Scientists and Engineers—1948–1954 National Surveys of Professional Scientific Salaries*, Los Alamos Scientific Laboratory of the University of California, Los Alamos, New Mexico. Percentages for 9- to 11-year experience group are average of annual percentages for three component groups.

creases were registered in 1953 and 1954, but there was a larger increase, especially for more experienced engineers, in 1955. Older research scientists and engineers experienced larger salary increases than younger scientists and engineers from 1948 to 1950 and in 1955, but on average the former's salaries have increased less rapidly in the postwar decade.

Only a few relevant salary or earnings series can be compared

[8] The similarity in annual movement and total change of the Endicott and Los Alamos series increases our confidence in their accuracy.

27

with those of engineers in the period since 1950 (Table 14). In the years immediately after the outbreak of the Korean War, salaries of new graduates in engineering rose at the same rate as those in fields like accounting and business, and as those of research scientists and engineers with little experience. All of these groups had larger increases than occurred in the average earnings of all manufacturing wage earners, but the difference was not large.

TABLE 14

Percentage Increases in Salaries and Earnings of Selected
Occupations, Various Periods, 1950–1956

	1950–1953	1950–1954	1950–1955	1950–1956
1. College graduates, average starting salaries				
Engineering	25.0	32.8	38.9	51.5
Accounting	24.8	32.4	39.5	47.9
Sales	25.4	30.8	40.0	49.2
General business	24.8	32.5	39.8	48.7
All fields	24.1	31.8	39.2	49.4
2. Research scientists and engineers with bachelor's degree, average salaries				
New graduates	27.0	31.7	41.2	
Graduates with one year's experience	26.2	33.1	39.8	
Graduates with 9–11 years' experience	21.1	24.0	37.9	
3. All Manufacturing Wage Earners, Average Earnings per Full-Time Employee	22.8	24.9	31.8	

Source: For manufacturing wage earners, Table 11 and *Survey of Current Business,* July 1956. For others, same as Table 13.

We may summarize these pieces of information on engineering earnings as follows. Since 1929, engineering salaries have declined substantially relative to earnings of all wage earners and relative to incomes of independent professional practitioners. Especially since 1939 engineering salaries have declined relative to the wage or salary income of the entire group of professional, technical and kindred workers, as well as relative to the working population as a whole. After the outbreak of the Korean War there was a minor increase in the relative salaries of engineers (and of other college-trained workers), but this was hardly more than a minor cross-current in a tide.

Relative to both the working population as a whole and the professions as a separate class, then, the record of earnings would suggest that up to at least 1955 there had been no shortage—in fact an increasingly ample supply—of engineers. But before we examine this conclusion more closely, it is necessary to consider whether the market for engineers' services is a good market in the technical economic sense. That is, do engineers fail to move to positions with higher salaries because of ignorance or inertia? Or do some employers have an appreciable degree of market control over salaries —an element of monopoly which distorts the movements of salaries over time? If the market for engineers' services has some imperfection such as these, movements of salaries are not an accurate index of scarcity in the economic sense.

More specifically, if engineers were not mobile among employers, then salaries would not be an accurate index of the state of the market because the offer of a higher wage would not necessarily attract an engineer away from another employer.[9] There is no direct information on the mobility of engineers among employers. However, of those members of the engineering profession in 1939 who remained civilians in the United States between 1939 and 1946, 25 per cent changed at least once the industry in which they were employed during this seven-year period, 30 per cent changed their State of employment at least once, 22 per cent changed from one type of engineering activity to another, and an unknown percentage changed employers in the same locality and industry. Fourteen per cent changed their branch of engineering and more than 20 per cent of all engineers worked at some time in their lives in a branch of engineering other than that in which they were trained.[10] The mobility of engineers among employers was undoubtedly higher than any of these indirect measures although less than their sum by the proportion of engineers who participated in two or more of the kinds of moves listed. Mobility was probably even higher among those engineers who entered the profession after 1939, and among the younger engineers who served in the armed forces. Some immobility undoubtedly exists, but in view of this

[9] But even in this case a higher wage would usually attract more engineers than a lower wage so a general increase in demand would still be associated with a general rise of salaries. But there would no longer be a single salary rate structure in the market, and in fact there would be no single market but instead a large number of loosely related markets.

[10] *Employment Outlook for Engineers*, p. 79. Data appear on census tabulating cards which show the geographic location of each engineer in 1935 and 1940 and again in 1949 and 1950. Analysis of these data would provide a measure of the geographic mobility of engineers in nonwar periods.

level of mobility among engineers and the substantial flexibility of choice open to new entrants into the profession, one would expect major salary and other inducements to be offered in industries or geographic areas with rapidly increasing demands for engineers.

Again, there might be a failure of competition, so that an increased demand for engineers did not lead to a rise in salary offers. The suggestion that employers may have been reluctant to compete on salaries presupposes some type of monopsonistic situation in the market, i.e., that some firms employed such a large portion of the engineering profession that any action on their part with respect to hiring and salaries would significantly affect the market price for engineering services.[11] But the fact is that the largest nongovernmental employer of engineers probably accounts for only about 2 per cent of the total number of engineers in the country, and other major employers account for substantially smaller percentages. Most engineers work for firms which employ insignificant proportions of the profession. Under these conditions, probably all firms have to match in some form or other the general market price for engineering services. Accordingly, general salary movement of engineers relative to those of other occupations should indicate the relative supply-demand balance in this market compared to that in the markets for other occupations.

It has been suggested that there may be an exception to the general prevalence of competition in the governmentally controlled industries. The Air Force retains the formal right to review the salaries paid by its contractors, and thus might hold down salaries in a substantial (but far from dominant) portion of the market.[12]

[11] Much current discussion implies that the individual employers have monopsonistic power over salary rates. For example, it is often said that salary rates for newly graduated engineers cannot be increased without increasing those of experienced engineers. But if the market is tolerably competitive, the salary rates of experienced engineers are fixed by the market and the individual employer will have to meet these rates (or accept lower quality engineers) whether he does or does not raise the rates for inexperienced engineers. This particular argument is also defective in that it fails to recognize the great reduction in the differentials paid for greater experience which has taken place in the last twenty-five years; see Appendix Tables A-3, A-7, etc.

Control over salary rates by individual employers has been suggested in *A Policy for Scientific and Professional Manpower,* National Manpower Council, 1953, p. 152. An agreement among aircraft manufacturers not to hire engineers from one another from 1950 to about 1953 was alleged, but no evidence of its effectiveness given, in Boeing Airplane Co. and Seattle Professional Engineering Employees Association, 110 National Labor Relations Board 147 (1954); see also *Business Week,* August 25, 1956, pp. 105–108.

[12] The Air Force Procurement Instructions (as revised January 2, 1956), Sec.

There is no evidence to suggest that this power is vigorously exercised.[13] If this power is exercised to even a minor degree, and no corresponding review is made of advertisements for engineers, the proliferation of advertisements for engineers would be largely explainèd.[14] But in any event such controls, whether public or private, over salaries paid by employers of a minority of engineers could not give rise to a shortage outside the industries practicing the salary control; i.e., there could be no general market shortage because of the salary control.

So we find no reason to reject the main implications of the data on the trend of relative earnings: the number of engineers has been growing more rapidly relative to the demand, in the past two and a half decades, than has been the case in the labor force as a whole. And since the differentials of engineers' earnings above those of the academically untrained labor force are still in excess of the costs of obtaining an engineering degree, we may expect this trend to continue in the future.[15]

It is true that after 1950 there was a short, and relatively minor, reversal in this movement of relative earnings of engineers. Engineers' salaries rose substantially for at least two years, and at a rate exceeding that in the independent professions and the labor force as a whole. This movement, obviously related to the expansion of military procurement after the outbreak of the Korean War and the associated increase in government expenditures for

---

54-905, 54-906, require, from contractors, justifying material for certain salary increases; other sections prohibit evasion through indirect salary increases (e.g., "fringe" benefits).

[13] A variety of tests, similar to those developed in the study of monopolistic product markets, could be employed (with fuller data than we possess) to test the effectiveness of either public or private wage control systems. The following examples will suggest their nature:

1. If the control system is effective, there will usually be much less dispersion of salary rates in the field where the controls are practiced than elsewhere. This corresponds to the finding that strict identity of prices in product markets is symptomatic of collusion. (See G. Stigler, *Theory of Price*, Revised ed., 1952, pp. 239 ff.)

2. If the control system is effective, the movements of salaries within the group will be more nearly simultaneous and more nearly equal than in other industries.

3. Elaborate systems of price differentials for various qualities (in our case, various types of training, classes of experience, etc.) will be necessary to reduce indirect competition through upgrading.

[14] See Appendix I.

[15] See Milton Friedman and Simon Kuznets, *Income from Independent Professional Practice*, National Bureau of Economic Research, 1945, Chap. 3.

31

private and public research, is the only basis we can find for the popular view that there was a shortage of engineers at that time, in comparison with other occupations.

It is clear that the increased demand for engineers for a short period after 1950 was not fully matched by a corresponding increase in supply. It is difficult, of course, to increase substantially the supply of engineers or other scientists with long academic training periods in a relatively short period. The major portion of current additions to the supply of engineers enter the profession via college training and the number of current graduates are determined by expectations ruling three or four years earlier. On the other hand, the number of nongraduates entering the profession through on-the-job training and upgrading can be speeded up more rapidly. And even a minimal degree of increased efficiency in the utilization of existing engineers substantially offsets a considerable degree of shortage in the production of new engineers, since the annual additions of new engineers to the profession are running at less than 5 per cent of the total.

Despite the temporary difficulties involved in meeting the increased demand for engineers and scientists after 1950, the modest relative increases in salaries of this group over the recent period cast considerable doubt on the existence of a shortage of such personnel of the magnitude that is implicit in much recent and some current discussions. A shortage of the dimensions often suggested would clearly have evidenced itself in perceptible changes in relative earnings of engineers and scientists since the late forties when the fear was just the reverse, i.e., that there were too many engineers. But in the five years after 1950 the increases in engineering and scientific salaries have been of essentially the same magnitude as those in other occupations, i.e., somewhat larger in the several years following 1950 and somewhat smaller, in many cases, after 1952. There may well be temporary shortages of personnel in certain geographic areas but we have found no evidence of any shortage of substantial magnitude.

Our conclusion that there is no evidence of a shortage of engineers will strike many readers as surprising and some as patently wrong. Although there always remains a range of defensible positions in matters like this, most disagreements probably stem from one of three sources. First, a "shortage" may mean a deficiency by some standard other than the market's. Since we have not investigated non-market concepts of shortages (which may be very important), our conclusion has no relevance to them (p. 23). Second, the finding that earnings of engineers have fallen relative to most other professions and to the general working population may be challenged. One would naturally wish that it rested upon fuller data —in particular, there is an urgent need for comprehensive data on the earnings of college graduates in business—and be supplemented by more precise analyses of "fringe" benefits. But the present statistical basis for the findings is impressive, and when that basis is widened, it is hardly probable that they will be so radically modified as to reverse direction. Finally, the conclusion rests upon the fundamental economic principle that increases in demand relative to supply will manifest themselves, in a free market, in a rising price relative to prices in other markets. One might raise questions of the willingness of engineers to change employers or of their knowledge of alternative positions, but these sometimes weighty questions seem, in light of our discussion of them, unimportant in the market for engineers. The more important question is whether the market is competitively free. There is no evidence, and scarcely any probability, of effective general salary-fixing by agreement among the great number of employers. There is a possibility, which we do not believe is large, that among defense contractors a sort of salary-fixing results from governmental procurement policies. We have indicated the empirical tests which would detect such salary-fixing; unfortunately they require data to which we do not have access (p. 31 n.). We may repeat that even if the procurement policies were found to constitute effective salary-fixing, the result would be, not a general shortage, but rather a shortage restricted to the industries participating in the salary-fixing. We hope, finally, that more work will be done on the problem of short-run shortages, but not to the exclusion of long-run determinants of supply and demand which is the real subject of the present study.

2. The Bureau of Labor Statistics Method of Prediction of Demand

A method (admittedly rough) of forecasting the long-run trend of demand for engineers was undertaken by the Bureau of Labor Statistics following the end of World War II.[16] In essence it amounted

[16] *Employment Outlook for Engineers*, Bureau of Labor Statistics, Bull. 968, 1949.

to relating the number of engineers to total employment in selected industries. The bureau's procedure for predicting the future gross demand for engineers involved three steps:

1. The calculation of the ratio of all U.S. engineers to the total labor force in mining, construction, manufacturing, transportation, and public utilities.
2. Prediction of the future labor force in these industries (on the basis of the trend in their ratio to the nonagricultural labor force).
3. Extrapolation of the ratio of engineers to the labor force in these industries.

TABLE 15

Total Engineers and the Labor Force in Five Industry Groups, 1890–1960

	ENGINEERS [a] (000)	LABOR FORCE IN FIVE INDUSTRY GROUPS (000)	ENGINEERS PER 100,000 LABOR FORCE	
			Ratio	*Percentage Increase in Ratio per Decade*
1890	26.8	7,800	344	
1900	41.1	10,459	393	14.2
1910	84.2	14,461	582	48.1
1920	129.9	18,075	719	23.5
1930	215.4	19,949	1,080	50.2
1940	261.4 [b]	20,399	1,282	18.7
1948 (estimated)	350.0	24,300	1,440	15.6
1960 (predicted)	450.0	26,500	1,700	14.8
1950 (actual)	475.4 [b]	24,418	1,947	51.9

[a] Excluding surveyors and metallurgists.

[b] The 1950 census volumes report a larger number of engineers in 1940 than was reported in the 1940 census. On a basis comparable to the 1950 census figure, the 1940 total was 291,465. For details, see Appendix B. We have here reduced the actual 1950 total of engineers of 529,947 (i.e. excluding surveyors and metallurgists) to a level equivalent to the ratio of 261,428 to 291,465 to achieve greater comparability with the 1940 figure used by the Bureau of Labor Statistics. Had we used the actual 1950 figure, the number of engineers in 1950 per 100,000 persons in the labor force in the five industry groups would have been 2,170 and the decade percentage increase in the ratio, 69.3 per cent.

Their basic data are presented in Table 15.[17] The actual figures for 1950, which we have added, are enough to show that the method is not reliable.

There appear to have been at least three reasons for the large underestimate of the expected demands for engineers. The first is

[17] *Ibid.*, pp. 12–13, 98.

that the estimated figure for engineers in 1948 was much too low. The BLS made this estimate of the then-current number of engineers by subtracting from the 1940 total of engineers (given by the 1940 census) an estimated number of deaths and retirements during 1940–1948 (derived on the basis of working-life tables) and adding the number of persons receiving first degrees in engineering during the eight years and a rough estimate of the "excess of [the] number of entrants [to the engineering profession] without engineering degrees over [the] number of engineers or engineering graduates leaving [the] profession for other employment."

It is clear that the major error in this calculation was in the last item, viz. the number of entrants to the profession through means other than graduation from an engineering school. For the period 1940–1948, the BLS estimated that the net additions from sources other than engineering schools at 15,500, and the gross additions at 35,000.[18] In all likelihood, the actual number of nongraduates entering the profession in those years was several times that figure. And no account was taken of the number of engineers who were not so employed in 1940 but who returned to the profession during the decade.[19] (We discuss this question in Chapter IV and Appendixes B and E.)

The second reason the predictions were unreliable is that individual industries within the total for the five industry groups are very uneven in their use of engineers. For example, we may present the following calculations for 1950 for the industry groups themselves:

	Per Cent of All Employed Engineers	Engineers as Per Cent of Employed Persons
Construction	14.81	2.26
Mining	2.34	1.30
Manufacturing	45.27	1.62
Transportation, utilities, etc.	11.17	1.33
Total	73.59	

[18] This estimate in turn was based on a rough estimate that there were an equivalent number of such entrants in the 1920's.

[19] Probably including the bulk of the 7,000 persons who reported that their usual but not current occupation in 1940 was engineering (see Alba M. Edwards, *Comparative Occupation Statistics for the United States, 1870 to 1940,* Bureau of the Census, 1943, p. 24).

These industry groups clearly differ considerably in their relative use of engineers, and industries within these industry groups, particularly within manufacturing which employs almost half of all engineers, differ among themselves even more sharply. Thus, shifts in the composition of the total labor force can have a substantial effect upon the employment of engineers. We examine this problem more closely in Chapter III.

The third reason the method used by the BLS proved unsatisfactory is apparent in the last column of Table 15—there is no discernible regularity in the trend of the ratios of engineers to the labor force. The ratio predicted by the bureau for 1960 is below the actual level for 1950. Yet it was not an unreasonable extrapolation if one placed heavy weight on the decade of the thirties.[20] Future predictions by this method must work with a sequence of percentage increases per decade of 23.5, 50.2, 18.7, and 51.9 in the ratio of engineers to labor force, and this is not a sequence which one can confidently extrapolate.

We have found one time series, however, which readily lends itself to this type of extrapolation. It is the percentage of the labor force who are engineers at alternate census dates. In 1890 this percentage was 0.12; it about doubled by 1910, when it was 0.24. By 1930 the percentage had again about doubled, to 0.47; and by 1950 it had doubled again, exactly to 0.94.[21] The deviations from a simple doubling of the percentage every twenty years are so small as to be easily accountable by errors in the data. It seems natural, therefore, to predict that the percentage will double again, and be 1.88 in 1970. Or, differently stated, the number of engineers would grow about 3.5 per cent per year, if there were no change in the size of the labor force.

Our faith in this interesting stability is small, however. One may question it statistically, for if the figures pertained to the twenty-year periods beginning with 1900, then the percentage would have more than doubled in the first period (from 0.15 in 1900 to 0.32 in

[20] Indeed, it is likely that the estimate of engineers in 1948, although derived directly, was acceptable to BLS because the resulting decade percentage rate of increase for the forties was of the same order of magnitude as that experienced in the thirties.

[21] We use engineers including surveyors for this series, in order to have a consistently defined group over the sixty years. Sources are: *Labor Force, 1890–1940:* Edwards, *op. cit.*, pp. 12, 104, and for 1950, *Census of Population, 1950,* Vol. II, Part 1, Table 50; *Engineers to 1930:* Edwards, *op. cit.*, pp. 49, 111; *1940 and 1950,* see Appendix B.

1920), and much less than doubled in the second period (to 0.57 in 1940). But more fundamental is the fact that we have no good reason to believe that this rate of increase will maintain itself. There has been retardation in the case of chemists (who were 0.10 per cent of the labor force in 1930 and 0.14 in 1950), and had there not been the vast war and postwar expansion of government financing of research, the proportion of engineers would surely have grown at a declining rate. It seems safer to predict that the proportion of engineers will rise at less than the previous rate from 1950 to 1970. However, we do not envy the task of future students of this problem if the percentage should double from 1950 to 1970.

3. The Engineers Joint Council Method of Prediction of Demand

The use of questionnaires to ascertain the plans of businessmen is now quite popular, and they have also been used to measure the future demand for engineers or scientists. The most extensive questionnaire study of the demand for engineers has been that of the Engineers Joint Council, which recently made three annual surveys of expected net additions to the engineering staffs of private and public enterprises.[22]

In each of the years 1952, 1953, and 1954, the council sent questionnaires to a large number of business firms and government agencies (1,100 in 1952, 2,000 in 1953). Responses were received from almost 400 firms and agencies, employing roughly one-fifth of the engineers in the country (see Table 16). There are serious, and unanswered, questions as to whether the sample is under statistical control, but we shall not open this Pandora's Box.

In each year the questionnaire asked for the number of engineers employed, the numbers of various types which were expected to be hired in the forthcoming year (i.e., new graduates, experienced

[22] We are greatly indebted to the council, and to its executive secretary Mr. W. T. Cavanaugh, for allowing us to use the company reports in the following study. In addition the council has made studies of the output of new graduate engineers, with a view to measuring the adequacy of supply, but we shall discuss only demand studies. The results of a fourth demand study by the Engineers Joint Council, conducted during late 1955 and early 1956, were released August 7, 1956.

Comparable techniques, but covering demands for a longer period in the future, were used in *Survey of Industrial Requirements for Professional Personnel, 1952–56*, Ottawa, Department of Labor, Economics and Research Branch, October 1954.

engineers working for others, engineers returning from the armed services), the number expected to be lost, and the expected net addition to the number of engineers during the year.[23]

We have examined the individual reports to see whether the various firms and agencies were able to give tolerably reliable estimates of their future requirements of engineers. Our basic test is that of comparing the predictions for a year, made at the beginning of that year, with the actual numbers employed at the end of the year, as reported in the succeeding year. This test is supplemented by an examination of the internal consistency of the estimates of the composition of engineers hired and lost.

TABLE 16

Response to the Engineers Joint Council Surveys, 1952–1954

	1952 [a]	1953	1954
Number of business firms and government agencies	399	376	377
Total employment	4,695,435	4,151,210	3,729,086
Total engineers employed	139,371	125,086	124,329

[a] Only 265 business firms and government agencies, employing a total of 98,557 engineers, provided returns with completely usable information on expected net increases in staff.

Source: Company reports for the 1952, 1953, and 1954 surveys of the Engineering Manpower Commission, Engineers Joint Council.

These tests, to which we shall turn immediately, are somewhat ambiguous because both the council and the respondents underwent a learning process. The questionnaires issued in 1952 were too laconic in their instructions; and many respondents did not take adequate care in filling them out. In particular, many firms reported that their net increase in engineering staff would equal (or sometimes even exceed) the numbers of new graduate and experienced engineers hired, i.e. that they would lose no engineers during the year. The fuller directions and the greater experience in filling the form led in 1953 to a substantial improvement in the quality of the returns.

Let us begin with the predictions of net increases in the numbers of engineers for 1952. We may compare the predicted increases of 265 firms and agencies, classified by ten broad industry categories, with the retrospective reports of 376 firms and agencies in the

[23] A copy of the 1954 form is reproduced in Appendix H, where we discuss certain details of the EJC studies.

TABLE 17

Comparison of Expected Net Accessions of Engineers and Realized Net Accessions, 1952, Total EJC Sample

INDUSTRY	1952 SURVEY				1953 SURVEY			
	Number of Firms and Govt. Agencies	Total Engineers Employed Jan. 1, 1952	Predicted Increase during 1952	Per cent Increase	Number of Firms and Govt. Agencies	Total Engineers Employed Jan. 1, 1952	Actual Increase during 1952	Per cent Increase
Chemicals	20	11,418	1,991	17.4	24	10,306	907	8.8
Machinery (except electrical)	48	6,932	993	14.3	58	3,848	242	6.3
Electrical machinery	16	21,061	3,106	14.7	34	26,844	2,462	9.2
Transportation equipment	17	10,765	1,770	16.4	26	17,578	2,098	11.9
Professional and miscellaneous services	4	1,428	142	9.9	12	2,495	183	7.3
Public utilities and communication	27	4,858	437	9.0	54	14,133	28	2.0
Primary metals and fabricated metal products a	23	5,022	734	14.6	42	4,915	94	1.9
Petroleum products, crude petroleum and natural gas	15	8,594	1,236	14.4	20	7,685	559	7.3
Transportation b	21	1,149	134	11.7	14	1,782	24	1.3
Total industry c	243	81,180	12,048	14.8	353	99,204	7,552	7.6
Government	22	17,377	2,933	16.9	23	17,449	−521	−3.0
Total industry and government	265	98,557	14,981	15.2	376	116,653	7,031	6.0

a Data on metal mining are included in the data from the 1953 survey.
b Only railroads are included in the 1953 survey data.
c Including data on industries not included in the table.

Source: *1952 Survey data:* "Need for Engineering Graduates in 1952," mimeographed, report on the Survey of the Engineering Manpower Commission of Engineers Joint Council, not dated, Table 5. *1953 Survey data:* "Distribution of Engineering Graduates and Demand for Engineers," 1953," *Electrical Engineering*, May 1954, Table IV.

succeeding year (Table 17). We find that the actual increase in the number of engineers was 6 per cent; the predicted increase was 15.2 per cent, or two and a half times as much. The firms in every industry category were much too optimistic in their estimates, but the errors were relatively smallest in electrical machinery and transportation equipment and professional and miscellaneous services, and the errors were relatively largest in primary metals and fabricated metal products, transportation, and government. Substantially the same poor record of predictions, and the same variation of error among industry categories, is found if the comparisons are restricted to 73 identical firms which reported in both years (Table 18).

TABLE 18

Comparison of Expected and Realized Net Accessions of Engineers, 1952, Constant Group Sample

INDUSTRY	NUMBER OF FIRMS	TOTAL ENGINEERING EMPLOYMENT JAN. 1, 1952	1952 ACCESSIONS	
			Expected Net	*Actual Net*
Chemicals	6	6,249	1,808	739
Machinery (except electrical)	6	496	67	18
Electrical machinery	9	19,483	3,218	1,651
Transportation equipment	2	2,813	520	629
Petroleum products	5	3,650	980	15
Primary metals and fabricated metal products	6	2,290	559	174
Paper products	4	445	37	4
Miscellaneous manufacturing	4	234	28	14
Railroads	6	721	122	−8
Public utilities and communication	21	10,227	657	213
Miscellaneous nonmanufacturing	4	848	122	−33
Total industry	73	47,456	8,118	3,416

Source: Company reports for the 1952 and 1953 surveys of the Engineering Manpower Commission, Engineers Joint Council.

The 1953 predictions of all respondents cannot be classified by industry category, but the aggregate figures reveal a great increase in the accuracy of the predictions (Table 19). For the predicted number was about 6,900 as compared with an actual increase of 6,500. If these firms and agencies had predicted the same rate of increase in the number of engineers as in the preceding year—that is, 6 per cent—the predicted increase would have been 7,500, or 9 per cent above the number predicted and 15 per cent above the actual number. To this extent the results were superior to simple extrapolation.

For the 73 firms and agencies that reported in all years, the general picture is essentially the same (Table 20). Actual net accessions were 3,137, whereas the predicted number was 3,085.

TABLE 19

Comparison of Expected and Realized Net Accessions of Engineers, 1953, Total EJC Sample

	1953 Survey	1954 Survey	1954 Survey Adjusted [a]
Number of firms and government agencies	376	377	—
Total engineers, employed, January 1, 1953	125,086	117,821	125,100
Predicted increase during 1953	6,692	—	—
Actual increase during 1953	—	6,508	6,900

[a] The number of engineers employed in January 1953 by the firms in the 1953 Engineers Joint Council sample was 6 per cent higher than the number employed in January 1953 by the firms in the 1954 EJC sample. Accordingly, the EJC raised all the results of the 1954 survey by 6 per cent.

Source: "Report of the ASEE Manpower Committee," mimeographed, American Society of Electrical Engineers, June 14, 1954.

TABLE 20

Comparison of Expected and Realized Net Accessions of Engineers, 1953, Constant Group Sample

INDUSTRY	NUMBER OF FIRMS	TOTAL ENGINEERING EMPLOYMENT JAN. 1, 1953	1953 ACCESSIONS Expected Net	1953 ACCESSIONS Actual Net
Chemicals	6	7,185	516	530
Machinery (except electrical)	6	440	32	35
Electrical machinery	9	24,432	1,498	1,709
Transportation equipment	2	3,187	346	394
Petroleum products	5	4,426	242	222
Primary metals and fabricated metal products	6	2,494	−77	12
Paper products	4	318	3	−1
Miscellaneous manufacturing	4	174	15	13
Railroads	6	649	35	11
Public utilities and communication	21	9,139	201	141
Miscellaneous nonmanufacturing	4	669	−32	−29
Total industry	73	53,113	2,779	3,037

Source: Company reports for the 1953 and 1954 surveys of the Engineering Manpower Commission, Engineers Joint Council.

The prediction was again somewhat better than that which would have been made by simply assuming the same additions as in the preceding year (3,416).

The chief difficulty in interpreting this large improvement in the 1953 over the 1952 predictions is that the task of prediction was presumably much easier in the latter year. The salary data discussed in Chapter II indicate that 1952 was of all recent years the one in which the largest increase in demand was experienced— the full impact of the expansion consequent upon the Korean War did not come until then. Did the predictions improve in 1953 because conditions were more stable, or because the questionnaires were better prepared and the respondents more careful in answering the questions?

We can form some notion of answer to this question by classifying the 73 firms into three classes: those whose ratios of the number of engineers employed at the end of 1953 to the number employed at the beginning of 1953 were 4 per cent or more above their comparable ratios for 1952, those whose ratios were at least 4 per cent below those in 1952, and those whose net accessions were within 4 per cent of those in 1952. If the 1953 predictions of the respondents whose net accessions of engineers rose or fell substantially from the preceding year are as good as the predictions of those whose net accessions changed less, we may ascribe the improvement in predictions to improvements in the method rather than to the easing of the task.

The results of this reclassification are somewhat surprising (see Table 21). The firms whose 1953 rates of growth in engineering employment were less than those in 1952 had substantially more accurate predictions in 1953 than did those firms whose growth rates were about the same in both years. The firms whose 1953 growth rates were greater than for 1952 also did relatively poorly in predicting 1953 accessions, but these firms, while almost as many in number as the other two groups, employed relatively few engineers. The results for this group, then, may simply be a function of poor coverage.[24] In any case, there is no evidence that firms that should have had a relatively easy task in 1953, i.e. those whose net accessions were made at about the same rate in both years,

[24] There is a second complication. Firms that had larger increases in engineering employment in 1953 than in 1952 overestimated 1953 accessions. Firms that had about the same net accessions in both years underestimated 1953 accessions.

42

were better able to predict than those that had different rates of growth in the two years.

The EJC questionnaires ask for an itemization of the types of engineers hired—new engineering graduates, graduates of earlier years, and engineers returning from military service—as well as losses, so it is possible to test also the accuracy of the predictions of the components of net accessions.[25] The business firms and government agencies we have examined were on balance quite accurate in their predictions of net realized accessions in 1953 (see Table 22), especially in the manufacturing industries. Nonmanufacturing firms actually hired only half the expected additional engineers, and government agencies obtained twice their expected increase in

TABLE 21

Comparison of Expected and Actual Net Accessions
for Three Groups of Firms, 1953

GROUP [a]	NUMBER OF FIRMS	NUMBER OF ENGINEERS EMPLOYED, JAN. 1, 1953	1953 ACCESSIONS	
			Expected	*Actual*
I (acceleration)	21	2,283	269	133
II (stable)	24	32,951	1,317	1,773
III (retardation)	28	17,879	1,193	1,131
Total	73	53,113	2,779	3,037

[a] Group I firms are those whose ratios of the number of engineers employed at the end of 1953 to the number employed at the beginning of 1953 were four per cent or more above their comparable ratios for 1952. Group II firms are those whose 1953 ratios were less than four per cent above or below their 1952 ratios. Group III firms are those whose 1953 ratios were four per cent or more below those in 1952.

Source: Same as in Table 20.

staff. Both of the latter groups, however, have little weight in this sample in terms of total employment of engineers or, particularly, in terms of total net accessions.

In terms of gross accessions, the forecasts of the total sample and of the three component groups were substantially accurate, as were their forecasts of losses of engineering staff.

For the components of gross accessions, however, we find a different picture. The smallest component, engineers returning from military service, was estimated almost precisely by the total sample,

[25] The EJC studies are in principle restricted to graduate engineers, but some companies explicitly and probably many companies silently included all engineers. Thus the three types of engineers listed above are not exhaustive.

TABLE 22

Comparison of Expected and Realized Gross Accessions (by Components) and Losses of Engineers, 1953

INDUSTRY	NUMBER OF FIRMS AND AGENCIES	TOTAL ENGINEERING EMPLOYMENT JAN. 1, 1953	1953 LOSSES		1953 HIRINGS OF NEW GRADUATES		1953 HIRINGS OF OLD GRADUATES		NUMBER OF ENGINEERS RETURNING FROM MILITARY SERVICE		1953 GROSS ACCESSIONS		1953 NET ACCESSIONS	
			Expected	Actual	Expected	Actual	Expected	Actual	Expected	Actual	Expected	Actual	Expected	Actual
Manufacturing														
Food	6	312	16	22	12	9	11	19	3	2	26	30	10	8
Textiles	4	608	33	30	45	29	29	38	5	4	79	71	46	41
Paper	5	331	14	21	10	15	2	2	4	3	16	20	2	−1
Chemicals	14	9,460	472	688	866	729	248	554	128	67	1,242	1,350	770	662
Petroleum	11	6,672	435	531	653	539	142	278	78	82	873	899	438	368
Rubber	2	1,598	77	32	178	109	2	3	12	4	192	116	115	84
Stone, clay and glass	4	506	36	24	43	50	20	15	8	1	71	66	35	42
Metals and metal products	15	2,810	182	187	194	171	15	15	24	24	233	210	51	23
Machinery (except electrical)	18	1,113	69	158	151	136	28	58	27	15	206	209	137	51
Electrical machinery	14	27,746	1,724	1,455	1,975	1,932	784	1,204	209	153	2,968	3,289	1,244	1,834
Transportation equipment	11	4,423	1,222	900	824	705	1,052	850	51	43	1,927	1,598	705	698
Instruments	5	3,610	386	288	717	356	258	430	37	63	1,012	849	626	561
Miscellaneous manufacturing	3	253	17	6	28	16	31	15	1	0	60	31	43	25
Total	112	59,442	4,683	4,342	5,696	4,796	2,622	3,481	587	461	8,905	8,738	4,222	4,396

TABLE 22 (continued)

INDUSTRY	NUMBER OF FIRMS AND AGENCIES	TOTAL ENGINEERING EMPLOYMENT JAN. 1, 1953	1953 LOSSES		1953 HIRINGS OF NEW GRADUATES		1953 HIRINGS OF OLD GRADUATES		NUMBER OF ENGINEERS RETURNING FROM MILITARY SERVICE		1953 GROSS ACCESSIONS		1953 NET ACCESSIONS	
			Expected	Actual	Expected	Actual	Expected	Actual	Expected	Actual	Expected	Actual	Expected	Actual
Non-manufacturing														
Railroads	11	1,606	51	133	92	90	12	42	12	12	116	144	65	11
Public utilities and communications	37	11,393	488	524	362	362	140	191	202	150	704	703	216	179
Mining and crude petroleum	5	477	38	46	50	24	11	16	3	3	64	43	26	−3
Miscellaneous services and construction	8	1,175	101	114	76	42	34	40	9	5	119	87	18	−27
Steamships and airlines	3	10	0	0	0	0	0	1	1	0	1	1	1	1
Total	64	14,661	678	817	580	518	197	290	227	170	1,004	978	326	161
Government	13	7,922	900	967	475	532	410	343	110	302	995	1,177	95	210
Grand Total	189	82,055	6,261	6,126	6,751	5,846	3,229	4,114	924	933	10,904	10,893	4,643	4,767

Source: Company and government agency reports for the 1953 and 1954 surveys of the Engineering Manpower Commission, Engineers Joint Council.

although this is a result of an overestimate by private firms and an underestimate by government agencies. In any case the numbers involved in this component were small.

The two major components of gross accessions, hiring of new graduates and hiring of old graduates, show the most striking deviations of realization from prediction of any element in the analysis. Private firms (both manufacturing and nonmanufacturing) substantially overestimated the number of new engineering graduates they would hire in 1953, and underestimated by the same margin the hiring of older engineers. Thus while firms correctly forecast losses and gross accessions, and therefore net accessions, they incorrectly predicted the distribution of gross accessions among new and old engineers. This result is somewhat puzzling, for the bulk of losses to individual firms, which were correctly predicted, consists of transfers of engineers to other firms. The acquisitions of such engineers, however, were substantially underestimated.

This pattern may simply be a result of internal inconsistency in the combined forecasts of business firms. Firms may have believed that they would recoup such transfers largely by hiring new engineering graduates, while in fact they found it impossible to do so to the extent predicted and had to resort in larger measure than predicted to hiring older engineers whose loss in turn was correctly foreseen by their original employers. Alternatively, the predictions may have been consistent but the firms in the sample might have been more aggressive in hiring older engineers than firms outside of the sample. If this were true and the latter had been questioned, they might well have substantially underestimated their actual losses of engineers. A third alternative is that a substantial number of persons who had never worked as engineers before were included in the "older engineers" hired in 1953. In other words, this category may include new entrants to the engineering profession, other than new graduates, who would not be included in the loss category.

The general impression we draw from this analysis of the predictions of the components of net accessions is that they were surprisingly good. They indicate that the predictions of net accessions were made with considerable care and consistency. For very short periods of time the questionnaire method could probably be brought to a useful level of precision.

CHAPTER III

FACTORS INFLUENCING THE DEMAND
FOR ENGINEERS AND CHEMISTS

THE demand for engineers and chemists is primarily a demand by the business sector of the economy. In 1950, the census reported 579,270 employed persons in these occupations, and of them only 54,630, or 9.4 per cent, were employed in public administration.[1] A considerable additional number of engineers work for governments in their enterprises—municipal utilities, naval repair yards, etc.— but their numbers are presumably determined by the same kinds of factors that influence employment in the corresponding private industries. Our analysis, therefore, will be concerned chiefly with the engineers and chemists in private business.

Our central problem is to explain why the number of engineers and chemists grew from 52,000 in 1900 to 625,000 in 1950—from 0.18 per cent of the labor force in 1900 to 1.11 per cent in 1950. And we should like an explanation which does not simply enumerate developments and institutions which certainly or with high probability increased the demand for these technological professions. Instead, we would like to be able to give at least rough estimates of the importance or unimportance of these developments. We shall find that we can do something in this direction, although some hypotheses escape even the roughest quantitative estimates.

We shall begin with a study of the role of the industrial composition of the economy in the rising demand for engineers and chemists. We find that it is a factor of some importance, but leaves unexplained a large part of the upward trend in numbers. We therefore examine several other possible factors, notably the expanding research interests of government. The purpose in these sections is to explain the long-term trend of demand; thereafter we examine the effects upon the demand for engineers and chemists of the short-run fluctuations in business conditions. Finally, we discuss the relationship between the net demand for engineers and the total (gross) demand for new entrants into the profession, which is larger by the losses of personnel from the profession.

---

[1] In addition a small number, usually estimated at about 2 per cent, were employed as teachers in higher education, and still smaller numbers are found in nonprofit organizations.

1. Industrial Patterns in the Use of Engineers and Chemists

It is natural to approach the problem of explaining changes in the past demand for engineers and chemists—and therefore to predicting their future course—by starting with the distribution of these occupations among industries. If we find large and stable differences among industries in the employment of technical personnel, we may be able to explain a considerable portion of the changing demand for such personnel. Everyone knows that there are large differences among industries in this respect: an engineer is an oddity in a department store, and a familiar sight in a factory producing machinery. We set forth these differences, in the detail that the census materials permit, in Table 23.

Even with the large differences observable among industries in the nature of their tasks and the manner in which they are performed, the differences in employment of technical personnel could be volatile and almost accidental. For example, if some chemical firms hired many chemists, and others relied extensively upon either other industries (such as the research firms) or other types of workers, where substitution is possible—then any underlying continuity of an industry's technology would not insure continuity of employment of technical personnel. The differences among industries would be a treacherous or at least a highly ambiguous basis for explaining the employment of technical personnel.

There is a good reason, however, for believing that the differences among industries in the employment of technical personnel are not greatly subject to such capricious influences: the interindustry differences have been relatively stable. Thus the correlation between the percentages of engineers and chemists to all employees in 1930 and in 1940 was 0.88 for 31 minor industry groups; the corresponding coefficient for 1940 and 1950 (for 39 minor industry groups) was 0.95. Particularly in the second decade, when the number of engineers and chemists rose from 350,000 to 610,000, the stability of the interindustry differences is most impressive.

The regression equation connecting the 1950 and 1940 industry ratios of engineers and chemists to total labor force was

$$\frac{\text{E\&C 1950}}{\text{Labor Force}} \times 100 = -0.581 + 1.435 \frac{\text{E\&C 1940}}{\text{Labor Force}} \times 100$$

where E&C denotes engineers and chemists. The various industries on average fell fairly close to this line of average relationship; in

TABLE 23

Chemists and Technical Engineers as a Percentage of Total Employment, Selected Industries, 1930–1950

	INCLUDING SURVEYORS			EXCLUDING SURVEYORS	
	Per Cent of All Gainful Workers 1930	Per Cent of Estimated Employment 1930	Per Cent of Total Employment 1940 (comparable to 1930)	Per Cent of Total Employment 1940 (comparable to 1950)	Per Cent of Total Employment 1950
. Mining, total	0.79	0.87	1.21	1.11	1.49
a. Coal mining	0.36		0.39	0.32	0.51
b. Petroleum and natural gas	1.03		2.25	2.01	3.13
c. Metal mining	1.81		3.06	2.99	2.94
d. Other, including quarried	1.67		1.47	1.45	1.34
. Construction	1.05	1.16	2.17	1.96	2.27
anufacturing a	1.34	1.47	2.04	2.04	3.10
urable goods a	1.19	1.26	2.03	2.03	3.13
. Iron and steel industries	1.11	n.a.	1.82	1.49	2.04
a. Blast furnaces, steel works	1.15		1.74	1.74	2.10
b. Other primary iron and steel	1.09		1.86	1.31	1.42 / 2.23 → 2.00
c. Miscellaneous iron and steel products					
. Nonferrous metal industries	1.43	n.a.	1.63	1.62	2.47
a. Primary nonferrous products	1.43		1.63	2.17	2.98
b. Miscellaneous nonferrous products				1.18	1.41
. Nonspecified metal industries	0.72	n.a.	2.57	1.31	2.24
. Machinery	3.12	n.a.	3.95	3.13	3.95
a. Electric machinery and equipment	3.47		4.55	4.55	4.94
b. Agricultural machinery	0.62		1.47	1.47	2.18
c. Office and store machinery	Included in 3c.		Included in 3c.	1.20	2.59
d. Miscellaneous machinery				2.65	3.62
. Transportation equipment	0.61	n.a.	1.61	1.59	3.16
a. Aircraft and parts	in 7d.		in 7d.	4.55	9.26
b. Motor vehicles and equipment	0.80		1.17	1.17	1.59
c. Ships and boats	0.48		1.20	1.15	1.97
d. Railroad and miscellaneous transportation equipment	0.15		3.64	1.46	2.72

TABLE 23 (continued)

	INCLUDING SURVEYORS			EXCLUDING SURVEYORS	
	Per Cent of All Gainful Workers 1930	Per Cent of Estimated Employment 1930	Per Cent of Total Employment 1940 (comparable to 1930)	Per Cent of Total Employment 1940 (comparable to 1950)	Per Cent of Total Employment 1950
8. Professional equipment and instruments	0.28		0.63	1.98	4.01
a. Professional equipment	Included in 5.		Included in 5.	} 3.15	4.11
b. Photographic equipment					5.86
c. Watches, clocks, time-pieces	0.28		0.63	0.63	1.20
Nondurable goods a	1.67	1.75	2.06	2.05	3.04
9. Food, drink, tobacco	0.40	0.42	0.53	0.53	0.88
10. Chemicals and allied products	5.23	5.36	4.81	4.80	6.70
a. Synthetic fibres	2.13		2.21	2.21	4.16
b. Paints, varnishes, etc.	3.85		6.10	6.10	6.04
c. Drugs and medicines	} 5.85		} 5.04	} 5.04	6.26 } 7.02
d. Miscellaneous chemicals					7.11
11. Petroleum and coal products	3.19	3.27	5.29	5.22	6.57
a. Petroleum refining	3.24		5.56	5.49	6.92
b. Miscellaneous petroleum and coal products	2.52		3.19	3.19	3.32
12. Rubber products	1.18	1.24	1.91	1.91	2.10
Transportation communications and other public utilities	1.06	1.09	1.26	1.28	1.41
13. Transportation	0.54	0.56	0.40	0.39	0.41
a. Air transportation	2.57		2.15	1.97	1.33
b. Railroads and express service	0.65		0.51	0.50	0.45
c. Streetcars and buses	0.79		0.44	0.44	0.41
d. Trucking and taxicabs	0.01		0.02	0.02	0.07
e. Warehousing and storage	0.72		0.39	0.39	0.86
f. Water transportation	0.44		0.22	0.18	0.24
g. Pipelines	0.87		2.64	2.53	4.90
h. Incident, transportation services	1.06		0.60	0.60	0.72
14. Communications	1.53	1.54	1.73	1.73	2.15
a. Postal service	0		0.03	0.03	0.03
b. Telephone	} 2.21		} 2.65	} 2.65	2.62 } 2.51
c. Telegraph					1.10
d. Radio and television	6.06		9.66	9.66	14.03

TABLE 23 (continued)

	INCLUDING SURVEYORS			EXCLUDING SURVEYORS	
	Per Cent of All Gainful Workers 1930	Per Cent of Estimated Employment 1930	Per Cent of Total Employment 1940 (comparable to 1930)	Per Cent of Total Employment 1940 (comparable to 1950)	Per Cent of Total Employment 1950
5. Utilities and sanitary services	3.54	3.63	4.96	4.35	4.06
a. Electric light and power	4.37		5.65	5.54	5.09
b. Gas supply	1.45		2.34	2.29	2.41
c. Water supply	n.a.		excl.	} 2.55	4.69 } 2.78
d. Sanitary services	n.a.		excl.		1.11
e. Not specified utilities	n.a.		excl.		
16. Professional and related services					
Including education	1.95	1.97	0.78		
Excluding education				1.21	1.48
a. Engineering architectural services	} 1.95	} 1.97	} 0.78	} 1.21	30.51 } 1.48
b. Other professional services					0.52
17. Education				0.14	0.37
a. Government	} Included in 16			} 0.14	0.32 } 0.37
b. Private					0.52
18. Public administration					
Including armed forces	2.57		2.44		
Excluding armed forces				2.59	2.68
a. Federal government				3.80	3.64
b. State government				1.97	2.02 } 1.74
c. Local government					1.64
Subtotal, above industries	1.37		1.64	1.58	2.13
All other industries [b]	0.10		0.14	0.12	0.25
Total, all industries					
Including armed forces	0.56		0.69		
Excluding armed forces				0.66	1.06

n.a. = not available.

[a] Includes industries listed under this heading; excludes manufacturing industries included in "All other industries" enumerated in footnote b.

[b] Includes agriculture, forestry, fisheries; the following manufacturing industries: lumber and wood products, glass products, stone and clay products, textiles and clothing, paper and printing, leather and leather products; and wholesale and retail trade, finance, insurance and real estate, business and repair services, entertainment and recreation, and personal services.

Source: Census of Population, 1930, 1940, and 1950 (for details, see Appendix B).

fact 90 per cent of the variance in the 1950 industry ratios is accounted for by this regression equation. The departures from the average relationship are too small to offer much of a clue to the factors affecting the relative employment of engineers but we may use them to study one disturbing factor.

Scientific personnel employed in industry may be divided into two classes: those engaged in functions related to current production, such as production supervision, testing, sales, and management; and those engaged in research. The distinction is of course somewhat imprecise, but it is implicitly recognized not only in the creation of separate research laboratories but also in the penchant of engineering societies for asking information on the members' type of work.[2]

We would expect scientific personnel engaged in production or management activities to be more closely geared in the long run to the industry's labor force than those engaged in research. If the distribution among industries of the rate of growth of research personnel differs from the distribution of and rate of growth of the remainder of scientific personnel, then a portion of the deviations of industries from the standard pattern of change in employment of engineers and chemists would be attributable to the growth in research activities. We have sought to test this possibility by four methods. We have compared the residuals from the regression equation given above (page 48) with:

----

[2] Among the activities reported in the 1946 Engineers Joint Council survey, the more important were:

Activity	Per Cent of Engineers
1. Technical administration-management	30.4
2. Nontechnical administration-management	3.6
3. Design	14.9
4. Applied research	6.8
5. Construction supervision	5.8
6. Teaching	4.4
7. Consulting (as employee)	4.2
8. Sales	4.1
9. Consulting (independent)	3.6
10. Operation	2.4
11. Analysis and testing	2.2
12. Production	2.1
13. Maintenance	1.9

Of these activities, numbers 4, 7, and 9 are presumably research, and possibly also number 3; most of the remainder would be more closely related to current production (see Andrew Fraser, *The Engineering Profession in Transition*, Engineers Joint Council, 1947, p. 24).

1. An estimate of the number of engineers engaged in research in each industry, based upon the 1946 reports of their activities.[3]
2. The growth in the number of engineers and chemists in research laboratories, classified by industry, from 1938 to 1950.[4]
3. The 1950 ratio of engineers and chemists in research laboratories in selected industries to the total number of engineers and chemists in these industries.
4. The ratio of total research engineers and chemists in selected industries to the total number of engineers and chemists in 1950.[5]

The data are so fragmentary that not more than ten industries can be studied by any one of these methods, and this is of course the reason so many approaches were followed.

A low degree of positive association is found between the regression residuals and estimates of scientific personnel in research made on each of these four bases. For example, the public utilities (other than telephone and telegraph) have a negative residual, and rank low in research personnel by our tests.[6] At the other extreme, transportation equipment (except motor vehicles) had a large positive residual and this industry had relatively many people in research.[7] The correlation, to repeat, was not high, but the largest residuals were in general agreement with expectations.

[3] *Employment Outlook for Engineers* (Bureau of Labor Statistics, Bull. 968, 1949) gives data on the activities of engineers in each major engineering field.
[4] *Industrial Research Laboratories of the United States,* National Research Council, 1950.
[5] Total research engineers and chemists were estimated by applying an expansion ratio to the number reported as working in industrial laboratories. This ratio was derived by comparing the total number of research scientists in each of the 20 largest firms in each industry, as reported to BLS in their 1951 study, with the number reported as working in industrial laboratories.
[6] Only 1.1 per cent of their engineers and chemists were in research laboratories in 1950 (the third measure above); only 3.5 per cent of their electrical engineers were in research (excluding design) in 1946 (the first measure); and research personnel in laboratories fell 26.8 per cent from 1938 to 1950 (the second measure).
[7] Thus engineers and chemists in research laboratories grew 3,535 per cent from 1938 to 1950 in this industry, and represented 16.2 per cent of all engineers and chemists in aircraft in 1950, although only 5.2 per cent in railroads, including equipment; total research engineers and chemists in the aircraft industry represented about 39 per cent of all the industry's engineers and chemists in 1950; and 22.6 per cent of the mechanical engineers in the entire transportation equipment industry (including motor vehicles) were engaged in research (excluding design) in 1946.

With more precise definitions of research and operating scientific personnel, and with better data, this hypothesis could be tested more conclusively, but it appears promising and may well account for most of the deviations from the standard pattern of industrial distribution of employment of engineers and chemists.

THE EFFECT OF CHANGING EMPLOYMENT WEIGHTS

The stability of the pattern of ratios of engineers and chemists to the labor force for the various industries is a useful piece of information in explaining changes in the demand for these groups. If industries employing relatively many engineers and chemists expand, and other industries contract, we are able to estimate the resulting effect upon total relative employment of these technological professions.

To be more specific, suppose that in 1930 we had predicted correctly the general distribution of the employed labor force among industries in 1940. Then we should have predicted that the number of employed engineers and chemists would rise from 0.56 to 0.61 per cent of the employed labor force, assuming no change in the ratio of engineers and chemists to total employment in each industry.[8] The actual 1940 figure was 0.69 per cent, so we have explained roughly $5/13$ of the growth of engineers and chemists relative to the labor force. A similar analysis for the decade 1940 to 1950 would have indicated a rise in the percentage from 0.66 to 0.79, whereas the actual increase was from 0.66 to 1.06.[9] Here our knowledge of the industry patterns explains $13/40$ of the growth of the engineers and chemists relative to the labor force.[10]

[8] Here we use the estimates based upon major industries in Table 23. They differ somewhat from the estimates based upon the more numerous and homogeneous minor industry groups, but are more comprehensive.

[9] The figure for 1940 differs between the two comparisons because of differing labor force concepts. The 1940 figure used in the comparison with 1930 includes surveyors among engineers and includes the armed forces in total employment. The 1940 figure used in comparison with 1950 excludes both.

[10] If one calculates the change in employment of engineers due to changing industrial structure, and subtracts it from the total change in employment, he gets an estimate of the effect upon employment of the rising ratios in most industries. If instead he calculates directly the effect upon employment of changes in the ratios, he gets another estimate. The latter will differ from the former ($11/13$ versus $8/13$ in 1930 to 1940, and $24/40$ versus $27/40$ in 1940 to 1950) unless changes in industry ratios and changes in industry structure are uncorrelated (see Irving H. Siegel, *Concepts and Measurement of Production and Productivity*, Bureau of Labor Statistics, 1952). For our purpose, the

These illustrative calculations indicate the limited scope as well as the usefulness of the knowledge of industrial patterns of employment. In the 1930 to 1940 decade $5/13$ (or 38.5 per cent) of the relative growth of engineers or chemists is explained; in the 1940 to 1950 decade $13/40$ (or 37.5 per cent) is explained. Thus roughly one-third of the relative growth of these occupations in the two decades can be explained by this approach, given a knowledge of the industrial composition of the labor force.

TABLE 24

Hypothetical Ratio of Engineers and Chemists to Total Labor Force, Assuming Industry Ratios Constant at the Average of Their 1930, 1940 and 1950 Levels, 1890–1950

Year	Ratio
1890	0.46%
1900	0.48
1910	0.58
1920	0.70
1930	0.71
1940	0.76
1950	0.88

Source: Industry ratios from Table 23. Industry employment or labor force estimates from *Census of Population, 1940* and *1950;* Daniel Carson, "Changes in the Industrial Composition of Manpower since the Civil War," in *Studies in Income and Wealth, Volume Nineteen,* National Bureau of Economic Research, 1949; Alba M. Edwards, *Comparative Occupation Statistics for the United States, 1870 to 1940,* Bureau of the Census, 1943; Solomon Fabricant, *The Trend of Government Activity in the United States since 1900,* National Bureau of Economic Research, 1952, and "The Changing Industrial Distribution of Gainful Workers," in *Studies in Income and Wealth, Volume Nineteen.*

We can perform a similar though cruder calculation for the entire period 1890–1950. If we compute the ratio of engineers and chemists to total labor force (or total employment) that would have existed in each decennial year since 1890 had each industry maintained its individual ratio at the average of its level for 1930, 1940 and 1950, we obtain the series in Table 24. With fixed industry ratios, the aggregate ratio of engineers and chemists to the labor force would have almost doubled over the 60 years, rising from about 0.46 per cent in 1890 to 0.88 per cent in 1950. This rise of 0.42 percentage

former estimate (which is used in the text) seems preferable: there is more information available to estimate changes in the industrial structure of the labor force than to estimate changes in the ratios.

points accounts for somewhat more than 40 per cent of the total change in the actual ratio over the six decades (Table 25).[11]

TABLE 25

Decade Increments in the Ratio of Engineers and Chemists
to the Labor Force, 1890–1950

	Actual Increments (1)	Increments Due to Changing Employment Patterns (2)	Residuals (col. 1 — col. 2) (3)	Col. 2 as % of Col. 1 (4)
1890–1900	0.04%	0.02%	0.02%	50.0
1900–1910	0.10	0.10	0.00	100.0
1910–1920	0.12	0.12	0.00	100.0
1920–1930	0.17	0.01	0.16	5.9
1930–1940	0.11	0.05	0.06	45.5
1940–1950	0.40	0.12	0.28	30.0
1890–1920	0.26	0.24	0.02	92.3
1920–1950	0.68	0.18	0.50	26.5
1890–1950	0.94	0.42	0.52	44.7

Source: Tables 23 and 24.

Although little weight can be attached to the precise values presented in Tables 24 and 25, both because the employment data are weaker in the earlier years and because we are forced to use a more limited and more broadly defined list of industries in this calculation, the outlines of the relationships are quite clear. Changing employment patterns, i.e. the more rapid growth of industries which employ relatively many engineers and chemists, accounted for the bulk of the change in the national ratio in the first three of the six decades, and for as little as a third of the aggregate change in the last three decades.

[11] There may have been a general positive correlation between changes in industry employment and changes in industry ratios. Accordingly, this procedure may assign to changes in employment patterns a somewhat larger share of the total change than would have been obtained had we been able to estimate the change in the aggregate ratio due to changing industry ratios and then derive the effect of employment changes as a residual. Further, the difference between the two methods of estimation may increase as we go back in time. But the broad conclusions are probably unaffected by this problem. In the two decades for which we can test this procedure, 1930–1940 and 1940–1950 (there are no industry ratio data before 1930), we have seen that the effect of changing employment weights is underestimated in one decade and overestimated in the other.

2. The Role of Government

The federal government has had a rapidly expanding program of research in the past fifteen years (see Chapter I, Section 3). This program has included some fields in which the government has been expanding its activities for many decades, but primarily it consists of research in areas related to national defense. Much of this research is conducted by private companies working on contracts with the federal government, and it is natural to ask: how much of the rising trend of employment in the technological professions is due to this governmental support?

Before 1940 the answer was that essentially none was due to governmental support. For the period since 1940 we may form an estimate along these lines: In the decade to 1950, governmental expenditures on research and development increased by $1.6 billions, whereas all expenditure on research and development increased by $2.5 billions.[12] Thus two-thirds of the increase in such expenditures was governmental, and so governmental research programs account for approximately two-thirds of the increase in employment of engineers and scientists in research and development, or roughly 50,000. If the employment on government contracts constituted a net addition to the demand for members of the technological professions, the government would be responsible for only about one-fifth of the increase in the total number of engineers between 1940 and 1950.[13]

The number of engineers and scientists working on government research contracts is not an exact measure of the addition such contracts make to the demand for these professions. At one extreme it might happen that private businesses first take on government research contracts, as a result become persuaded of the benefits of research, and then embark upon private research also—so that the government contracts serve a sort of pump-priming function. At the other extreme, research that the businesses had been conducting on their own account might simply be shifted to public contracts,

[12] See Table 6. The figures are for the decade 1941 to 1951 since data are not available for 1940.

[13] This may be restated in the terms we employed earlier (p. 54): Engineers and chemists were 0.66 per cent of the labor force in 1940, 1.06 per cent in 1950. In the absence of the governmental employment, on research programs, the ratio would have been about 0.98 in 1950, and substantially unchanged in 1940. Of the rise of 0.40 percentage points (from 0.66 to 1.06) changes in industry composition accounted for 0.13 points and governmental employment 0.08 points—the two together account for half the rise in the ratio.

so these contracts would constitute no net additional demand. Of course both of these extremes are wholly improbable, but so too is the intermediate situation in which the public research constitutes exactly a net addition to total research.

Perhaps the most efficient, and certainly the most direct, way to discover the extent of substitution of public for private research would be to trace the history of research programs of a suitable sample of companies, including some which had experienced large increases and decreases in government contracts. Such a study has not yet been made, however, so we must glean what information we can from a comparison of research programs of private firms at a given time.

Through the cooperation of the Bureau of Labor Statistics we have data on governmentally supported and privately supported research in 1951 for nearly all of the 1,564 manufacturing firms who reported their industrial research and development activity in a recent survey.[14] These manufacturing firms accounted for about nine-tenths of the dollar volume of research in all private businesses reporting to the BLS, and the survey covered perhaps 85 per cent of the nation's research by business, so our sample covers about three-quarters of all privately conducted research (i.e., nongovernment and nonuniversity research) in the United States. For most of these firms we know (1) size of firm, measured by total employment, January 1952; (2) engineers and scientists on government research as a percentage of total employment, January 1952; (3) engineers and scientists on private research as a percentage of total employment, January 1952; and (4) corresponding figures on the operating cost of research (public and private separately) as a percentage of total sales, 1951.

Perhaps the simplest direct test of possible substitution of public for *private* research is given by comparing the percentage of technological professional workers to all employment for firms with and without government research (Table 26). One may say, as a rough first generalization, that if relatively fewer technological professionals are hired for *private* research by those firms that engage also in public research, then it would appear that public research is partly substituted for private research.

And this proves to be the case. In every industry category except

[14] *Scientific Research and Development in American Industry*, Bureau of Labor Statistics, Bull. 1148, 1953.

two (photographic equipment and supplies; paper and allied products), the percentage of engineers and scientists in private research to total employment is lower for firms with government contracts than for those firms without contracts. If we strike an average by weighting the industry ratios in Table 26 by the total employment

TABLE 26

Average Ratio of Engineers and Scientists Engaged in Private Research to Total Employment in Manufacturing Firms, by Industry, January 1952

Industry	*Ratio of Engineers and Scientists Engaged in Private Research to Total Employment in Manufacturing Firms* [a]	
	Firms with Government-Supported Research	Firms with No Government-Supported Research
Chemicals	3.1%	3.8%
Petroleum	1.6	2.5
Electrical machinery	0.8	1.8
Motor vehicles	0.4	1.5
Aircraft	0.4	1.9
Other transportation equipment	0.2	0.8
Professional and scientific instruments (except photographic)	1.6	3.6
Photographic equipment and supplies	1.6	1.5
Food and kindred products	0.5	1.2
Textile mill products and apparel	0.4	0.9
Paper and allied products	0.7	0.7
Rubber products	1.1	1.4
Stone, clay and glass products	0.7	1.2
Primary metal products	0.6	1.2
Fabricated metal products	0.4	1.3
Machinery (except electrical)	1.0	1.7
All other manufacturing	0.5	1.1

[a] Excluding those firms whose ratios of engineers and scientists on public or private research to total employment exceeded 10 per cent.

Source: Company reports underlying *Scientific Research and Development in American Industry,* Bureau of Labor Statistics, Bull. 1148, 1953.

in each industry, we find that research engineers and scientists on private work were 0.7 per cent of all employment in firms having government contracts, 1.4 per cent in firms having no government contracts. But the engineers and scientists who worked on government contracts were 0.8 per cent of all employment in firms with government contracts, so we can say—as a first approximation—that seven-eighths of professional employment on government research contracts represents a substitution of public for private re-search.[15]

Even before we begin to qualify this rough estimate, we should notice that "substitution" is the economist's generic word for a whole class of phenomena, and does not simply mean that the government begins to pay for an activity that previously was privately paid for. It may be difficult to supervise efficiently, or to implement the small-scale experiments of, more than a given number of scientists, and then when a firm accepts a government contract, it is compelled to abandon some researches in which it was previously engaged. To what extent "substitution" is literally a transfer of finance without a change of activity we have no way of knowing.

Two objections to the inference drawn from Table 26 readily come to mind: the first is that some other factor—perhaps industrial heterogeneity—is at work; the second is that our reporting universe is possibly strongly biased. Unfortunately there is only one other factor (size of firm) that we may examine, and we do this below in connection with a test of bias. The possible biases in reporting deserve fuller discussion.

At one extreme, we might ask every firm in manufacturing in the United States for the type of information given in Table 26. We should then find that the percentages would not change much for the firms engaged in government research, since most such firms are now in the sample. On the other hand, most firms having no government research contracts also engage in no private research, so the figures in the second column of Table 26 would fall drastically.[16] Then we would be inclined to infer that government contracts serve a pump-priming function. This is of course an improper universe of firms to consider, simply because the vast majority of firms do not and under present conditions should not and will not

[15] When one makes a comparable analysis with the ratio of operating costs of research to sales, a quite similar pattern is found. But it differs in two noteworthy respects: (1) In five industry categories the operating cost ratio of private research for firms with government research is equal to or slightly higher than the ratio for firms with only private research; and (2) the ratios are more nearly equal in most industries. There is no reason to expect costs to be in strict proportion to scientific personnel, but these differences suggest that our seventeen manufacturing industry categories are uncomfortably wide for our purposes.

[16] Assume there were 50,000 research workers in private research in manufacturing in January 1952. Then they amounted to about 0.3 per cent of total employment in manufacturing.

engage in any kind of formal research requiring the services of engineers and scientists.

At another extreme, one may consider only those firms which are presently engaged in *both* private and public research—the total sample of 1,199 [17] contains 260 firms engaged in only government research, and 602 firms engaged only in private research. We have made this tabulation, and in general substitution is now almost absent (see Table 27). For we find that the higher the ratio of engineers and scientists in private research to total employment, the higher

TABLE 27

Average Ratios of Engineers and Scientists Engaged in Government-Supported Research and Private Research to Total Employment in Manufacturing Firms Engaging in Both Types of Research, by Industry, January 1952 [a]

Ratio of Scientists and Engineers in Government-Supported Research to Total [a] Employment	Ratio of Scientists and Engineers in Private Research to Total Employment								
	Chemicals	Petroleum	Electrical Machinery	Aircraft	Professional and Scientific Instruments	Textiles and Apparel	Rubber	Fabricated Metal Products	Machinery (except elec.)
0.1–0.4%	3.2%	1.1%	1.2%	0.3%	1.0%	0.4%	1.3%	0.7%	1.1%
0.5–0.9	5.4		0.8	0.7	2.4	1.3	0.7	1.0	1.6
1.0–1.9	4.8	1.5	1.4	0.8	2.3			0.8	1.6
2.0–3.9	5.1	4.1	1.3		4.0		4.0		1.6
4.0–5.9	6.8		1.8	4.3	3.0				
6.0–7.9			1.6		3.9				
8.0–9.9					6.7				
10.0 or greater			6.5		5.6				

[a] Excluding those cases in which only one firm fell into a class interval and a few cases with extreme ratios.

Source: Same as in Table 26.

on average is also the public ratio. But here the objection is that firms which already engage in private research on a large scale are more likely to get large government contracts. Moreover, here we omit all firms which wholly abandoned private research when they received government contracts, and there may have been some such firms among the 260 that did only government research.

The best we can do is to take into account the size of each firm,

[17] This is the total number of firms for which ratios of employment of scientists and engineers on public and on private research to total employment were available.

measured by total employment. The sample should be much more reliable for the largest size of firm (5,000 or more employees), where the coverage of the underlying universe is the fullest. This comparison indicates that the substitution effect, which seems very large in the smallest firms, more than vanishes in the largest firms (see Table 28). We do not interpret this as strong evidence of a complementary ("pump-priming") relation of public to privately financed research, because the coverage of the largest firms is by no means complete. But the comparison does suggest strongly that the crude estimate of substitution derived from the aggregate data grossly exaggerates the forces making for a substitutive relation.

TABLE 28

Engineers and Scientists on Private Research as
Per Cent of Total Employment, 1952

Employment of Firm	Firms with Government Research	Firms with No Government Research
Under 500	0.7%	3.0%
500 to 5,000	0.8	1.8
5,000 or more	0.7	0.5
All	0.7	1.4

Source: Same as in Table 26.

3. The Upward Trend of Demand

We have found that roughly $\frac{4}{10}$ of the increase in the ratio of engineers and chemists to total employment is due to changes in industrial structure—to the more rapid growth of industries which employ relatively more of the technological professions. A small additional part of the increase in their employment is due to the expansion of government research in the period after 1940, for it appears that this research has been largely a net addition to private research. But this leaves us with half or more of the relative increase in the ratio of these professions to total employment still to be explained.

The ratio of engineers and chemists to total labor force has risen at different rates over the range of industries. The growth has been most rapid in those industries in which the ratio had already reached the highest level, in 1940, so that over time the differences among industries have been increasing. The coefficient of variation of industry ratios for 39 minor industry groups (see Table 23) was 84.2 per cent in 1940, 106.5 per cent in 1950.

There are two main possible explanations of this rising absolute and relative trend of demand. The first is that reductions in the relative cost of highly trained personnel have led to the substitution of this class of workers for skilled or unskilled workers. The second is that changes in the technology of production have increased the relative demand for highly trained personnel. One or both of these main forces presumably account for most of the upward drift we have not explained.

For the last quarter century the cost of engineers—their salaries—has fallen relative to that of the working population as a whole, as we showed in Chapter II. It is probable that this trend began much earlier, for the rapid growth of trained engineers began much earlier. Through a variety of channels this relative reduction in the cost of trained personnel probably led to the substitution of such personnel for other classes of workers.

Direct substitution—the transfer of the identical task from another type of worker to an engineer—probably has been limited chiefly to the transfer of tasks involving much technological knowledge from supervisory and highly skilled workers to the professionally trained engineers.[18]

Indirect substitution was probably much more important. The growth in formal training of engineers merely parallels that of the entire working force: the increase in the average period of schooling, and the virtual disappearance of immigrant labor, have greatly reduced the relative supply of wholly manual and nonresponsible labor. As a result, unskilled labor has become relatively expensive, and thus fostered mechanization of routine tasks. The extensive substitution of capital for labor probably involves also the substitution of professional workers, who install and maintain the increasingly intricate forms of capital, for the laborers whose tasks have been taken over. One may conjecture that differences among industries in the relative employment of the technological professions broadly parallel differences among industries in the amount of durable producer goods employed per worker.

The effect of technological and scientific progress upon the demand for scientifically trained workers is universally remarked. It is platitudinous to observe that scientific knowledge is rapidly ac-

---

[18] It would probably require close analysis of the functions of the engineer and chemist to determine the areas and measure the extent of direct substitution. Our statistical experiments in measuring substitution as against broad classes of skilled operatives have been uninformative.

cumulating, that this knowledge is rendering production methods more complex and making the best methods of any given time more quickly obsolescent—and so creating a demand for the trained engineer and scientist. Thus a recent Bureau of Labor Statistics survey of the demand for chemists and chemical engineers found that the development of more complex methods of production (e.g., the shift from batch to continuous processing) and more complex products (e.g., antibiotics) were the most important factors, in the opinion of the companies interviewed, in increasing their demand for scientifically trained personnel.[19]

But there is no warrant for the assertion that a rising demand for scientifically trained personnel is part and parcel of modern industries, or that any simple extrapolation of past trends is likely to yield good results. The layman, at least, believes that commercial production and scientific research are closely associated in chemical and electrical industries. And it is true that the ratio of engineers and chemists to total employment is high in chemicals and petroleum refining (6.7 and 6.9 per cent respectively in 1950). But there is no uniformity or stability in patterns among the chemical industries: the ratio has risen continuously in petroleum refining, it fell slightly from 1940 to 1950 in paints and varnishes, and it rose only after 1940 in drugs and miscellaneous chemicals (see Table 23). Again: the ratio has been high in the electrical industries, but it has fallen since 1940 in the electric utilities while rising slowly in electrical machinery and rising rapidly in radio and television.

But conversely there is good reason for believing that the differences among industries are governed by powerful technological and economic forces, and are not accidental or spurious. Our analysis of the 1953 data of the Engineers Joint Council reveals the following ratios of engineers to total employment:

	Quartiles		
	Q_1	Q_2	Q_3
Railroads	0.002	0.003	0.005
Primary metals and fabricated metal products	.008	.018	.027
Petroleum refining	.031	.047	.067
Public utilities	.031	.047	.053

[19] "Demand for Personnel in the Chemical Professions, a Preliminary Report on a Pilot Survey of the Chemical, Petroleum, and Rubber Industries," processed, Bureau of Labor Statistics, June 1954.

There is substantial variation in the ratio among firms in an industry, so it is evident that technological considerations do not dictate a unique role for engineers, but these intra-industry differences are often vastly smaller than the differences among industries. The relative roles of economic choice and technological necessity in determining the demand for engineers, one may conjecture, would be much illuminated by closer studies of the differences among plants of a given company, and differences between American and (say) British or German employment practices.

The determination of forces governing the employment of scientific personnel in research is surely even more complex. Industrial research is still a relatively recent development, and much of it must still be based more upon a reading of the future than a lesson drawn from the past. But the future is easily misread, and the contemporary industrial differences in research programs may change radically in the light of experience. The differences among industries, and within industries among firms, in the employment of scientific personnel on research are probably considerably larger than the differences in the employment of such personnel for current production. We present some abbreviated distributions for four industries in Table 29; they may overestimate the differences among firms because they take no account of research performed for the companies on contract by commercial laboratories specializing in research.

TABLE 29

Distribution of Number of Companies and Employment in Companies Carrying on Research, by Ratio of Research Engineers and Scientists to Total Employment, in Four Industries, January 1952

Research Engineers and Scientists as Per Cent of Total Employment	Industrial Chemicals		Drugs and Medicines		Electrical Machinery		Machinery	
	Per Cent of Companies	Per Cent of Employment	Per Cent of Companies	Per Cent of Employment	Per Cent of Companies	Per Cent of Employment	Per Cent of Companies	Per Cent of Employment
Less than 1.5	12.8	7.7	14.1	14.3	26.7	59.1	52.4	66.3
1.5–2.9	23.1	62.5	18.3	55.0	22.2	30.1	19.9	28.0
3.0–4.4	17.9	13.7	11.3	3.6	15.4	6.1	7.8	3.0
4.5–5.9	7.7	3.4	12.7	20.7	10.4	2.3	5.4	1.6
6.0 and greater	38.5	12.7	43.7	6.4	25.3	2.3	14.5	1.1
Total Number of Companies and Total Employment in Sample	78	233,409	71	99,014	221	1,315,350	166	433,830

Source: Same as in Table 26.

It is worth observing that technological research makes extensive demands on the technological professions only in those industries whose techniques are fairly closely related to natural sciences. In many of the largest industrial categories the techniques are essentially pragmatic rather than scientifically based: in trade or the service industries, for example, the role of the technological professions is wholly incidental. Since industrial categories such as trade and services have been growing more rapidly than manufacturing or mining, it is at least one-sided and at most positively wrong to equate progress with a growing relative role of the technological professions in economic life.

4. *Short-Run Changes in Demand*

One would not expect that the demand by business firms for the services of engineers and chemists would necessarily respond in substantial amount to or even be in the same direction as short-run changes in business conditions. The functions performed and positions held by most engineers and scientists are somewhat removed from those areas of business operation most directly affected by short-run economic fluctuations. This distinction is most evident with regard to research workers whose activities are presumably governed by longer-run goals of the business firm, but it also applies in considerable degree to those engineers who perform administrative functions. It is not customary to hire and fire administrative employees, in response to short-run changing economic fortunes, to the degree to which employment of workers directly engaged in production is varied. These considerations are perhaps less important for engineers who are engaged in operation, testing, production, and maintenance functions, but these constitute a relatively small proportion of all engineers (see p. 52, supra).

We have made several rough tests of the degree of relationship between alternative measures of short-run changes in business activity and changes in the employment of engineers and scientists. The number of such tests and their degree of precision is severely limited by the paucity of data on employment by individual business firms of engineers and scientists. However, although the results of our experiments are somewhat ambiguous, they tend to support our expectation that there is no simple and general short-run relationship between business activity and employment of scientific personnel.

Our tests took two forms. First, using data reported to the Engineers Joint Council in their surveys of demand for engineers, we were able to determine the percentage change in engineering employment between January 1953 and January 1954 of 100 firms for which we could also obtain information from Moody's Manuals on volume of sales in 1952 and 1953. These 100 firms were classified into 13 industries. For each industry, we correlated the 1952–1953 percentage changes in sales by individual firms with the 1953–1954 percentage changes in engineering employment in the same firms. In only one industry (public utilities) was the relationship statistically significant; even here, less than one-fifth of the variation in changes in engineering employment was "accounted for" by changes in sales volume.

Second, the Bureau of Labor Statistics provided us with data on the percentage changes in employment of research engineers and scientists between January 1951 and January 1952 in roughly the twenty largest firms in each of three industries (machinery, nonelectrical; electrical machinery; chemicals), and with similar data on changes in employment of research engineers and scientists working on privately supported research. Data on the percentage changes between 1950 and 1951 in sales, profits before taxes, and profits after taxes of these firms were also collected. For each industry, we measured in turn the degree of correlation between each of these three measures of change in business activity, on the one hand, and each measure of change in research activity, on the other. For the machinery industry, none of the relationships tested was statistically significant.[20] For the electrical machinery industry, only one relationship proved to be statistically significant; a little more than half the variation in changes in employment of research personnel on private projects was associated with changes in sales volume ($r = 0.76$). For the chemical industry, two relationships were statistically significant; about half of the variance of changes in both total and private research employment was associated with changes in sales volume ($r = 0.73$ and 0.71).[21]

Although our attempts at measurement have been quite limited in scope, the results suggest that short-run changes in demand for

[20] In fact, they tended to show an inverse relationship between changes in business activity and changes in research employment.

[21] We also correlated percentage changes in sales, profits before taxes, and profits after taxes between 1947 and 1951 with the ratio of engineers and scientists (on private projects) to total employment in each firm in January 1952. Only the chemical industry showed significant positive correlations: $r = 0.60$ for profits before taxes, and $r = 0.59$ for profits after taxes.

engineers and scientists are not closely associated with changes in business activity.

5. *The Gross vs. Net Demand for Engineers*

If between two dates the number of engineers in the United States is to increase by 10,000, then more than 10,000 must enter the profession in the intervening period. Two types of losses from the profession must be made good: deaths and retirements from the labor force; and departures from engineering for other types of work.[22] We consider these losses in turn.

Estimates have been made elsewhere of current death and retirement rates for engineers [23] but it is possible to make new estimates based largely on more recent census information.

Engineers are slightly younger than most other professional or technical groups so that their losses through death and retirement are probably somewhat smaller in relation to their total numbers than would be true for other professions. Thus, the median age of all engineers in 1950 was 37.9 years, as compared with 39.0 years for all professional, technical and kindred workers.[24] Engineers were younger than 12 of the 20 other occupations in this group distinguished by the census, and, indeed, were younger than all of the traditional professions, viz. accountants, architects, clergymen, college teachers, dentists, lawyers, pharmacists, physicians, and school teachers. Chemists and other natural scientists were even younger than engineers, with median ages of 34.9 years and 35.1 years respectively.

[22] The boundaries of professional engineering work are quite vague, as we have already remarked. Sales engineers, for example, often consider themselves to be active engineers, and so too do many persons with engineering training who are in nontechnical administration.

[23] See *Effect of Defense Program on Employment Outlook in Engineering,* Bureau of Labor Statistics, Supplement to Bull. 968, August 1951, p. 4. These estimates, published in 1951, are slightly lower than our estimates. But these BLS estimates merely reproduce those in *Employment Outlook for Engineers* (p. 42), published in 1949 and derived from the 1940 number and age distribution of engineers as given in the 1940 census and the estimated additions to the supply of engineers between 1940 and 1946. Since both the BLS estimates and our estimates are based on the same set of tables of working life, the difference in level of current estimated deaths and retirements is a function of the fact that there were more engineers in 1950, as reported in the 1950 census, than the BLS forecast (in 1949). Possibly some minor differences may arise because of differences between the age distribution given by the 1950 census and that implicit in the BLS forecast. For deaths and retirement rates used, see the table on working life of urban white males in *Tables of Working Life,* Bureau of Labor Statistics, Bull. 1001, 1950, p. 22.

[24] *Census of Population, 1950,* Vol. II, Part 1, Table 127, p. 273.

Assuming that all those who were engineers in 1950 will remain engineers until they die or retire, and that new entrants consist solely of engineering graduates with bachelor's degrees,[25] we estimate that total deaths and retirements from the engineering profession averaged around 9,000 per year in the early 1950's, are currently averaging about 10,000, and will rise to about 12,000 by 1960. The annual ratio of deaths and retirements to the total number of engineers is between 1.6 and 1.7 per cent.

The losses from engineering on the score of occupational change are more difficult to estimate with the information presently available. Because of the manner in which the information is collected, it is convenient to consider here as a loss to the profession those persons who, upon graduation from an engineering school, never enter the profession—although it would be somewhat more appropriate to consider this kind of loss as a deduction from supply than as an addition to gross demand.

A variety of sample studies in the past three decades suggest that the number of new engineering graduates who do not enter the profession has been about 5 to 10 per cent of all graduates.[26]

Probably all of these surveys underestimate the losses because they are based upon questionnaires, and graduates who have left engineering were less likely to receive and respond to such questionnaires.

The most detailed information with regard to the activities entered by new college graduates of all disciplines was collected by the National Scientific Register and the Commission on Human Resources and Advanced Training in 1952 and covered a sample of

[25] Since the bulk of deaths and retirements occur at the older age levels, any error in the assumed annual flow of new college-trained entrants is of minor importance. However, there is some slight degree of underestimate involved in these figures since we have not taken into account deaths and retirements of future non-college-trained entrants, some of whom enter the profession at advanced ages.

[26] A 1924 survey of the classes of 1922, 1923 and 1924 showed 11.9 per cent in nonengineering activities (*Report of the Investigation of Engineering Education, 1923–29*, Society for the Promotion of Engineering Education, 1930, p. 257). Of a sample of engineers graduated between 1925 and 1929, 5.3 per cent reported themselves in nonengineering employment in 1929 (*Employment and Earnings in the Engineering Profession, 1929 to 1934*, Bureau of Labor Statistics, Bull. 682, 1941, p. 54). About 3.5 per cent of the graduates of 1939–1946 were engaged in nonengineering employment in 1946 (*Employment Outlook for Engineers*, p. 43). A survey of Stanford graduates showed that 6.7 per cent of the classes of 1947 and 1948 had left engineering by December 1948 (*ibid.*, p. 44). A survey of 1950 graduates indicated that 10 per cent of those with civilian jobs were outside engineering in the spring of 1951; *Effects of Defense Program on Employment Outlook in Engineering*, p. 4.

all 1951 graduates. Analysis of the data by Dael Wolfle provides more precise knowledge of the activities engaged in by new graduates in the first year after graduation than has hitherto been available.[27] Only 71 per cent of those men who received first degrees in engineering in 1951 were actively engaged in engineering work in 1952. Another 18 per cent were in the armed forces and a further 4 per cent were in full-time graduate study. About 3 per cent were working in professional fields other than engineering; 2 per cent were in business; 1 per cent were in subprofessional work; and 1 per cent had left the labor force.

Active engineers thus represented about 93 per cent of the new male engineering graduates with civilian jobs. Presumably the bulk of those in military service and in graduate school would also enter the engineering profession upon their discharge or graduation. If these men were distributed in their initial civilian jobs as were those who directly entered employment following graduation, then about 93 per cent of all new first-degree graduates in engineering in 1951 entered engineering work immediately or within three or four years. Thus the loss to the engineering profession of those new graduates who do not enter the profession upon graduation amounted to 7 per cent—and this figure is likely to hold in the future in periods of high demand for engineers' services.

The final category of loss to the engineering profession consists of engineers who transfer into other lines of work during their active working life. Data are even more fragmentary on this form of loss. The BLS survey of the engineering profession in 1946 indicated that about 3 per cent of the engineers active in engineering work in 1939 were engaged in nonengineering activities in 1946, or a rate of transfer out of the profession of almost one-half of 1 per cent per year.[28] This probably represents a low estimate of current transfers, both because of nonreporting by inactive engineers in the 1946 survey and because of the very high level of demand for engineers during the war years. Indeed, there were undoubtedly a significant number of returns to the profession during the war by former engineers who had been unable to obtain engineering work during the depression.

A survey of the 1953 occupational distribution of the graduates of the classes of 1930, 1940, and 1951 of two large universities was

[27] Dael Wolfle, *America's Resources of Specialized Talent*, Harper, 1954, pp. 62–71, 99.
[28] *Employment Outlook for Engineers*, p. 43.

conducted by the National Scientific Register and the Commission on Human Resources and Advanced Training. The results of this survey were converted into an estimate of the 1953 occupational distribution of all living college graduates (under the age of seventy) by Dael Wolfle and his staff.[29] Of all engineering school graduates:

- 64 per cent were in engineering work in 1953
- 3 per cent were in other professional fields
- 10 per cent were in business
- 5 per cent, in administration, outside of business and elementary or secondary education [30]
- 10 per cent, in nonprofessional work
- 2 per cent, in full-time graduate study
- 5 per cent, not in the labor force

The graduates who were not in the civilian labor force included those retired, whose loss we treated earlier, and those in military service, who presumably would return to the profession upon discharge. Similarly, those in graduate study presumably would engage in engineering activities upon receipt of an advanced degree. Further, of the 15 per cent in business and in administration a very substantial proportion undoubtedly considered themselves actively engaged in engineering work or drawing heavily upon their engineering background, as Wolfle observes. Thus, of the total number of living graduates of engineering schools in 1953, excluding only those who were retired, possibly 21 or 22 per cent were engaged in nonengineering work.

Of this total, we have seen that perhaps 5 to 7 per cent have never engaged in engineering at all. The remaining 14 to 17 per cent actually left engineering employment to enter other lines of work. Since engineers in 1953 had a median age of about 36 years, and since the typical graduation age is 22, this total of transfers implies an annual rate of transfer out of the profession of about 1 per cent or slightly higher.[31]

The estimate of 1 per cent loss through transfer probably is a

---

[29] Wolfle, op. cit., pp. 49–61, 302–307. ". . . the actual numbers in the three graduating classes [were] differentially weighted to approximate the age distribution of all living college graduates" (p. 302).

[30] College presidents and deans, directors of laboratories, etc.

[31] We have no data on the rate of loss to the profession of engineers who did not graduate from engineering school. It is possible that the nongraduates have a lower rate of transfer out than graduates, since entrance of the former into the profession in many cases is the result of many years of effort and represents their peak of professional attainment.

high estimate for the current period since it includes the substantial numbers who left the profession during the depression.[32] The most reasonable estimate lies somewhere between the one-half of 1 per cent rate derived by BLS in 1946 and the 1 per cent rate derived from Wolfle's data, say about three-quarters of 1 per cent per year.

There is no evidence as to whether younger or older engineers have a higher rate of transfer out of the profession. The only recent survey which reports on the proportion of engineering graduates, classified by year of graduation, who have left the engineering profession is one conducted by Stevens Institute of Technology on its alumni.[33] This survey presents data on every fifth class from 1902 to 1952. When the proportion in each class reporting nonengineering work in 1954 has been adjusted for that proportion which probably entered nonengineering work immediately upon graduation, the implied annual rates of transfer out of the profession show no clear pattern when related to years since graduation (for detail, see Appendix G).

To sum up, then, each year during the present decade the engineering profession has losses of about 1.6 or 1.7 per cent through death and retirement and perhaps 0.75 per cent through transfers to other lines of work. Further, about 7 per cent of the new engineering graduates in each year immediately enter nonengineering work. On this basis, we may estimate total losses at almost 17,000 in 1950, slightly more than 17,000 in 1955, and rising to 20,000 or 21,000 by 1960 and perhaps to about 27,000 or 28,000 by 1970. Of this latter total, about 60 per cent will be accounted for by death and retirement, about 30 per cent by transfers out of the profession, and the remainder by new graduates entering other lines of work.

To meet the demand for replacements for these losses, and the demand for the net future increments to the profession, three sources of supply will be called upon. These sources include: (1) new engineering school graduates; (2) graduates of other disciplines; and (3) others who are not college graduates but who may enter the profession through on-the-job training or other kinds of noncollegiate education. The prospects for the supply of engineers from these sources will be discussed in Chapter IV.

[32] At least 50,000 engineers under the age of 35 in 1930 left the profession during the thirties, according to calculations based on the 1930 and 1940 censuses of population (see *Employment Outlook for Engineers*, p. 87).

[33] *A Report on Engineering Careers*, reprint from *Stevens Indicator*, Stevens Institute of Technology, October 1954, p. 8.

CHAPTER IV

THE SUPPLY OF ENGINEERS

IN THE past the engineering profession has been able to grow at a very high rate, and even to raise the educational level of its entrants. The primary reason for this great increase in supply, even with salaries falling relative to the working population, is that it was highly remunerative for a young man to get college training. The additional earnings over those of a high school graduate compensated manyfold for the additional costs of college training.

This is still true, although to a lesser degree. In 1950 the average income of an engineer was about $5,300 per year, whereas the average income of a male with high school education was about $3,200.[1] The additional costs of college training—of which the largest component is four years' postponement of income—would be about 25 or 30 per cent of the earnings of a high school graduate.[2] Since the differential is about 65 per cent, it is still quite remunerative to get college training for engineering, and we may expect numbers to continue to grow.

To this broad conclusion one must make one major qualification: It may not be possible to recruit the same quality of young men in the future, for total demands for highly trained individuals are now both high and growing. We discuss this at a later point.

But this broad answer to the question of future supply is only a beginning. One wishes also to know the future roles of college-trained and other engineers, the extent of graduate training, the appropriateness of the choice of field for specialization, and the like. We turn to these questions.

Entrants to the engineering profession may be classified into two general groups. One group consists of those with four or more years of college training, and holding at least a bachelor's or first professional degree, usually but not invariably from an engineering school. It is this group about which most discussion of additions to the supply of engineers centers. The second group comprises those who have entered the profession with less than four years of

[1] *Census of Population, 1950,* Vol. II, Part 1, Table 129; *Census of Population, 1950,* Special Report P-E 58, *Education,* Table 12.
[2] For a detailed discussion of this problem, see Milton Friedman and Simon Kuznets, *Income from Independent Professional Practice,* National Bureau of Economic Research, 1945.

college training. These engineers may have had several years of college, or have graduated from noncollegiate technical institutes or may simply have been trained on the job. We have already noticed (in Chapter I) that there is some controversy over the proportion of this group which should be called engineers.[3] And yet, even today a substantial part of the engineering profession is drawn from noncollegiate ranks.

In 1940 about 57 per cent of the employed male engineers and the experienced male engineers seeking work had attended college for four or more years (Table 5, Chapter I).[4] About the same division between graduate and nongraduate engineers was found in each of the three main branches of engineering: civil, electrical and mechanical. In the remaining branches (among which chemical engineers were the largest single group), the college-trained portion was somewhat higher. In 1950, after what was apparently a large influx of nongraduates into the engineering profession during and after the war, the proportion of engineers with four or more years of college dropped to about 55 per cent.[5] Graduate engineers accounted for 53 per cent of mechanical (including aeronautical) and civil engineers, and 55 per cent of electrical engineers. The remaining branches again had a larger proportion of graduate engineers, 61 per cent.

1. College-Trained Engineers

The dominant method of preparing for the engineering profession is through college training, usually at an engineering school. The future number of engineering graduates will be determined by the numbers of persons reaching college age, the proportion of such persons attending college, and the proportion of the latter choosing to study engineering. The number of persons reaching college age will increase substantially over the next decade and a half—by almost two-fifths from 1955 to 1965 and almost three-fifths by 1970 (see Chapter V). The proportion of college-age population attending college has risen more or less steadily over time and there is

[3] See also Dael Wolfle, *America's Resources of Specialized Talent*, Harper, 1954, pp. 95, 96.

[4] With definitions comparable to those in 1950. The percentage as reported in the 1940 census was slightly higher—about 61 per cent (see Chapter I, note 11).

[5] Special unpublished tabulation of the census manpower occupations card file for the Bureau of Labor Statistics and sponsored by the National Science Foundation. Dael Wolfle suggests slightly different percentages for 1940 and 1950: 56 and 58 per cent, respectively (Wolfle, *op. cit.*, pp. 95-96).

little reason to believe that it will not continue to do so, provided sufficient facilities and staff are made available. If there were no change in the distribution of college students by area of specialization, these two factors would produce a very substantial increase in the future number of engineering graduates.

The proportion of college graduates specializing in engineering is the difficult and interesting component of supply. The number of first degrees in engineering grew continuously in each half-decade between 1900 and 1950, reaching an all-time high of 159,600 in 1946–1950 (Table 30). The ratio of first degrees in engineering to

TABLE 30

Number of Bachelor's and First Professional Degrees in Engineering and Ratio to Total Bachelor's and First Professional Degrees, 1901–1955

	Number of First Degrees in Engineering	Annual Average Number of En- gineering Degrees	Per Cent of Total First Degrees
1901–1905	4,900	980	3.3
1906–1910	7,500	1,500	4.3
1911–1915	12,500	2,500	6.0
1916–1920	20,100	4,020	9.3
1921–1925	37,100	7,420	10.3
1926–1930	38,800	7,760	7.0
1931–1935	54,800	10,960	8.0
1936–1940	62,600	12,520	7.6
1941–1945	68,500	13,700	8.8
1946–1950	159,600	31,920	11.3
1951–1955	143,118	28,624	8.9

Source: Dael Wolfle, *America's Resources of Specialized Talent*, Harper, 1954, pp. 292–295; *Earned Degrees Conferred by Higher Educational Institutions*, Office of Education, Circulars 418 and 461, December 1954 and 1955.

all first degrees has also shown a rising trend but with considerably more irregularity. The ratio increased from 3 and 4 per cent in the first decade of this century to 9 to 11 per cent since 1940. There have been two bulges in this trend, one after each war, which were followed by a temporary decline in the relative importance of engineering degrees, although never back to prewar levels. After the decline in the late twenties, the ratio started rising again, and the same phenomenon is occurring now.[6]

For lack of data, we cannot discuss in detail the degree of future attractiveness (financial or otherwise) of engineering as

[6] *Ibid.*, p. 98; also *Engineering Enrollments and Degrees, 1952*, Office of Education, Circular 364, 1953, pp. 1 and 2.

compared with other occupations that college graduates engage in. In Chapter II, where we compared engineering incomes and incomes of other occupations, we found in general a fall in relative incomes of engineers over the last twenty-five years. But these comparisons were largely restricted to the entire labor force, on the one hand, and to the major independent professions, on the other. The former group is essentially not college-trained and the latter's training usually exceeds by several years the standard four-year engineering program. While these comparisons were valid for the purpose then at hand, they yield little information on the changes in engineering income relative to those in other occupations which most entering college students consider alternatives to engineering. For this comparison we would need data on incomes over a reasonably long period of those occupations in which most college graduates engage or, more precisely, on incomes of graduates themselves. And such data are not available.

For the very recent past, Endicott's data on starting salaries of college graduates (Chapter II, and Appendix A) show no important change in salaries of newly graduated engineers relative to other new graduates entering the business world since 1948. But starting engineers throughout this period commanded a higher salary than other graduates.[7] Such a premium is likely to exercise a continuing incentive for students to shift towards engineering.

Pending the accumulation of wider information on incomes of college graduates, we may employ simple extrapolations of the engineering degree ratio to derive at least rough orders of magnitude of the likely number of future engineering graduates. Under this procedure, of course, the major part of the expected increase in engineering graduates will be a result of the increases in college age population and college enrollments.

In Appendix D we develop several projections of the future number of engineering graduates to 1970. We there use both expected total population and expected male population [8] reaching college graduation age as bases for applying ratios of graduation age population receiving degrees and ratios of degree recipients in engineering. In essence our conclusions are that if the proportion of the graduation age population receiving degrees rises only

[7] For example, in 1954 the average starting salary for new engineering graduates was $345, compared with $315 for graduates in accounting, $314 for graduates entering sales work; $310 for general business trainees, and $328 for other fields (see Appendix A).

[8] Nearly all engineers are males.

moderately, and if the ratio of engineering degrees to total first degrees remains essentially at present levels (or increases very slightly), the number of engineering graduates will reach about 35,000 in 1960, almost 50,000 in 1965, and 60,000 or more in 1970. If the proportion of graduation age population receiving degrees increases to 1970 at the annual rate it grew between 1930 and 1950,[9] and if the proportion of degrees accounted for by engineering graduates rises at the 1930–1950 annual rate, there will be 40,000 or more engineering graduates in 1960, 60,000 or more in 1965 and as many as 80,000 to 90,000 in 1970. We may contrast these estimates with the annual average number of first degrees in engineering during the twenties of almost 8,000; during the thirties, of 12,000; during the forties, of about 22,000; and during the early fifties, of about 29,000.

It would be desirable, we repeat, to examine the determinants of occupational choice among college students, but we shall not enter upon this large subject here. But it should be emphasized that the roles of income, stability of employment, subsequent breadth of choice of industry or type of work, and similar factors have not yet been examined quantitatively.

2. Graduate Degrees in Engineering

The number of master's degrees in engineering has risen substantially over the last three decades, from less than a thousand per year in the twenties to four to five thousand per year in the late forties and early fifties (see Table C-6, Appendix C). Surprisingly, there has been no upward trend in the ratio of master's degrees awarded each year to bachelor's degrees awarded in the preceding year. Since the late twenties, this ratio has fluctuated about the 10 per cent level, rising above it during the early thirties, falling substantially below during the war, rising above it again during the first postwar years, but returning to it once again in the early fifties.[10] One might expect the proportion of engineers with bachelor's degrees going on to a year of graduate training to rise

[9] We exclude veterans from the data on population and degree recipients in 1950 (see Appendix D).

[10] See Appendix Table C-6; also Henry H. Armsby, "Current Trends in U.S. Colleges and Universities: Production of Engineers" and Herbert S. Conrad, "Current Trends in U.S. Colleges and Universities: Production of Scientists," both in *Symposium on Scientific and Specialized Manpower*, Department of Defense, Research and Development Board, June 15–16, 1953, pp. 23, 29–30. Armsby uses the 10 per cent ratio in his projections of master's degrees in engineering, while Conrad employs a 9.8 per cent ratio.

somewhat in the future, in view of the growing importance of the research function among engineers and the great increases in demand for engineering services in the aeronautical, nuclear energy and electronic fields. But the past growth in these areas does not seem to have had any perceptible influence in this direction.

The number of engineers obtaining the Ph.D. degree has always been small, reaching an annual rate of more than 100 only after World War II (Table 31). By the early fifties, about 550 doctor's

TABLE 31

Number of Doctor's Degrees in Engineering, 1911–1955

	Number	Average Annual Number	Ratio to Number of Bachelor's Degrees
1911–1915	10	2	0.1
1916–1920	20	4	0.1
1921–1925	60	12	0.2
1926–1930	150	30	0.4
1931–1935	340	68	0.6
1936–1940	320	64	0.5
1941–1945	230	48	0.3
1946–1950	1,180	236	0.7
1951–1955	2,763	553	1.9

Source: Dael Wolfle, *America's Resources of Specialized Talent*, Harper, 1954, pp. 294–295, 300–301; *Earned Degrees Conferred by Higher Educational Institutions*, Office of Education, Circulars 418, 461, December 1954 and 1955.

degrees in engineering were being awarded annually. Unlike the situation with regard to master's degrees, the ratio of doctor's degrees in engineering to bachelor's degrees has shown an upward movement over time, rising from 0.1–0.2 per cent in 1911–1925 to 0.4–0.6 per cent in 1926–1940, and to 0.7 per cent in 1946–1950. In the early fifties this ratio reached 1.8 per cent, although a portion of this rise was a reflection of the very large college graduating classes several years earlier, classes larger in size than those now being graduated. Although the number of engineering doctorates being awarded is still small, so small in fact that they probably can be disregarded in analysis of the general engineering supply problem, they undoubtedly are of importance in certain highly specialized fields and for additions to college teaching rolls. It is likely that the growth not only in the numbers of doctorates but also in the proportion of recipients of bachelor's degrees going on to Ph.D. training will continue.[11]

[11] Engineering doctorates now account for a perceptible proportion of all doctorates, rising from about 1 per cent of all doctorates around 1920 and

3. *The Distribution of Bachelor's Degrees by Field*

In 1952, the most important field of specialization for new engineering graduates was mechanical engineering, accounting for about a quarter of all bachelor's degrees awarded in that year (Table C-7, Appendix C). The next largest fields were electrical engineering, with slightly more than a fifth of all degrees, and civil engineering, with slightly less than a fifth. Chemical engineers represented almost a tenth of all new graduates; and mining engineers, only a little more than 1 per cent. About a quarter of all first degrees in engineering could not be allocated to specific fields or were in minor engineering fields.

The proportions of all first degrees in engineering accounted for by civil and electrical engineering degrees followed essentially similar paths of movement after the late twenties: a continuous decline through the thirties, and a rise during the forties. The share of civil engineering degrees experienced a rise from 1941 to 1946, a drop during the next two years, and a further substantial rise from 1948 to 1952. The share of electrical engineering degrees was fairly stable (at its trough level) through the war and rose sharply from 1947 to 1950, with a decline in the next two years.

Degrees in chemical and mechanical engineering followed almost the reverse pattern: their share rose through the thirties and into the war, and declined after the war. Chemical engineering degrees followed precisely this path, while mechanical engineering degrees differed slightly in two respects. Their share remained at a constant level through much of the thirties and started to rise after 1938, reaching a peak in 1947.

The share of engineering degrees accounted for by mining engineering was extremely small throughout this period and declined steadily with almost no reversals.

Data are available on the relative earnings of engineers in the various specialties for benchmark dates during the period 1929–1946. These data permit us to give at least a broad answer to the question of whether the distribution of engineering students among the major fields responds over time to the changes in demand for specialists in the several fields. In principle, one would expect occupational choice to be largely determined by the discounted values of expected life earnings in alternative occupations, compared with the discounted costs of entering these occupations.

---

2 per cent around 1930 to 5.6 per cent in 1946–1950 and 6.7 per cent in 1951–1953 (Wolfle, *op. cit.*, pp. 298–299).

Among engineering fields, educational costs are approximately equal, so that choice should be a function of earnings alone. We here use the movement of median salaries of engineers with 9 to 11 years' experience as an index of the movement of the discounted life earnings of engineers in the several specialties.[12]

If entrants to the engineering profession are influenced in their choice of field by relative changes in present values of life earnings in the several engineering fields, the proportion of entrants in each field will vary in response to salary differentials. If nothing else changed and if sufficient time elapsed to permit this equilibrating process to reach completion, salaries among the fields would approach equality or at least reach some stable relationship whose differentials would compensate for the "net disadvantages" of each specialty. Thereafter the distribution of new entrants would be such as to maintain this equality or stable relationship in earnings. However, relative demands for the various specialties have shifted so much in this period, that one would not expect a long-run equilibrium to be attained.[13] As a result we are forced to limit our analysis to investigation of the degree to which the distribution of new entrants responded to changes in salary differentials.

In Table 32 we rank the four largest engineering fields in terms of percentage increase in salary in each field and in terms of the percentage increase in the share of first degrees in each field.[14] Since

[12] In Appendix A, we develop data on salary level at benchmark dates between 1929 and 1946 of three groups of engineers in each major field: those with less than a year's experience, those with 9 to 11 years' experience, and those with 30 to 34 years' experience. Changes in salary rates at each of these experience levels will be reflected in changes in the discounted value of life earnings, with weights related to the reciprocal of the discount factor at each experience level. Since the discount factor for our group of older engineers is quite large, the effect of differential changes in salary rates at this experience level is relatively small. The weight of differential movements in salary rates of younger engineers is much larger but the differences in salary movement among this group for the period under study are quite small. Accordingly the relative changes in intermediate engineers' salary rates probably provide a reasonable index of shifts in discounted values, since the differences in salary movement for this group are substantial and the discount factor is only moderate.

[13] But the salary differentials among the major fields have declined perceptibly since 1929. Thus in 1929 the ratio of the median salary of graduate engineers with 9 to 11 years' experience in the highest paying field to that in the lowest paying field was 1.28. In 1946, the corresponding ratio was 1.16 (see Appendix A).

[14] The salary data combine the information in Appendix A on salary rates for graduate engineers and for all engineers on the assumption that rates for both groups changed in parallel fashion. In the sources from which the degree data are obtained, degrees in minor and "other" engineering fields account for

an engineer decides on his professional field some time before he receives his degree, shifts in degrees should lag behind changes in prospective income. The lag is probably less than a full four years, since there is substantial flexibility in the early years of engineering school. An engineering student is not heavily committed to a field until his second or, more likely, his third year at college. Accordingly, the comparisons in Table 33 generally involve a lag of two years between the initial or terminal year for income data and the

TABLE 32

Ranking [a] of Engineering Fields by Percentage Increase in Base Salary of Engineers with Nine to Eleven Years' Experience, and by Percentage Increase in Share of First Degrees, Various Periods, 1929–1948

Salaries, 1929–1934	Degrees, 1932–1936	Salaries, 1934–1939	Degrees, 1936–1941	Salaries, 1939–1946	Degrees, 1941–1948
Civil	Chemical	Mechanical	Mechanical	Civil	Civil [b]
Electrical	Mechanical	Chemical	Chemical	Mechanical	Electrical
Mechanical	Civil	Electrical	Electrical	Electrical	Mechanical
Chemical	Electrical	Civil	Civil	Chemical	Chemical

[a] Ranked from high positive increases to high negative increases.
[b] The average share for 1947 and 1949 substituted for the share for 1948.
Source: *Salaries:* Appendix Tables A-9 and A-10.
    Degrees: Appendix Table C-7.

corresponding initial or terminal year for degree data, e.g. 1934–1939 for incomes and 1936–1941 for degrees.[15] An inspection of the data suggests that a lag of a year more or less than the one we used would yield similar results.

For the last half of the thirties and again for the first half of the forties, there is a high positive association between changes in salary differentials among the major fields and lagged changes in

---

roughly about a fifth of all degrees granted each year since 1932; such degrees are not included in the degree calculations, although all engineers in minor fields are reclassified into one of the five major fields in the income data. The major field of mining engineering is not included in the analysis; this field accounted for a very small proportion of all first degrees in engineering (less than 4 per cent since 1934 and less than 3 per cent since 1938) and this share declined almost continuously over the period under study. Minor changes in the number of such degrees reported or in the classification of such degrees as between mining engineering and minor engineering fields could have a major impact on the share of total degrees accounted for by this field, since the level of the share is so low. Accordingly, it seemed advisable to restrict the analysis to the four large fields, each of which accounted for at least 9 or 10 per cent of first degrees.

[15] Since 1931 data for degree shares were not available, 1932 figures were used.

the distribution of degrees. The ranking of fields by percentage changes in salaries for 1934–1939 is matched precisely by the ranking of fields by percentage changes in degree shares for 1936–1941. The association between the two rankings is not perfect for 1939–1946 (1941–1948 for degrees) but is still high, with only one reversal of rank.[16]

In the first period (1929–1938 for salaries and 1932–1936 for degrees), there is essentially an inverse relationship between the two rankings (the rank correlation coefficient is -0.8). Indeed, if we combine civil and electrical engineering, on the one hand, and mechanical and chemical engineering, on the other, we obtain an inverse relation; degrees in these two pairs of fields, it will be remembered, had different patterns of change after 1929.

But in this earliest period (and in this period alone) average incomes of engineers in different fields are not fully measured by median salaries of employed engineers. Of all the years for which income data are available, only in 1932 and 1934 was there substantial unemployment in the engineering profession. In 1929 and again in 1939, and still again in 1946, the reported level of unemployment was under 1 per cent. In 1932 and 1934 unemployment was reported at 10 and 9 per cent respectively.[17] Measurement of changing economic incentives in this period, then, must take account of the degree of likelihood that a new graduate would obtain employment in his chosen field.

If the four major fields are inversely ranked by their percentage of unemployment in 1934, the following list is obtained: chemical, mechanical, electric and civil.[18] This ranking is the same as that for changes in degree shares for 1932–1936, except for the reversal of electric and civil engineering. If changes in degree shares are taken for 1932–1935, the largest percentage decline in share of total

[16] The coefficient of rank correlation is 0.8. The same coefficient holds for a comparison of ranks for 1939–1943 (1941–1945 for degrees). In the two periods running into World War II, mechanical engineering degrees are out of rank; this exception may be due to the exclusion from the degree data of minor engineering fields that properly belong in this category. The differences in percentage change in salaries between 1943 and 1946 are too small to permit analysis of the responsiveness of degree distribution.

[17] *Employment and Earnings in the Engineering Profession, 1929 to 1934,* Bureau of Labor Statistics, Bull. 682, 1941, p. 93.

[18] Although the unemployment rate for electrical engineers in 1934 was only fractionally higher than that for mechanical engineers (7.4 per cent as against 7.3 per cent), "increases of nonengineering employment [between 1929 and 1934] were particularly important to electrical engineers" (*Employment and Earnings in the Engineering Profession, 1929 to 1934,* pp. 52, 93).

first degrees is in civil engineering, and the ranking of changes in degree shares is identical with the inverted ranking of fields in terms of unemployment.

It appears clear, therefore, that economic incentives have played an important role in attracting engineering students toward those fields in which demand has been high and increasing.[19]

4. *Other College-Trained Entrants into the Engineering Profession*

A substantial component of the current supply of college-trained engineers consists of persons trained in nonengineering fields who enter the engineering profession upon graduation or at some later time. The largest single group of such entrants consists, of course, of persons who majored in the natural sciences while in college. The remainder are scattered widely over other fields of college training.

Estimates have been made by the Commission on Human Resources and Advanced Training of the occupational distribution in 1953 of all living college graduates (under the age of 70) who had trained in each major field of undergraduate study.[20] By combining these estimates with other estimates by the Commission of the number of living college graduates (under 70) in each of these fields,[21] we are able to determine the relative magnitude of this component of college-trained engineers.

According to these estimates, about 28,000 persons who had received bachelor's degrees in the natural sciences were actively engaged in engineering in 1953. About 12,000 of these were trained in the physical sciences (primarily physics and mathematics), about 9,000 in chemistry and about 7,000 in the earth sciences (primarily geology).[22] There were also another 30,000 persons trained in other fields (except engineering) who were functioning as engineers in 1953. The largest single group of these were the 10,000 persons who had received bachelor's degrees in education,

[19] If we plot the data underlying Table 32 on a scatter diagram, it appears that an engineering specialty with a percentage increase in salary 10 per cent greater than that for all others will increase its share of degrees by about 6 or 8 per cent. However, we are not inclined to press the precision of this estimate, because we have only eight observations (four in each of two periods), and one of these deviates considerably from this line of relationship.

[20] Based on a survey of the occupational distribution in 1953 of the graduates of 1930, 1940, and 1951 of two large universities (see Chapter III for details).

[21] Wolfle, *op. cit.*, pp. 295, 304.

[22] "Of the 31 per cent of chemistry undergraduates who entered other professions 26 per cent went into medicine and most of the rest into engineering. . . . Nearly all earth scientists who entered other professions became engineers" (*ibid.*, p. 57).

presumably in science and mathematics teaching. The remainder were distributed widely over other fields of study.

The 58,000 engineers with college training in fields other than engineering comprised about 9 per cent of the total number of engineers and about 16 per cent of the number of college-trained engineers in 1953.[23] To put it another way, the number of engineers with college training outside of engineering was equal to almost one-fifth of the number of active engineers with engineering degrees.[24]

A second study, conducted jointly by the National Scientific Register and the Commission on Human Resources and Advanced Training, deals with the occupational distribution in 1952 of college graduates of June 1951 and was based on a 20 per cent sample of all 1951 graduates. It was found that about 71 per cent of the 41,000 persons who received bachelor's degrees in engineering in 1951 (or 29,100) were actively engaged in engineering work in 1952 (see Chapter III for further details). These engineers, however, represented about 93 per cent of those graduate engineers with civilian jobs in 1952. In addition, about 5,000 persons who received bachelor's degrees in other fields in 1951 were engaged in engineering in 1952. The largest single group, again, consisted of natural science degree holders (about 2,000); the remainder were scattered over the remaining fields of study, including about 700 with degrees in education and 900 with degrees in business and commerce.[25]

Thus the number of bachelors in fields other than engineering who entered the engineering profession within a year after graduation equalled almost one-eighth of all recipients of first degrees in engineering in 1951, and about one-seventh of all 1951 college graduates who immediately entered engineering. And these nonengineering graduates represented an addition of about one-sixth to the engineering graduates of 1951 who entered the profession in their first year following graduation. Indeed, the total of the nonengineering graduates who entered the profession, the recipients of advanced engineering degrees, and the recipients of bachelor's degrees in engineering who immediately entered engineering work amount to about 7 per cent more college graduates starting

[23] *Ibid.*, p. 96.
[24] Some of the former, of course, had received graduate training in engineering (*ibid.*, p. 39).
[25] Based on unpublished tabulations for the National Science Foundation. Similar results were found for holders of master's degrees.

engineering work in 1951 than the number who received bachelor's degrees in engineering in that year.[26]

Accordingly, it is reasonable to expect that, if there is in the future a rising demand for engineering services, the number of nonengineering graduates entering engineering work will constitute an addition of 10 to 15 per cent to the number of bachelor's degrees in engineering. This would suggest that perhaps 4,000 to 6,000 college graduates in fields other than engineering will enter engineering work in 1960 and perhaps 6,000 to 12,000 in 1970.[27]

5. *Limitations on the Supply of College-Trained Engineers*

Unless the able young men find it more difficult than less able men to enter college—that is, unless college selection is perverse—one would expect a rise in the proportion of people entering college to be associated with a fall in their native capacity. But the important questions are: how much (if at all) does the quality decline; and can any one large profession insulate itself from a general decline?

On the former question—the average level of ability of all college entrants—there is no good historical information. Writers on this subject, once they reach a critical age, are inclined to observe a decline over time, and it would be improper to dismiss this as pure nostalgia. But one may conjecture that changes are small: the vast proportion of additional college students will come from intelligence levels which largely overlap those already attending, and presumably still with a minimum intelligence score of about 110.

According to Wolfle, graduating engineers place third out of the twenty major fields of undergraduate study, when ranked according to median scores on intelligence tests.[28] Students in the physical sciences and in chemistry rank higher, with median scores of 127 and 125, followed by the median score of 124 for engineers.[29] The remaining groups vary from a median score of 124 for law and 123 for English down to 113 for home economics and 112 for physical education. Thus it might appear that any substantial expansion of

[26] But 8 per cent less than the number receiving engineering degrees at all levels in 1951 (Wolfle, *op. cit.*, p. 63).

[27] The numbers are unlikely to be higher than these because the high projections of engineering degrees are based on a rate of growth in the ratio of engineering to total first degrees that involves some diversion of students to the engineering field during college, rather than afterward.

[28] Wolfle, *op. cit.*, p. 199.

[29] The scores are based on the Army General Classification Test scale (*ibid.*, pp. 317–320).

engineering enrollments, relative to other enrollments, would involve recourse to students of lower caliber.

But the range of median scores among fields is quite small, while the range of scores within each field is very large. While median scores for all fields range from 127 to 112 (127 to 118 for the top 18 fields), the middle 50 per cent of engineering graduates range from 132 to 117 and the middle 80 per cent, from 140 to 110. In 17 of the 20 fields, the top 50 per cent of the graduates rank higher (in many cases, considerably higher) by this measure than the lowest 25 per cent of engineering graduates, and the top 25 per cent, higher than the median score for engineers. Even in the two lowest-ranking fields (home economics and physical education), the top 25 per cent place higher than the lowest 25 per cent for engineers.

On the basis, then, of general intellectual aptitude, there should be no large deterioration in quality of engineering students with a moderate expansion of the proportion of undergraduates specializing in engineering, providing the level of demand and resulting financial incentives warrant such an expansion. It will be more difficult, however, to maintain the same share of engineers of the highest abilities. There may be difficulties in terms of limitations of specialized abilities or quality and breadth of high school training or nonmonetary incentives, but about these we know little. Indeed, further investigation of the limits of the supply of college-trained engineers should focus precisely on such questions.

6. Nongraduate Engineers

The component of the supply of engineers about which we know the least and about which controversy flourishes is that composed of persons without a college degree. As we have seen, two-fifths or more of the profession (by census definitions) fell into this category in both 1940 and 1950.

We can roughly estimate that nongraduate engineers entering the engineering profession in the twenties accounted for about two-fifths of the gross number of entrants during that decade or, in other words, that they represented an addition of perhaps two-thirds to the number of engineering graduates entering the field.[30] In the thirties and again during the forties, nongraduates accounted for about one-third of total gross accessions and equalled about one-

[30] *Employment Outlook for Engineers*, Bureau of Labor Statistics, Bull. 968, 1949, p. 41; Appendix E.

half of the number of entering graduates.[31] Clearly, nongraduates have formed a large component of the supply of new engineers over the last thirty years. There is no reason to believe that this component of supply will diminish rapidly in the near future. Accordingly, any attempt to measure the current or prospective supply of new engineers that is restricted to engineering and other graduates considerably understates the magnitude of new accessions. If the ratio of nongraduates entering the profession to new engineering graduates remains at the same level as in the last twenty years (or declines only moderately), we may expect the former to reach 15,000 to 20,000 per year around 1960 and 30,000 or more around 1970.

In view of the quantitative importance of nongraduates in the engineering profession, it is surprising that so little is known about the ways in which they enter the profession and the kinds of functions they perform. It is, of course, hard to collect information about nongraduate engineers. It is obviously simpler to work with data on engineering degrees granted and even to collect data on the work history of recipients of such degrees. It is also hard to define an engineer. Although it is generally assumed that any engineering graduate (or indeed any college graduate) who reports himself as engaging in engineering work is an engineer, there is much less unanimity about nongraduates who so report themselves. In fact, the disagreement with regard to the 1950 census count of engineers essentially centers about the question of what proportion of the nongraduate engineers there reported were engineers and what proportion were really subprofessionals. With no clear definition of what constitutes an engineering position, the task of collecting information on the number, duties and means of entrance of nongraduate engineers becomes extremely difficult.

It is clear that information about nongraduates would help us greatly in measuring supply. Perhaps some limited field studies of engineering staffs of corporations employing large numbers of engineers might yield sufficient initial data on the ways in which both employers and employees define engineering work to clarify the definitional problem. Further questionnaire studies, then, could obtain direct information on the numbers of nongraduates, the duties they perform, and the ways in which they entered the profession.

[31] *Employment Outlook for Engineers,* pp. 41, 87; Appendix E.

Even though our understanding of the character of the nongraduate component is very limited, some information is available from special tabulations of the 1950 census and other sources. Of the 45.5 per cent of employed engineers with less than four years of college in 1950, more than one-third had attended college for some period of time, another one-third had completed four years of high school, and the remaining slightly more than one-quarter had completed less than four years of high school (Table 33).

TABLE 33

Percentage Distribution of Employed Engineers by Age and Years of Schooling, 1950

YEARS OF SCHOOL COMPLETED	TOTAL EMPLOYED	AGE				
		14–19 Years	20–24 Years	25–34 Years	35–44 Years	45 Years and Over
High School						
1–3 years	12.2	0.1	0.4	1.9	3.3	6.6
4 years	15.7	0.1	0.9	4.6	4.7	5.3
College						
1–3 years	17.6	a	1.1	5.6	5.4	5.5
4 years	40.2	a	2.8	16.5	9.9	11.0
5 or more years	14.3	a	0.7	5.8	4.1	3.7
Total	100.0	0.3	6.0	34.4	27.3	32.0

a Less than 0.05 per cent.
Note: Items do not necessarily add to totals because of rounding.
Source: Appendix Table F-2.

The 1950 census count of engineers included younger men who reported themselves as engineers but who had little or no college training. The 1940 census specifically excluded from the technical engineering category any person under 35 who had completed less than four years of college training; it has been estimated that 20,500 persons were excluded from the engineering category by this ruling. Had the 1950 census employed the same definition, between 75,000 and 80,000 fewer engineers would have been reported. However, the very young engineers (by 1950 census definitions) with very little schooling do not bulk large in this group (Table 33). Thus only 1.5 per cent of those counted as engineers in 1950 were under 25 years of age and had completed no years of college, and only 2.6 per cent were under 25 and had completed less than four years of college. The nongraduates were most important in the older age groups. Almost five-sixths of those engineers with less than

88

four years of high school were 35 or older, and more than half were 45 or older.

The greater age of non-college-trained engineers is of course due primarily to the fact that competent training in applied science is acquired more rapidly by formal education than by experience. Moreover, there will be relatively few college-trained engineers who transfer to this work after (say) the age of forty, but there are a considerable number of non-college-trained workers who do so.

The younger engineers with little or no college training were fairly equally represented in nearly all of the branches of engineering (Table 34). Of all the specialities, chemical engineers had the

TABLE 34

Per Cent of Employed Engineers under 25 and under 35 Who Had Completed No Years of College and less than 4 Years of College, by Field of Specialization, 1950

	NO COLLEGE TRAINING		LESS THAN 4 YEARS OF COLLEGE	
FIELD OF SPECIALIZATION	*Under 25*	*Under 35*	*Under 25*	*Under 35*
Aeronautical	0.9	9.4	1.9	21.9
Chemical	0.9	4.0	1.6	7.5
Civil	2.2	7.5	3.6	13.3
Electrical	1.9	9.3	3.4	16.9
Industrial	1.0	10.2	1.7	18.1
Mechanical	1.2	7.8	2.1	14.0
Metallurgical	2.5	10.2	3.6	16.7
Mining	1.5	6.7	2.1	10.3
Other	1.1	7.7	2.0	15.5
All engineers	1.6	8.0	2.7	14.8

Source: Appendix Tables F-2 to F-11.

smallest proportion of those under 35 years of age who had not attended college or had completed less than four years of college. The highest proportions of those under 35 with no college training and with less than four years of college training were found in industrial, metallurgical, aeronautical and electrical engineering.

When we compare the proportions of all nongraduates (not merely those under 35) in the various engineering fields in 1950, we find that the three largest fields (civil, electrical, and mechanical, including aeronautical) were all at about the same level, with 45 to 47 per cent having completed less than four years of college (Table 35). A fourth group, comprising chemical, industrial, and mining and metallurgical engineering, had only 38 per cent with less than four years of college; within this group, chemical engineering had the lowest proportion of nongraduates, only 30 per cent. A final category of engineers "not elsewhere classified" was divided equally between graduates and nongraduates.

TABLE 35

Percentage Distribution of Employed Engineers by Field of Specialization and Years of Schooling, 1950

Field of Specialization	Less than 4 Years of College	4 or More Years of College
Civil	47.2	52.8
Electrical	45.0	55.0
Mechanical (including aeronautical)	47.1	52.9
Chemical, industrial, and mining and metallurgical	38.3	61.7
Other	50.0	50.0
All engineers	45.5	54.5

Source: Appendix Tables F-2 to F-11.

It is difficult to compare the changes in the graduate-nongraduate composition of the several fields between 1940 and 1950. There were some changes in definition among the fields. Also, in 1940 all engineers were classified into one of six fields, while in 1950 a substantial number of engineers were classified into a seventh category, viz. engineers "not elsewhere classified." [32] The 1940 counterpart of each of these engineers was apparently included in one of the major engineering fields in the 1940 census tables. [33]

However, if we disregard this category and deal solely with the groups we can identify in both 1940 and 1950, we find that the proportion of nongraduates increased by between 6 and 9 percentage points in each field over the decade. The much smaller

[32] In 1940, the education data on engineers were presented in terms of three fields, civil, electrical and mechanical, and a fourth which combined chemical, industrial, and mining and metallurgical. An examination of the index of occupations used in the 1940 census revealed that aeronautical engineering was then treated as a component of mechanical engineering. The unpublished age-education tabulations of the 1950 census present separate data for civil, electrical, mechanical, chemical, industrial, mining, metallurgical, and aeronautical engineering and for 72,000 engineers not elsewhere classified. We can add aeronautical engineering to mechanical engineering and combine chemical, industrial, mining, and metallurgical engineering to approximate the 1940 classifications, but we are still left with the n.e.c. engineers whom we are unable to distribute among the already-specified fields.

[33] Thus acoustical engineers in 1940 were considered civil engineers but fell into the n.e.c. category in 1950.

increase [34] in the proportion of nongraduates in the profession as a whole resulted from the fact that these substantial increases in the nongraduate proportion within each field were largely offset by the more rapid growth of the fields with a high proportion of graduates. Thus the combined group of chemical, industrial, mining and metallurgical engineering, with only 29 and 38 per cent nongraduates in 1940 and 1950, increased by 176 per cent over the decade, while both civil and mechanical engineering, with 41 and 47 per cent nongraduates in 1940 and 1950, grew only 41 and 57 per cent respectively during the ten-year period. Electrical engineering, with 38 and 45 per cent nongraduates in 1940 and 1950, grew by 85 per cent over the decade.

Finally, we may add a word about the functions most typically performed by nongraduates. In a 1946 study the Engineers Joint Council obtained data on the distribution of professional society members (with differing educational backgrounds) among approximately thirty different functions.[35] These data suggest that nongraduates were distributed widely among the functions performed by graduates and, with one or two exceptions, in rather similar proportions. There were some differences which are enlightening but in almost no case was there any indication that nongraduates cannot or do not perform functions engaged in by persons with bachelor's or higher degrees in engineering.

The largest number of privately employed engineers are engaged in technical administration-management; about one-third of both graduates and nongraduates are so occupied.

The following five functions (in order of importance) accounted for another third of privately employed society members: design, development, applied research, construction supervision, and university or college teaching. About the same proportion of nongraduates were engaged in design activities as of members with bachelor's degrees (15 to 17 per cent as against 18 per cent); for holders of doctorates the figure was only 7 per cent. A smaller proportion of nongraduates were active in development and applied research (6 to 8 per cent) than bachelors (15 per cent), and, particularly, than holders of advanced degrees (22 to 30 per cent). Some 19 per cent of the Ph.D's and 10 per cent of the master's degree holders were engaged in teaching, while only 1.5 per cent

[34] Or the slight decrease, according to Wolfle (*op. cit.*, pp. 95–96).
[35] Andrew Fraser, *The Engineering Profession in Transition,* Engineers Joint Council, 1947, p. 26.

of the bachelors and 1 per cent of those with some or no college training were so engaged. The proportions engaged in construction supervision were inversely related to education level. Only 1 per cent of the Ph.D's and only 2 per cent of the masters were performing this function, while 4 per cent of the bachelors, and 6 per cent of those with less than full college training were engaged in this activity.

Thus for those functions in which about two-thirds of the society members were engaged, nongraduates were somewhat more concentrated in technical management and construction supervision than graduates and somewhat less concentrated in development and applied research (particularly in relation to holders of advanced degrees). Both nongraduates and bachelor's degree holders had much smaller proportions in teaching than did advance degree holders and somewhat larger proportions in design.[36]

The remaining society members were scattered over more than twenty functions and only in maintenance and operation (in which nongraduates were more concentrated than bachelor's degree holders and, particularly, advanced degree holders) and in basic research (in which the reverse was true) were there marked differences in education levels.

It would appear, then, that nongraduates engage in activities that are essentially similar to those of graduate engineers, particularly those of engineers with four years of college training who comprise the bulk of the college-trained profession. But nongraduates are more likely to be found in administrative or operational positions and less likely in research or teaching positions.

[36] A similar pattern is found in the distributions of a broader sample of engineers, i.e. not restricted to society members (*Employment Outlook for Engineers*, pp. 99–100).

CHAPTER V

SUPPLY AND DEMAND FOR
MATHEMATICIANS AND PHYSICISTS

THE numbers of mathematicians and physicists in the United States are not large: the 1950 census reported only 7,359 mathematicians and 11,520 physicists.[1] We propose to study chiefly the even smaller number of persons in these sciences who possess a Ph.D. In 1951 the number of living Ph.D's in mathematics was about 2,100 and the number in physics about 3,500.

These professions do not constitute a significant fraction of the nation's labor force. They do constitute a significant share of the highest stratum of intellectual ability in the population, however, and large relative increases in their numbers probably would involve an appreciable lowering of the number of superior members of other professions. Our reason for choosing to study the factors determining the numbers of mathematicians and physicists is not, however, to emphasize either their unusual capacities or the strategic role they play in the advance of natural science.

Instead, we choose these fields because they pose a very different problem in analysis from that encountered in engineering and chemistry. Most mathematicians and physicists are college teachers, as can be seen from the summary of employment of the Ph.D's included in the 1951 National Registers.[2] There are significant proportions in industry (see Table 36), but the universities are the predominant source of demand for their services. Despite the small size of these two professions, together they are approximately as large as any of the other pure sciences except chemistry, and therefore as good a group as any for the study of supply and demand forces.

1. *Demand Factors*

The educational demand for mathematicians and physicists is broadly determined by the average number of college students per teacher of these subjects, and the trend of enrollments. Certain

[1] Unpublished tabulations of the 1950 census of population, prepared for the National Science Foundation, Bureau of the Census, June 23, 1953.

[2] Since only about two-thirds of the living Ph.D's in each field were included, there is an unknown but possibly appreciable bias in the figures. It is generally believed that the emphasis upon membership in professional societies led to fuller reporting of college teachers.

financial data must also be taken into account, but this simple classification of demand factors will permit a discussion of the main determinants of demand by universities and colleges.

TABLE 36

Distribution of Mathematicians and Physicists with Ph.D.'s among Fields of Employment, 1951

Field of Employment	Mathematicians	Physicists
Colleges and universities	87.4%	58.4%
Manufacturing	3.7	25.0
Government	6.2	10.7
Other	2.7	5.9
Total	100.0	100.0

Source: *Manpower Resources in Mathematics*, National Science Foundation, 1954, p. 18. *Manpower Resources in Physics, 1951*, Office of Education, 1952, p. 39.

a) FACULTY-STUDENT RATIOS

Since there is no comprehensive and continuous information about the composition of college and university faculties by branch of instruction, we have collected such information for three types of institutions in three well-spaced years. These data, expressed as ratios to total enrollments, are summarized in Table 37. The thirty-five institutions were chosen with such objectives as achieving variety in location and quality of institution, but the largest and the best known institutions are much overrepresented.[3] Our chief interest in these data, however, is methodological: they illustrate a type of information which could easily be collected on a large scale, and for a considerable period in the past.

The faculty-student ratios display no strong trend over the last quarter century. The ratio for mathematicians fell sharply from 1939 to 1951, but this was due entirely to a reduced ratio in liberal arts colleges—the ratio was stable in universities. On the other hand the ratio for physicists rose in the whole period, but the rise was restricted to state universities. It would be easy to rationalize the

[3] The institutions chosen are as follows: *State Universities:* California, Colorado, Illinois, Kansas, Maryland, Michigan, Missouri, Nebraska, Washington, Michigan (State), Ohio (State), Purdue, and Texas Agricultural and Mechanical College. *Private Universities:* Baylor, Boston, Columbia, Duke, New York, Northwestern, Notre Dame, Western Reserve, Yale, Southern California, California Institute of Technology, and Massachusetts Institute of Technology. *Private Liberal Arts Colleges:* Amherst, Antioch, Bates, Beloit, Bowdoin, Centre, Colby, Dartmouth, Grinnell, Haverford.

changes that we observe, but they are not sufficiently general to deserve much confidence.

TABLE 37

Faculty per 1,000 Students in 35 Colleges and Universities, Selected Years

	MATHEMATICS		PHYSICS	
	Average	Standard Deviation of Average	Average	Standard Deviation of Average
1925–1926	3.31	0.14	2.57	0.18
1938–1939	3.32	0.10	2.71	0.17
1950–1951	2.86	0.12	2.87	0.20

Source: Basic data for 35 state universities, private universities, and liberal arts colleges from *American Colleges and Universities,* American Council on Education, 1928, 1940, 1952. Means and standard deviations were calculated for each type of school separately, and these were combined with total enrollments in the three types of schools used as weights; enrollment data are from *Atlas of Higher Education in the United States* (John D. Millett, editor, Columbia University Press, 1952, Tables 21 and 22).

Until faculty-student ratios are collected for more years and more schools—and both types of extension can readily be made—one might take the ratios as 3.3 in mathematics and 2.8 in physics in making at least rough predictions of future faculty requirements. But it is possible also to search more deeply for the factors which govern the faculty-student ratio, and we shall sketch some of the variables which we have investigated. They fall into two classes: enrollment characteristics; and financial data.

Enrollment characteristics

One would expect the ratio of mathematics (or physics) faculty to students to be higher, the larger the fraction of students enrolled in mathematics (or physics) courses. Enrollment data, classified by field, are not available for the individual institutions, so we studied instead the percentage of degrees conferred in physical sciences, mathematics, and engineering in 1950. The 1951 faculty-student ratios proved to be fairly highly correlated with the percentage of such degrees: the correlation coefficient was 0.714 for mathematics teachers and 0.750 for physics teachers. This would suggest that in predicting the future ratio of faculty to students in these areas one should make some allowance for the drift of students toward the physical sciences and engineering.[4]

[4] In 1926–1930, bachelor's degrees in the physical sciences (including mathematics) and engineering accounted for 10.0 per cent of all first degrees;

95

We also investigated the share of graduate students in total enrollment in 1950 in these thirty-five institutions. Graduate students are taught in small classes and require much more individual attention from teachers, so the larger the share they are of the student body, the more faculty should be required. (Unfortunately we could not segregate the graduate students specializing in mathematics or physics.) For all graduate students, our expectations were not confirmed: the correlation coefficient was −0.071 for mathematics and 0.191 for physics.

We also studied the change in enrollment from 1948 to 1950. A university cannot quickly reduce the number of its faculty when enrollments drop: some of the faculty are appointed for indefinite tenure; and hardly any can be dismissed as suddenly as enrollments may decline. And when enrollments rise, classes can be allowed to increase in size more quickly than the institution can, or desires to, make long run commitments for more staff. This expectation that the faculty-student ratio will be higher in schools whose enrollments have fallen than in schools whose enrollments have risen is known to hold for the experience of American institutions in the postwar period, but it is not confirmed for mathematics or physics: the respective correlation coefficients are 0.140 and 0.095. It should be noted that even when the short-run changes in enrollments are influential, they are relevant only in short run predictions of the faculty-student ratio. This single test, admittedly not complete evidence, suggests that adjustments for short-run fluctuations in enrollments are not necessary in predicting short-run changes in the number of mathematics and physics teachers.

All of the correlations we have so far given are simple correlations, and some change markedly when other variables are introduced. But we shall postpone discussion of the partial correlations until the financial characteristics of the employing institutions are discussed.

---

in 1931–1935, 11.0 per cent; in 1936–1940, 10.4 per cent; in 1941–1945, 11.7 per cent; in 1946–1950, 13.9 per cent; in 1951–1953, 11.9 per cent. This rise is due to the growing importance of engineering degrees, rather than to growth in science degrees. The proportion of doctorates in the physical sciences and engineering has grown more rapidly; for the same periods, the comparable percentages are 10.5, 10.9, 10.8, 8.6, 14.1, 16.2. For this degree, only engineering has shown a large relative growth (Dael Wolfle, *American Resources of Specialized Talent*, Harper, 1954, pp. 292–293, 298–299).

Financial characteristics

Two financial characteristics of the employing institutions of higher education have been examined: the level of income; and the amount of research funds.

The wealth of an institution has an obvious effect upon the ratio of faculty to students: the wealthy institution can afford to have smaller classes (and also, what we here ignore, better trained teachers). We measure income of the educational institutions by their total current receipts less receipts from auxiliary enterprises and sales of goods and services (most of which recoup expenditures upon these activities). One uniformly obtains a very high correlation between income per student and the faculty-student ratio: 0.753 for mathematicians, and 0.928 for physicists.

Finally, a considerable number of university faculty are employed in research work, and with the large expansion of grants from the federal government this source of university employment has been growing rapidly. We have sought to measure it by expenditures upon "organized research," per student, in 1950.[5] Again very high correlation coefficients were obtained; 0.666 for mathematicians, and 0.911 for physicists.

Looking back over this list of five possible influences upon faculty-student ratios, we have found three that appear significant: the percentage of degrees conferred in natural sciences, mathematics and engineering; the income per student; and research grants per student. But there are high intercorrelations between some of the factors we examined,[6] so multiple regressions were also calculated. Eliminating variables which were statistically nonsignificant in the first regression equation, we obtained:

$$M = 0.0084 - 0.049\,G - 0.032\,R + 0.0031\,Y + 0.041\,D$$
$$\qquad\quad (0.015)\quad (0.0011)\ \ (0.0007)\quad (0.013)$$
$$P = 1.334 - 0.068\,G + 0.0022\,R + 0.0013\,Y + 0.013\,D$$
$$\qquad\quad (0.018)\quad (0.0013)\quad (0.0008)\quad (0.016)$$

[5] We also examined the federal contracts for research per student for the same year. Federal grants are so closely correlated with total research funds ($r = 0.990$) that there is no need for considering them separately.

[6] The correlation between income per student and research funds per student was 0.979, and holding all the other factors we have mentioned constant it was 0.696. It would have been preferable to measure research expenditure as a percentage of total expenditure, but the calculations are laborious, and we did not redo them.

where the standard errors are given below the regression coefficients, and

> M = mathematics teachers per 1,000 students, 1951
> P = physics teachers per 1,000 students, 1951
> G = percentage of graduate to all students, 1950
> R = expenditures on organized research per student, 1950
> Y = income (except from enterprises) per student, 1950
> D = percentage of degrees conferred in natural sciences, mathematics, and engineering, 1950

These regression equations explain most of the variation among schools in the faculty student ratios: the multiple correlation coefficient (adjusted for degrees of freedom lost) is 0.895 for mathematicians, 0.947 for physicists.

Yet the economic significance of some of the regression coefficients is at least as limited as their statistical significance. It is not easy to explain why those institutions with relatively *few* graduate students have relatively *high* faculty ratios especially since the proportion of graduate degrees granted in the natural sciences is higher than the proportion of first degrees.[7] One expects research expenditures to favor physicists more than mathematicians, as our equations suggest, but the sign of the regression coefficient for mathematicians is opposite to what we expect.

The chief suggestion one may wring from this exploratory statistical work—aside from the obvious one that much more work needs to be done in this area—is that perhaps the upward drift of the faculty-student ratio in physics is a genuine phenomenon. The cross-sectional analysis suggests that the growth of organized research favors employment of physicists in universities, and we know that there has been a continuous growth in this type of expenditure in universities for two decades.

b) THE TREND OF COLLEGE ENROLLMENTS

In addition to estimates of the future faculty-student ratio, one must have also estimates of future enrollments in order to predict the demand of institutions of higher education for mathematicians

---

[7] Conceivably, there may be an inverse relationship among institutions between the proportion of all students enrolled in graduate programs and the proportion of mathematics students enrolled in graduate programs, since mathematics departments perform a service function for such major undergraduate departments as engineering.

and physicists. We set forth the main facts upon which such a prediction must be made in Tables 38 and 39.

TABLE 38

College Enrollments, 1900–1954

	Enrollments (000)	Per Cent of Population 18–21 Inclusive
1900	237.6	4.01
1910	355.2	4.84
1920	597.9	8.14
1930	1,100.7	12.19
1940	1,494.2	15.32
1946	1,214.8 a	12.74
1948	1,360.5 a	14.67
1950	1,730.0 a	19.65
1952	1,878.3 a	21.92
1954	2,180.8	25.70

a Excluding veterans, who numbered 462,100 in 1946; 1,256,800 in 1948; 929,000 in 1950; and 423,600 in 1952.
Source: *Biennial Survey of Education,* Office of Education.

There has been a steady increase in the proportion of the population aged 18–21 attending institutions of higher education, at the rate of almost a doubling of the proportion every twenty years (see Chart 1). Although there were reductions in the proportion in the thirties due to depression, and in the forties due to war and the subsequent postwar flood of veterans, there is little evidence of retardation in the growth of college enrollments relative to population. It would not be very bold to predict that the proportion would be three-tenths by 1965—in the absence, of course, of radical limitations imposed by war or threat of war.

TABLE 39

Estimated Population of College Age (18–21), 1940 to 1965

Year	Population (000)
1940	9,753.5
1950	8,805.0
1955	8,537.1
1960	9,459.9
1965	11,765.3

Source: Data for 1955 to 1965 are number of persons 18–21 inclusive, in the absence of deaths or immigration.

The growth of the population of college age reflects the changes in the birth rate of twenty years before, in the absence of catastrophic mortality or mass immigration such as we have not experienced for several decades.[8] We are now at approximately a trough in the number of persons aged 18 to 21 (see Table 39), but soon the number will increase substantially: by 11 per cent from 1955 to 1960, and by 38 per cent from 1955 to 1965.

Let us join these two predictions for 1965—an increase of almost two-fifths in the proportion of college age population, with perhaps three-tenths of this group attending college. Then college enrollments will be roughly 3.5 millions in 1965, or 75 per cent above the record levels of 1954. One can easily defend an alternative estimate that is somewhat higher or lower—especially somewhat higher—but only developments of a magnitude for which we have no precedents in recent history would justify a prediction of only a small increase in college enrollments.

Since we have found that there is no strong tendency for the faculty-student ratio to change in mathematics, we can predict that

[8] It is conventional to follow the Office of Education in relating college and university enrollments to the population aged 18 to 21. Actually a very considerable number of college students come from outside this range; in October 1954 the figures were:

Age	Students in College or Professional School
14 to 17	151,000
18 to 19	758,000
20 to 24	924,000
25 to 29	425,000
30 to 34	155,000

Source: "School Enrollment: 1954," processed, Bureau of the Census, Series P-20, No. 54, January 20, 1955, Table 5.

The lack of a broader age base, perhaps with weights proportional to enrollments, suggests short run predictions on this basis cannot be accepted with great confidence. A broader age base would tend to yield slightly lower forecasts of college enrollments. To demonstrate this we have computed two indexes. One is based on the number of persons who will be in the 18–21 age bracket in each year 1950–1970, derived from corrected birth registrations. The other is based on the number of persons, aged 17–24, who will attend college in each year 1950–1970, if the proportions of persons at college at each age in this eight-year bracket remain at their 1950 levels (derived from corrected birth registrations and data on college enrollments by age brackets in the *Census of Population, 1950,* Vol. II, par. 1, Chap. C). The first index moves in proportion to the changes in the numbers of persons in the age bracket 18–21; the second, in proportion to the age bracket 17–24, weighted by the proportions attending college in 1950. With both indexes computed to a 1950 base, the first index reaches 110 in 1960, 139 in 1965 and 163 in 1970; the second index reaches 106 in 1960, 133 in 1965 and 159 in 1970.

at least as a first approximation, colleges and universities will require about three-fourths more mathematicians in a decade. If there is a moderate upward tendency in the faculty-student ratio in physics, the college and university demand will increase somewhat more rapidly than in mathematics. Since our analysis of the faculty-student ratio in particular rests upon very tentative and almost illustrative calculations, we are not inclined to press these predictions in detail, but they surely are tolerably reliable so far as general orders of magnitude go.

Chart 1

College Enrollments as Percentage of Population 18–21 Inclusive, 1900–1954

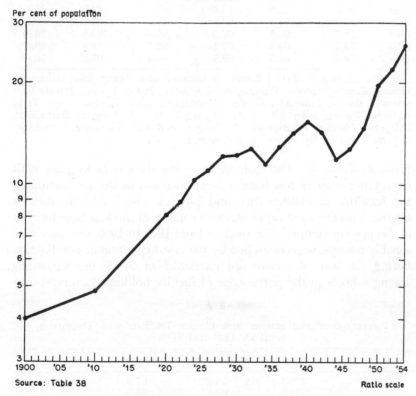

Per cent of population

Source: Table 38

Ratio scale

There remains one further question in principle: is there a college demand for fully trained mathematicians and physicists—by which we mean those possessing the doctorate—or is the demand readily met by the employment of those with lesser formal training?

101

The history of the composition of the faculty possessing the doctorate in a small sample of institutions is presented in Table 40 and summary figures for a somewhat larger group of institutions are

TABLE 40

Percentage of Mathematics and Physics Teachers with Doctorates in 21 Institutions, 1900–1954

	MATHEMATICS			PHYSICS		
	State Universities	Private Universities	Liberal Arts Colleges	State Universities	Private Universities	Liberal Arts Colleges
1900	45.2	47.4	35.6	26.1	66.2	50.0
1910	49.5	64.7	35.0	39.8	92.2	69.0
1920	66.1	51.5	46.7	48.8	53.0	67.2
1930	63.6	62.8	48.2	61.5	64.0	82.1
1940	67.4	73.3	67.6	77.8	81.7	90.8
1945	78.7	67.2	67.3	65.0	79.8	73.0
1950	73.5	59.3	64.1	85.1	76.4	83.3
1954	74.5	82.5	62.1	90.2	87.7	76.9

Source: Catalogues of the following institutions: *State Universities:* California, Indiana, Kansas, Missouri, Washington, Louisiana (State), Purdue; *Private Universities:* Brown, Columbia, George Washington, Johns Hopkins, New York, Western Reserve, Yale; *Liberal Arts Colleges:* Antioch, Colgate, Dartmouth, Lafayette, Oberlin, Swarthmore, Washington and Lee. Unweighted averages of percentages for the individual institutions.

given in Table 41. The main drift of the data is in keeping with expectations: there has been a large increase in the proportion of the faculties in mathematics and physics who hold the doctor's degree, with the most rapid increase coming in the first two decades of the present century. The decline from 1940 to 1950, one may reasonably assume, was compelled by the vast expansion of enrollments during the war. We have not examined in detail the variations among schools in the percentage of faculty holding doctorates—an

TABLE 41

Percentage of Mathematics and Physics Teachers with Doctorates, 1930, 1940 and 1950

	Mathematics	Physics
1930	59.2	67.9
1940	69.1	82.9
1950	66.3	81.8

Source: Covers same 35 institutions that are used in the faculty-student analysis. Weighted averages, with enrollments as weights.

inquiry that could be conducted in a manner similar to the earlier study of inter-school variations in the faculty-student ratio. But it seems probable from the historical record that there will be a moderate upward drift in the proportion of mathematicians and physicists in universities holding the doctorate, so that the demand for fully trained members of these professions will increase moderately more than the demand for all teachers.

One investigation of the composition of university faculties was made because it was naturally suggested by general economic theory: that the numbers of more experienced faculty members are smaller when their relative salaries are higher. Unfortunately it was necessary to accept academic rank as a measure of experience (and ability), and this may well have been a serious or fatal defect in the investigation: the weak institution may have lower standards for the higher ranks relative to the lower ranks. But for the forty-eight land-grant institutions for which we could get 1952 data on numbers and salaries (for the entire institution, not mathematics and physics only), there is no evidence that the institutions substitute less experienced for more experienced teachers when the latter's salaries rise relatively.[9]

2. *The Supply of Mathematicians and Physicists*

In a broad way it may be stated that there cannot be a serious problem of supply of faculty in institutions of higher education. For the very presence of a much increased demand (that is, a much increased student body) carries with it a much increased supply of trained individuals. Indeed there has been much more concern with the problem of finding appropriate employment for a rapidly increasing population of highly trained persons than in finding teachers to train them.

To this broad generalization there are obviously several qualifications. The first is that the supply of highly trained individuals (say, possessors of doctorates) need not keep exact pace with current college enrollments, so that for a time there may be a relative scarcity of such teachers. Since the average doctorate in physics is received

[9] The correlation coefficient between the ratio of the number of full and associate professors to assistant professors and instructors and the corresponding ratio of average salaries was 0.06. Similarly, there was little relationship between the ratio of the number of full (and associate) professors to assistant professors (and instructors) and the average salaries of all faculty members. The data were made available by the Office of Education.

about six years after the bachelor's degree, the period of shortage of highly trained individuals can obviously be at least this long.[10]

But the proportion of college graduates going on for advanced degrees has been rising. Graduate students were 4.3 per cent of all college and university enrollments in 1930, 7.1 per cent in 1940, and 8.9 per cent in 1950, and presumably this upward movement will continue. The pool of new doctorates will therefore at least keep pace with current enrollments.

It will still be possible for the supply of teachers of given competence and experience to shrink relative to teaching demands whether because of increased competition from employers in industry and government, or from the even longer lag in developing a large number of experienced mathematicians and physicists. It is obviously almost impossible to discuss in quantitative terms the deterioration of faculty standards that might arise in staffing the much larger number of classrooms of a decade hence. Since the enrollments are increasing less rapidly than from 1940 to 1948, and it is not anticipated that there will be a virtual suspension of advanced training such as occurred then, one can say that the deterioration should be substantially less than it was in the immediate postwar period.

The second qualification of our broad generalization that the demand and supply of college teachers move together is that there can be an imbalance between the demands and supplies of any one kind of highly specialized personnel. A large expansion of enrollments in courses in mathematics may be matched, but not appropriately staffed, with a large increase in the number of qualified teachers of modern language.

One may give both a specific and a general answer to this question of whether specialists are trained in proportions corresponding to the demands for them, i.e., in such proportions that the salaries of the various kinds of specialists move in parallel fashion. The specific answer is that there is no reason to doubt that so far as mathematics and physics are concerned, there will be at least an adequate proportion of doctorates in these fields. Since 1940 there has been a substantial increase in the relative number of doctorates taken in

[10] For the average delay between receiving bachelor's and doctor's degree in physics, see D. E. Scates, B. C. Murdoch, and A. V. Yeomans, *The Production of Doctorates in the Sciences, 1936–1948,* American Council on Education, 1951, p. 133.

these fields.[11] The enormous growth of the public interest in physics and mathematics, and the rise in the prestige, and probably in relative monetary earnings, of doctorates in these fields are such that there is no presumption that there will be a relative inadequacy of specialists in these fields. On the contrary, it is other fields, such as the humanities, that have reason for concern.

The general question—do specialists choose their fields in such a way as to maintain a relative balance of supply of the fields (measured by earnings)—is more difficult to answer. We do not have the data to determine whether there are large fluctuations in the relative salaries of professors in the various disciplines, and in the absence of such data all complaints of shortages—as we have already noted in the discussion of engineering shortages—must be viewed as highly subjective, and possibly quite imaginary.

Even over periods of say five years the numbers in any one branch of the professions cannot be increased greatly unless it is possible to plan the expansion years in advance: the period of training puts a minimum length upon the period of readjustment of the rate of recruitment. The question naturally arises—is it possible to recruit instead the experts from related sciences when one science needs to expand rapidly?

The answer to this question is rendered especially difficult by the fact that we do not possess definitions of the various sciences which are satisfactory for our purposes. The conventional boundaries, like physics, mathematics and chemistry, are the product partly of historical experience (and hence are slowly changing) but also of convenience in university and professional organization. A more suitable division for our purposes would be one constructed perhaps on the basis of the similarity of the formal education. Thus if physics and physical chemistry had the same training to the extent of 80 per cent of their graduate work, and for physics and geology the common training were only 20 per cent, we could say that the former pair of disciplines were much closer than the latter pair. Indeed if we found that the common training for two branches of physics was less than 80 per cent, we could say that physics and physical chemistry were closer in training than say acoustics and classical physics, and predict greater mobility in the former case.

[11] In 1941–1945, 7.0 per cent of all doctorates were in the physical sciences (physics, metallurgy, mathematics); in 1946–1950, 8.5 per cent; in 1951–1953, 9.5 per cent (Wolfle, *op. cit.*, p. 298).

As it is, to be told that of a sample of the better known physicists in 1949, some 37 per cent had worked in another general field such as chemistry, electronics, and mathematics is fundamentally ambiguous.[12] Electronics may simply be a branch of physics—it is so treated in another government study of the same time [13]—so the occupation mobility may be misstated, or at least represent an unknown amount of real mobility.

The National Scientific Registers have been examined in both physics and mathematics for educational background.[14] In both disciplines there is relatively little mobility among those with doctorates. Of the physicists with a Ph.D., 89 per cent had the degree in physics; in mathematics the corresponding percentage was 93. Of course at lower levels of training there is greater movement, so, for example, only 70 per cent of the physicists with a bachelor's degree had taken that degree in physics, and another 17 per cent had engineering degrees.

One cannot complete this type of calculation and estimate how many Ph.D's in physics are still in this line of work but a part of the answer we seek can be found in the two studies just referred to. They allow the following tabulation:

| | Ph.D. Conferred in | |
	Mathematics	Physics
Employed in mathematics	1,360	38
Employed in physics	34	2,621

These fragments of information suggest that it is valid to treat the various disciplines separately when one is dealing with periods of time too short to allow major additions by recruiting graduate students.

[12] *Occupational Mobility of Scientists,* Bureau of Labor Statistics, Bull. 1121, 1953, p. 16. Some of the shifts are spurious, or at least misleading: thus when a physics professor becomes dean of sciences, a shift to the separate discipline of general science was recorded.

[13] *Manpower Resources in Physics, 1951,* Office of Education, June 16, 1952, p. 5.

[14] *Ibid.; Manpower Resources in Mathematics, 1951,* National Science Foundation, December 1, 1953.

APPENDIX A

ENGINEERING EARNINGS

In this appendix we summarize the available data on engineering earnings. The data cover varying periods between 1894 and 1955 and are classified in various ways. We present:

1. Sample studies of engineering income, at different experience levels and for the several major specialties.

2. Income data from the 1940 and 1950 censuses.

3. Annual data on starting salaries for engineers and salaries of research engineers and scientists for recent years.

SAMPLE STUDIES

Five major sample studies of engineering incomes covering various nonoverlapping periods between 1894 and 1953 are available. The coverage and detail of the data in these sources differ considerably but it is possible to derive from them series describing the income behavior of the engineering profession or significant components thereof for major portions of the last sixty years. Although no single series covers the entire period, the several series are sufficiently comparable to permit broad conclusions about the level and changes in engineering income over the entire period, except for the years between 1924 and 1929.

Data Sources

The first source is the Report of the *Investigation of Engineering Education*, which presents data on earnings of graduate engineers (i.e., engineers who had received at least a first degree in engineering) at benchmark dates between 1894 and 1924.[1] The data were apparently collected during the academic year 1924/25 and were based on questionnaires distributed to the graduates of a "representative group of engineering colleges in the United States and Canada." Graduates of engineering schools in Canada represent a very small fraction of the combined number in the United States and Canada, as low as 1 or 2 per cent in the thirties. The data can therefore be treated as if they pertained solely to U.S. graduate engineers.

[1] *Report of the Investigation of Engineering Education*, Society for Promotion of Engineering Education, *A Study of Engineering Graduates and Non-Graduate Former Students*, Bull. 3 of the Investigation of Engineering Education, 1930, pp. 226–271.

Questionnaires were distributed to graduates of the classes of 1922 and 1923 and 1924 at 43 institutions and to graduates of the classes of 1884, 1889, 1894, 1899, 1904, 1909, 1914 and 1919 at 34 institutions. The response of the group of recent graduates was about one-half, while the response of the older graduates was about one-third. The report indicates that the returns covered approximately one-sixth of all engineering graduates in the classes 1922–1924, but that the coverage for older graduates was much smaller. Simply on the basis of the number of institutions included in the sample, one might estimate the coverage of the older groups at around 8 or 10 per cent. The committee felt, however, "that the method of sampling by classes of each fifth year and of institutions representing the various types and geographical locations of engineering colleges gives a fair cross-section of the older graduates."

The data are given in terms of annual earnings of engineering graduates of each class at various experience levels. We converted annual to monthly incomes to conform with the data from other sources. About one-fifth of the older graduates (i.e., graduates of classes earlier than 1922) and about one-tenth of the recent graduates were engaged in nonengineering work. For years after 1924 only the incomes of engineers from engineering work are reported.

The second source of data on engineering incomes is BLS Bulletin 682, *Employment and Earnings in the Engineering Profession, 1929 to 1934.*[2] The tabulations in this Bulletin were based on a questionnaire survey in 1935 of all the nation's professional engineers who could be located. The questionnaires were distributed to a total of 173,000 engineers, including all current and former members of engineering societies, all engineers registered with 32 state boards of engineering examiners who are not included in the membership lists, and all engineers who received degrees from engineering schools in 1930–1934 who were not included in either the membership lists or the examining board rosters. The total of 173,000 engineers represent about two-thirds of the estimated total of engineers in the United States in 1935.[3] About one-third of the questionnaires were returned with usable information.

The report suggests that there was a minor bias in the data for older engineers because names were obtained from engineering so-

[2] *Employment and Earnings in the Engineering Profession, 1929 to 1934*, Bureau of Labor Statistics, Bull. 682, 1941.

[3] Estimated by BLS by summing the 1930 census total for technical engineers and the number of first degree engineering graduates between 1930 and 1934, and subtracting estimated deaths of engineers between 1930 and 1934.

ciety rosters; members of such societies are not fully representative of all engineers. A similar minor bias exists for the group of younger (post-1929) engineers since recent entrants into the profession who had not received a first degree from an engineering school were probably underrepresented. However, tests (against 1930 census data) of the distribution of the returns by age, geographical location and professional specialty of the reporting engineers indicated that in these respects the collected data were representative of the entire engineering profession, with the single exception that the younger group (i.e., post-1929 entrants to the profession) was overrepresented in the total returns. Accordingly, in all tabulations which combined data for the two groups, the weight of the younger group was reduced to its proper level.

In addition to other data, the survey collected information on total earned income of respondents "from salaries or personal services in both engineering and nonengineering work" for the calendar years 1929, 1932 and 1934, and on the average monthly rate of income from "engineering work for time actually employed" during the same years. The monthly rates, rather than annual incomes, are used here, for several reasons. First, there was considerable unemployment among engineers during 1932 and 1934.[4] Accordingly, annual incomes of engineers during those years reflected both the salary rates at which they were employed and the proportion of each year in which they were employed. Second, some respondents who entered the profession in 1929, 1932 or 1934 reported their actual income during their first professional year, which may have been for work during only a portion of the year. Third, the monthly rates were restricted to engineering work while the annual incomes covered both engineering and nonengineering work. Although some engineering graduates always leave the field of engineering deliberately and indeed may even contemplate this departure in choosing to study engineering, for many engineers during the thirties the choice was not voluntary.

Thus, we concentrate in the present analysis on monthly salary rates for engineering work in the data for 1929–1934. Equivalent data were available for 1939–1946 and are here used, and only data on income from engineering work are available for 1953. Only in

---

[4] While unemployment among professional engineers was less than 1 per cent in 1929, 1939, 1943, and 1946, it was as high as 10.1 per cent in 1932 and 8.5 per cent in 1934 (*Employment and Earnings in the Engineering Profession, 1929–1934*, p. 18; and Andrew Fraser, *The Engineering Profession in Transition*, Engineers Joint Council, 1947, p. 54).

the period before 1929 do incomes include earnings in nonengineering work.

The third and fourth sources of data on engineering incomes stem from a survey conducted in 1946 by BLS in cooperation with the Engineers Joint Council and the National Roster of Scientific and Specialized Personnel. The mailing list for this survey was derived from the files of the National Roster which included the names of about 200,000 engineers, originally derived from the membership lists of the professional societies, state boards of engineering examiners, schools of engineering, and the occupational questionnaires filled out in connection with Selective Service registration of all male civilians aged 18 to 64. These persons had been sent National Roster questionnaires and the returns had been screened to eliminate those who were deemed not qualified as engineers. BLS estimated that there were about 300,000 engineers in the United States in 1946; the Engineers Joint Council estimated 317,000.[5]

The Roster registrants were classified by age, educational level, and engineering specialty and a sample of 20 per cent of the engineers in each group were sent questionnaires by BLS. The Engineers Joint Council wished to obtain similar information from the members of its six constituent societies so the same questionnaires were sent to all persons on the membership lists of these societies. All persons who were included in both the sample from the National Roster and the membership lists for the EJC were sent only the EJC questionnaire but their returns were marked and included in the summary data for the Roster sample.

About 42,000 questionnaires were mailed to the Roster sample in September 1946; about 25,000 returns were received—a 59 per cent response. The summaries for the Roster sample excluded those engineers answering the questionnaire who were in the armed forces, outside the United States, or engaged in nonengineering work. The results of the survey were presented in a BLS Bulletin, entitled *Employment Outlook for Engineers.*[6]

The survey obtained information from respondents on annual income in 1939 and 1943 (but not 1946) from "salaries or personal services in both engineering and nonengineering work, including fees and bonuses," and on monthly salary rates (exclusive of fees

---

[5] See Appendix E for discussion of the varying estimates of the number of engineers in recent years.

[6] *Employment Outlook for Engineers,* Bureau of Labor Statistics, Bull. 968, 1948.

and bonuses) for 1939, 1943 and 1946 "for the time actually employed in engineering work." The monthly rates were obtained inclusive and exclusive of overtime compensation; actually it was found that overtime compensation provided substantial supplements to income in 1943 only and the tabulations for this year alone are presented inclusive and exclusive of overtime.

To test the representativeness of the data, the returns were compared with the full Roster sample and with the 1940 census data with regard to distribution by engineering field, age and educational status. In general, the conformity was found to be good, notwithstanding slight overrepresentation of the younger age groups, minor discrepancies in the distribution by engineering specialty, and some overrepresentation of engineering graduates. It was concluded that "a presentation of earnings disregarding experience and education would not be distorted to any extent, because the high proportion of younger and hence lower-paid engineers would probably be offset by the too high proportion of graduate engineers who earn, on the average, more than those with less education."

No attempt was made in the tabulations to correct for these minor biases. Rather, data were in general presented separately for each field of engineering and for different experience levels. Although this procedure eliminated biases in the data presented in the Bulletin, it created difficulties for us, since it proved impossible in almost all cases to aggregate the data to provide information on incomes of all engineers or all graduate engineers. In fact, only in 1946 could median and quartile monthly salary rates for all engineers be derived. In no year could median or quartile annual incomes be obtained.

An earlier report summarized the information obtained by the Engineers Joint Council from a circularization of this questionnaire to the 87,000 engineers who were members of their six constituent societies in May 1946.[7] Returns were received from 47,000 engineers or 53 per cent of the total. The basic tabulations in the report were based on returns from those engineers who maintained continuous residence as civilians in the United States over the seven-year period 1939–1946, about 83 per cent of the total returns.[8]

The report compared the 1939 distribution of EJC respondents by age, geographic location, professional specialty and industry with

[7] Fraser, *op. cit.*
[8] Data on incomes were given separately for those engineers who were civilians in 1939 and 1946 but were in the armed forces in 1943.

corresponding distributions of all technical engineers in the 1940 census, and the rate of growth in the number of engineers between 1939 and 1946 (as indicated by the sample returns) with the rate of growth independently estimated from such data as engineering degrees. Although younger engineers were slightly overrepresented in the sample and there was some discrepancy between the two distributions by industry, the report concluded that the composition of the reporting engineers was adequately "representative of all professional engineers who maintained continuous residence as civilians in the United States, over the period 1939 to 1946" and that the returns from this group could be taken as describing the economic changes in "the entire engineering profession, or its several general fields of employment" over the seven-year period.

The EJC report on incomes of society members of 1939–1946 was issued in 1947. The BLS report covering incomes of all engineers in the same period was not published until 1949. It is interesting to note that both reports said that their samples were representative of all engineers, although BLS added a note of caution on the over-all figures, and that both reports included sections on changes in income of engineers between 1929 and 1946 in which each tied its data to the data gathered in the 1935 BLS survey. Actually, a comparison of salaries given in the two reports for 1946 indicates that society members tend to have somewhat higher salaries than all engineers; this is particularly true at the upper end of the respective income distributions, and holds in nearly all comparisons of salaries by professional field and experience level.

The BLS collected the same data as did the EJC (identical questionnaires were used) but published a much larger quantity. Income distributions for all engineers, graduate and nongraduate engineers, engineers classified by years of experience and by public and private employment were available in the BLS report in nearly all cases for the three years 1939, 1943 and 1946, and medians and quartiles are presented later in this appendix. We use only the monthly salary rates for 1939–1946.

The final major study of engineering incomes analyzed here is that of the Engineers Joint Council for 1953.[9] It provides data on incomes of engineers employed in industry, in government and in educational institutions. Companies and government agencies were asked to make reports covering their employees, while for engineers employed in education, the reports were made by each

[9] *Professional Income of Engineers,* Engineers Joint Council, 1954.

individual faculty member. No questionnaires were sent to self-employed engineers. This survey was designed to cover only graduate engineers and the questionnaires specifically requested this limitation. But in our analysis of the actual returns (see Chapter II) we discovered that some companies explicitly included nongraduate engineers; others undoubtedly did the same without so indicating on the report form. Unlike the 1946 EJC study, this report was not restricted to members of engineering societies; the varying coverage at different educational levels is not known.

Returns were received from 295 companies employing 65,000 graduate engineers, estimated by the EJC to represent about 18 per cent of all engineers employed by industry. Twelve government agencies, employing 4,000 graduate engineers or about 4 per cent of publicly employed engineers, submitted reports. Data were received from almost 3,000 college staff members, or about 30 per cent of all engineers employed in engineering education.[10]

For engineers employed by industry and government, data were collected on annual salaries, defined as "base salary including cost of living allowance, if any, and bonus if considered part of salary but not including payments for overtime work." This definition accords with that for monthly salary rates used in the 1935 and 1946 surveys (except for some uncertainty about the treatment of bonuses). For college teachers, both annual salaries and total income from the practice of engineering were obtained. In this appendix all annual salaries are converted to monthly rates. We discuss the reliability of this study below.

A new salary study, conducted for the EJC and covering the year 1956, was reported in the *New York Times* (January 18, 1957) after this book went to press. Some of the results are referred to briefly in footnote 24, below.

Classification of the Income Data

With a single exception, all the income data available are in the form of medians, with most sources also providing quartiles and occasionally upper and lower deciles. For most analytical purposes the arithmetical mean incomes would be preferable to medians but they are not available.

[10] These coverage estimates imply an estimate for total privately employed engineers of 362,000, for publicly employed engineers (exclusive of the armed forces) of 97,000, and for engineering faculties of 10,000, or a grand total of about 469,000 engineers in the United States in 1953.

The several sources present income data in various classifications, e.g. all engineers, graduate or nongraduate engineers, engineers classified by years of experience, publicly or privately-employed engineers, engineers classified by specialty. Incomes for the separate components of the engineering profession are of interest and are presented here. Further, since data for neither the over-all group of engineers nor any of its components are available at all dates, the income behavior of the profession for the entire period can be followed only by shifting attention from one classification to another.

TABLE A-1

Median and Quartile Base Monthly Salary Rates of All Engineers, 1929–1946

	First Quartile	Median	Third Quartile	Ratio of Inter Quartile Difference to Median	Ratio of Third Quartile to First Quartile	Index of Median Salary (1929 = 100)	Index of Median Salary (1939 = 100)
1929	$215	$289	$415	0.69	1.93	100.0	
1932	167	235	334	0.71	2.00	81.3	
1934	148	210	304	0.74	2.05	72.7	
1939	196	277	411	0.78	2.10	95.8	100.0
1943	251	334	469	0.65	1.87	115.6	120.7
1943 [a]	272	354	480	0.59	1.76	122.5	127.9
1946 [b]	319	409	553	0.57	1.73	141.5	147.7
1946 [c]	311	392	506	0.50	1.63	135.6	141.5

[a] Base salary plus overtime.   [b, c] See source note, below.

Source: 1929, 1932, 1934: *Employment and Earnings in the Engineering Profession, 1929 to 1934*, Bureau of Labor Statistics, Bull. 682, 1941, p. 162. 1939, 1943, 1946 [b]: Calculated from frequency distributions in Andrew Fraser, *The Engineering Profession in Transition*, Engineers Joint Council, 1947, pp. 74–75. Restricted to members of the six principal engineering societies. 1946 [c]: *Employment Outlook for Engineers*, Bureau of Labor Statistics, Bull. 968, 1949, p. 49.

Salary Rates for All Engineers and for Graduate Engineers, 1929–1953

Table A-1 presents median and quartile base monthly salary rates for all engineers for benchmark years between 1929 and 1946. Salary rates declined through 1934 and rose steadily thereafter. In 1934 median engineering salaries were slightly more than a quarter below their 1929 level but by 1939 they had almost recovered to the 1929 level. In 1943 salaries were about 16 per cent higher than in 1929 and 21 per cent higher than in 1939 (23 and 28 per cent including overtime); in 1946, between 36 and 42 per cent higher than in 1929

114

and between 42 and 48 per cent higher than in 1939, depending upon which of two estimates of median salaries in 1946 is used.

One estimate of salaries in 1946 covers solely members of the six principal engineering societies and one covers all engineers without regard to society membership. The median salary for the latter group was about 4 per cent less than the median for the group of society members; the two quartiles were similarly lower for the total group. Comparisons of engineers classified by professional field and experience level corroborate the fact that society members tend to have slightly higher salaries than other engineers, and are particularly numerous at the upper end of the income distribution.

The data for 1929–1934 are derived from a study which leaned heavily on society memberships for its mailing list. The EJC report for 1939–1946 was restricted solely to society members. The BLS survey for 1946 was based on the National Roster list of engineers in which society members were augmented by engineers located through Selective Service registration. The 1946 BLS study, therefore, probably had the widest coverage of the three. It is reasonable to assume that the movement of engineering salaries in 1929–1934 as reported by BLS and the movement of salaries in 1939–1946, as reported by the EJC, are approximately accurate. It should be recognized, however, that salaries of experienced engineers do not always move in strict proportion to those of inexperienced engineers, and, thus, movements of salaries of society members (who have greater experience—including in this term educational experience) are not strictly accurate for all engineers. We notice differential movements among the various experience classes below (see Tables A-3 and A-6–8). The chief effect is probably that the 1939–1946 rise is underestimated moderately. In addition, it is likely that the level of salaries in 1939–1946, as reported by the EJC is slightly higher than would have been indicated by a sample comparable to that for 1929–1934. Similarly, the level of salaries in 1946, as reported by BLS, is probably slightly lower than one derived from a sample comparable to that for 1929–1934. Thus, the actual increase in salary rates from 1929 to 1946 lies between 36 per cent and 42 per cent and the increase from 1939 to 1946, between 42 and 48 per cent.

Two measures of relative variability of incomes are available: the ratio of the interquartile difference to the median and the ratio of the upper quartile to the lower quartile. Both measures show a rise in relative variability of engineering salaries between 1929 and 1934 and a probable further rise to 1939. Variability dropped sharply during the war (the drop would be even greater if overtime were included) and dropped further by 1946. In that year, the relative variability of engineering salaries was substantially below that in any year since 1929. The rise in variability between 1929 and 1939 appears to be largely a function of the differential movement of engineering salaries at various experience levels. The decline since 1939 is due to the narrowing of the salary differential for experience and the decline in salary variability within each experience level.

TABLE A-2

Median and Quartile Base Monthly Salary Rates of Graduate Engineers, 1946 and 1953

	First Quartile	Median	Third Quartile	Ratio of Inter Quartile Difference to Median	Ratio of Third Quartile to First Quartile	Index of Median Salary (1946 = 100)
1946	$319	$405	$527	0.52	1.66	100.0
1953 a	418	518	682	0.51	1.63	127.9

a Excludes engineers on college faculties, estimated in the source to comprise about two per cent of all engineers, and all self-employed engineers.

Source: 1946: Calculated from frequency distribution in Andrew Fraser, *The Engineering Profession in Transition,* Engineers Joint Council, 1947, pp. 82, 83. Restricted to members of the six principal engineering societies. 1953: Monthly equivalents of annual rates given in *Professional Income of Engineers,* Engineers Joint Council, 1954, p. 12.

Table A-2 compares salary rates in 1946 and in 1953 for graduate engineers. The data show a 28 per cent increase in median salaries between these two years, so engineering salaries were about 75 or 80 per cent higher in 1953 than in 1929 and about 80 to 90 per cent higher than in 1939. This may be some slight understatement of the increase between 1946 and 1953, in view of the restriction of the 1946 data to members of professional societies, but society members are much more representative of graduate engineers than they are of all engineers.

A slight decline in relative variability of engineering salary rates is indicated between 1946 and 1953, but the drop is so small as to be untrustworthy in view of the differences in coverage of the data. Indeed, if one adjusted the 1946 measures of variability by the ratio of income variability for all engineers to that for all society members (from Table A-1), the uncorrected data would show a slight rise in variability between 1946 and 1953.

Salary Rates Classified by Years of Experience, 1929–1946

All studies of engineering salaries, and indeed most studies of professional incomes, stress the important effect of years of experience on individual earnings. In all professions, a substantial and increasing premium is paid for experience until one reaches an age ranging from 45 to 60 when a peak is reached. There is usually some reduction of incomes after this peak. The importance of income differentials resulting from varying years of experience in the engineering profession is illustrated in Table A-3. In 1946, engineers with less than one year of experience had a median monthly salary rate of $231; engineers with 9–11 years' experience, $395; engineers with 30–34 years' experience, $550.

TABLE A-3

Median and Quartile Base Monthly Salary Rates, by Years of Experience, for All Engineers, 1929–1946

	First Quartile	Median	Third Quartile	Ratio of Inter Quartile Difference to Median	Ratio of Third Quartile to First Quartile	Index of Median Salary (1929 = 100)	Index of Median Salary (1939 = 100)
				Under 1 Year			
1929	$130	$149	$174	0.30	1.34	100.0	
1932	89	111	137	0.43	1.54	74.5	
1934	91	110	129	0.35	1.42	73.8	
1939	110	128	156	0.36	1.42	85.9	100.0
1943	164	183	216	0.28	1.32	122.8	143.0
1943 a	195	218	251	0.26	1.29	146.3	170.3
1946	206	231	259	0.23	1.26	155.0	180.4
				9–11 Years			
1929	245	304	396	0.50	1.62	100.0	
1932	192	239	300	0.45	1.56	78.6	
1934	169	212	262	0.44	1.55	69.7	
1939	206	250	314	0.43	1.52	82.2	100.0
1943	269	325	413	0.44	1.54	106.9	130.0
1943 a	290	351	428	0.39	1.48	115.4	138.7
1946	333	395	470	0.35	1.41	129.9	157.7
				30–34 Years			
1929	297	419	608	0.74	2.05	100.0	
1932	241	341	488	0.72	2.02	81.4	
1934	212	307	441	0.75	2.08	73.3	
1939	311	434	669	0.82	2.15	103.6	100.0
1943	359	485	720	0.74	2.01	115.7	111.7
1943 a	370	492	727	0.73	1.96	117.4	113.3
1946	414	550	813	0.73	1.96	131.2	126.6

a Based on salary plus overtime.

Source: 1929, 1932, 1934: *Employment and Earnings in the Engineering Profession, 1929 to 1934*, Bureau of Labor Statistics, Bull. 682, 1941, p. 167. Estimates for 9–11 years' experience and 30–34 years' experience interpolated. 1939, 1943, 1946: Andrew Fraser, *The Engineering Profession in Transition*, Engineers Joint Council, 1947, p. 41. Restricted to members of the six principal engineering societies.

The magnitude of these experience differentials suggests two ways in which a series on engineering incomes, drawn from data not classified by years of experience, might yield a distorted or incomplete picture of the movement of incomes in this profession. First, a change in the experience composition of the profession will result in a change in reported median salaries of the entire profession, although there may have been no actual change in salary rates for engineers at given experience levels. Second, there may be disparate movements in salary rates for different experience levels. As a result of these two possible complications, it is general practice to present income series for engineers with specified years of experience.

Three such series are presented in Table A-3 (and Chart A-1) and following tables. One series is for inexperienced engineers, viz. those with less than one year's experience. A second series covers engineers with substantial experience, viz. 9–11 years' experience. The third series covers engineers with 30–34 years' experience, i.e. engineers at about their peak of earning capacity.

Two notes of caution must be given in the interpretation of these data. First, years of experience are measured by the time elapsed since an engineer started his first professional job (in the 1939–1946 data) or by the difference between the age of an engineer and the median age at which graduate engineers receive a first professional degree (in the 1929–1934 data). Thus, periods of unemployment or work in another occupation are implicitly counted here as engineering experience. Second, the experience level data for 1929–1934 are, as just noted, based in part on the median age at which graduate engineers receive a first engineering degree. Nongraduates may, on the average, enter the profession at a somewhat later age than graduate engineers.

All three series show a decline in salary rates to 1934 and a steady rise thereafter. The three classes of engineers had a decline in salaries of about the same proportion between 1929 and 1934, but the older engineers had a more substantial recovery in salary rates by 1939 than either of the two younger groups.[11] Thus, salary rates

[11] Unemployment among engineers was extremely low in 1929 and 1939 and of course negligible thereafter. During 1932 and 1934, when engineering unemployment was substantial, unemployment rates were highest both among the very young and the very experienced engineers. Thus, engineers under the age of 25 in 1932 reported a 17 per cent unemployment rate and engineers over 50, a rate of 11 per cent. Less than 9 per cent of engineers between 31 and 50 years of age were unemployed. Similarly, in 1934, engineers under 25 had a 14 per cent unemployment rate; engineers over 52, a 12 per cent rate; and engineers between 25 and 52 a rate between 7 and 8 per cent.

Chart A-1

Indexes of Median Salaries for All Engineers and for Engineers at Stated Experience Levels, Selected Years, 1929–1953

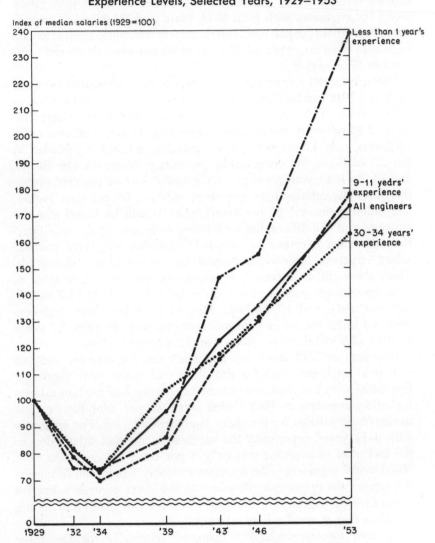

Index of median salaries (1929=100)

Less than 1 year's experience

9-11 yedrs' experience

All engineers

30-34 years' experience

Source: Table A-8

for engineers with 30–34 years' experience were slightly higher in 1939 than in 1929, while engineers with less than one and with 9–11 years' experience were still earning substantially lower salaries in 1939 than in 1929. Between 1939 and 1946 percentage increases in salaries were inversely related to experience level, so that salary levels for engineers with both 9–11 years' and 30–34 years' experience were about 30 per cent above 1929 levels while inexperienced engineers were receiving salaries about 55 per cent above the comparable 1929 level.[12]

The substantial narrowing of the experience differential between 1939 and 1946 can be seen more clearly when salaries are related to a 1939 base (Table A-3). By 1943 younger engineers' salaries increased 43 per cent, intermediate engineers, 30 per cent, and older engineers, only 12 per cent. When overtime in 1943 is included in the calculations, the comparable percentage increases are 70, 39, and 13. By 1946, younger engineers' salaries were 80 per cent higher than in 1939, intermediate engineers' salaries, 58 per cent higher, and older engineers', 27 per cent higher. It will be noted that the narrowing of the differential took place early during the war (particularly when overtime is included) and that the early postwar salary structure largely maintained the war-created differentials. Thus, the ratio of intermediate engineers' median salary rates to rates for younger engineers was 2.0 in 1939, 1.8 in 1943 (1.6 including overtime), and 1.7 in 1946. Median rates for older engineers were 3.4 times the salaries for younger engineers in 1939, 2.7 times in 1943 (2.3 including overtime), and 2.4 times in 1946.

Overtime in 1943 was more important for the younger and less well paid engineers than for the older and better-paid engineers. Engineers with less than one year of experience had median salaries including overtime in 1943 which were 19 per cent higher than median base salaries for the same group in that year. For engineers with 9–11 years' experience the increase in median salary due to the inclusion of overtime was only 8 per cent; for engineers with 30–34 years' experience, the increase was only 1 per cent. Similarly, the ratio of the upper quartile salary to the lower quartile salary for each of the three groups in 1934 was lower for base salaries including overtime than it was for base salaries alone.

Relative income variability changed erratically for the three

[12] The data for 1939–1946 are restricted to society members while those for 1929–1934 have wider coverage. The actual increases between 1929 and 1946, thus, are probably somewhat greater than those indicated in the text and table.

groups of engineers between 1929 and 1939, but declined consistently between 1939 and 1946. For both the younger and the older engineers, the two measures of variability were higher in 1939 than in 1929. Younger engineers' incomes rose in variability between 1929 and 1932, declined by 1934 and remained at about the same level through 1939. Variability of older engineers' salaries declined between 1929 and 1932 and rose steadily through 1939. Intermediate engineers, however, experienced a decline in variability of salary rate throughout the 1929–1939 period. For all three groups variability in incomes was substantially lower in 1946 than in 1939.

In every year, relative (as well as absolute) income variability increased with years of experience. Thus, in 1929 the ratio of the interquartile difference to the median for younger engineers was 0.30; for intermediate engineers, 0.50; for older engineers, 0.74. In 1946, the comparable ratios were 0.23, 0.35, and 0.73. This is in accord with a priori expectation, since the longer an engineer works, the more opportunity is afforded for individual ability (as well as random factors) to affect earnings.

Engineering Earnings, Classified by Years of Experience, 1894–1924

When attention is restricted to graduate engineers, it is possible to extend the analysis of incomes, classified by years of experience, back of 1929 (in at least one case to 1894) and forward to 1953. Tables A-4 to A-6 perform the first function; Table A-7, the second.[13]

There is some question as to the reliability of the pre-1929 data and serious question as to their comparability with data for following years. Although the estimate of median starting earnings for graduate engineers with less than one year's experience was lower in 1924 than in 1929, reported median earnings in the earlier years were 6 per cent higher for graduate engineers with 9–11 years' experience and 48 per cent higher for graduate engineers with

[13] Indexes of monthly earnings of graduate engineers show almost the same movements between each benchmark year from 1929 to 1946 as were shown in Table A-3 for all engineers. This conformity suggests that the movements (if not the levels) of incomes for graduate engineers can be taken to represent adequately the movements of income for all engineers in at least the later years of the pre-1929 period and in the post-1946 period, when data for all engineers are not available. The conformity is extremely close for the younger and intermediate engineers and only slightly less so for the older engineers. However, while salary rates for nongraduate engineers approximate those for graduates at younger experience levels, they tend to fall below rates for graduates at the older levels.

30–34 years' experience. A decrease in salaries of engineers at specified experience levels is totally unreasonable for these years.[14] In
fact one would have expected some increase in view of the high
levels of prosperity and investment during the late twenties.

There are three possible reasons for this apparent movement.
First, with the exception of the younger engineers (for whom starting salaries are apparently reported), all of the pre-1929 data relate
to total earnings, while the data for later periods are based on salary
rates for engineering work. Thus, the earlier data include bonuses
and, particularly, fees for outside engineering work, as well as outside earnings in nonengineering work. But in 1929 and 1939, annual
earnings of engineers did not exceed 12 times base monthly salary
rates by more than 5 per cent, except possibly at the highest experience levels.[15] This difference in coverage, then, accounts for only a
portion of the apparent decline in engineering incomes between
1924 and 1929.

Second, the pre-1929 data relate to all engineering graduates,
regardless of whether or not they were engaged in engineering
work. About one-fifth of the reporting engineers who graduated
before 1922 and about one-tenth of the reporting graduates of the
class of 1922, 1923 and 1924 were employed in work of a nonengineering nature in 1924. However, at most experience levels
graduate engineers employed in engineering work in 1929 earned
more than graduates engaged in nonengineering work.[16] In isolation,
this difference in coverage, then, should have yielded a rise in income between 1924 and 1929.

We are left, then, with the presumption that there was, in addition,
some selective bias in the sample for the pre-1929 data which pre-
cludes a comparison of the levels of income reported before 1929

[14] The decline between 1924 and 1929 was found at each experience level
(for which data were available) between 5 years and 30 years, and increased
with increasing experience. At the 1 to 2-year level, earnings in 1924 were 10
per cent lower than in 1929. At the 5-year level, earnings in 1924 were 1
per cent higher than salaries in 1929; at the 10-year level, 6 per cent higher;
at the 15-year level, 16 per cent higher; at the 20-year level, 13 per cent
higher; and at the 30-year level, 42 per cent higher.

[15] *Employment and Earnings in the Engineering Profession, 1929–1934*, pp.
140, 170; Fraser, *op. cit.*, pp. 41, 43.

[16] Of the seven experience levels between 1–2 years and 25–32 years in
1929, graduates engaged in engineering had higher median earnings than
graduates in nonengineering work at six levels. The excess declined from 15
per cent at 1–2 years' experience to zero at 13–16 years, amounted to minus
10 per cent at 17–24 years, and was three per cent at 25–32 years. *Employment
and Earnings in the Engineering Profession, 1929–1934*, p. 151.

with those reported for 1929 and following years. It also appears that we cannot compare the experience differentials of the two periods, since the bias seems greatest at the upper levels of experience.[17]

However, there is no evidence of strong bias in the *movement* over time of the reported incomes of engineering graduates with specified years of experience. This is particularly true at the younger experience levels where there is always considerably less salary variability and where outside earnings play a smaller role.

In Table A-4 are shown annual earnings of engineering graduates at various specified experience levels for the period 1894–1924, derived from data in the *Report of the Investigation of Engineering Education*. When graphed, earnings at the several experience levels show quite similar movements, particularly so at the lower levels. The internal consistency of the data supports the view that they can be accepted as depicting at least the broad movements of engineering incomes over the three decades in question.

When the earnings data are converted to indexes with a 1924 base (Table A-5), the major movements can be more readily traced.[18] Earnings of engineering graduates (at least at the younger experience levels) increased between 100 and 150 per cent between the end of the nineteenth century and 1924, with the bulk of this increase occurring during World War I and the immediate postwar years. The median percentage increase between 1894–1896 and 1904–1906 (for those experience levels reporting) was about 20 per cent. This rise is equivalent to about a 1½ to 2 per cent compound annual rate. The median increase for the decade 1904–1906 to 1914–1916 was 11 per cent, or about 1 per cent compounded annually, with nearly all of this increase coming in the second half of the period. For the half-decade 1914–1916 to 1919–1921, covering the first World War, the median rise was 33 per cent, or about 6 per cent compounded annually. For the somewhat shorter period 1919–1921 to 1924, the increase was 14 per cent or between a 3 and 4 per cent compound rate per year.

There was perceptible narrowing of the experience differentials over the two or three decades prior to 1924. Starting salaries in

[17] Thus, while relative income variability at less than one year's experience was about the same in the 1924 and 1929 data, at 9–11 years' experience it was slightly higher in 1924 than in 1929, and at 30–34 years it was substantially higher in the 1924 income data than in the 1929 data.

[18] The 3-year experience class is omitted since no earnings data for the base year, 1924, were available for this group.

1899 were 41 per cent of their 1924 level while earnings of engineering graduates with five years' experience in 1899 were 52 per cent of comparable earnings in 1924. Similarly the ratios of earnings in 1909 to earnings in 1924 were 0.49 for starting engineers, 0.53 for

TABLE A-4

Annual Earnings of Engineering Graduates, Classified by Years since Graduation, 1894–1924

	STARTING SALARY	YEARS SINCE GRADUATION							
		1	2	3	5	10	15	20	30
1894	$ 600								
1895		$ 900							
1896			$1,000						
1897				$1,200					
1899	600				$1,500				
1900		800							
1901			1,075						
1902				1,380					
1904	720				1,600	$2,400			
1905		900							
1906			1,200						
1907				1,300					
1909	720				1,530	2,700	$3,600		
1910		900							
1911			1,200						
1912				1,366					
1914	800				1,800	2,500	4,000	$5,000	
1915		1,000							
1916			1,200						
1917				1,600					
1919	1,300				2,400	3,000	4,000	6,000	
1920		1,800							
1921			2,000						
1922	1,320			2,200					
1923	1,440	1,800							
1924	1,476	1,800	2,100		2,860	4,000	5,000	5,500	$7,500

Source: *Report of the Investigation of Engineering Education, 1923–1929,* Society for the Promotion of Engineering Education, 1930, Vol. I, p. 261.

engineers with five years' experience, 0.68 at the ten year level, and 0.72 for the fifteen year level.

The bulk of this narrowing occurred during the first World War; there was some reversal of the movement during the immediate postwar years. Thus, the increase in earnings at the starting level and at one and two years' experience ranged between 61 and 80 per cent between 1914–1916 and 1919–1921, while the increase for engineering graduates with 10, 15, and 20 years' experience ranged between zero and 20 per cent. During the following period (1919–1921 to 1924), the comparable ranges were zero to 14 per cent for the younger engineers and 25 to 33 per cent for the intermediate engineers (excluding those with 30 years' experience, who showed a slight decline).

TABLE A-5

Indexes of Annual Earnings of Engineering Graduates, Classified by Years since Graduation, 1894–1924 (1924 = 100)

| | STARTING SALARY | YEARS SINCE GRADUATION | | | | | | |
		1	2	5	10	15	20	30
1894	40.7							
1895		50.0						
1896			47.6					
1899	40.7			52.4				
1900		44.4						
1901			51.2					
1904	48.8			55.9	60.0			
1905		50.0						
1906			57.1					
1909	48.8			53.4	67.5	72.0		
1910		50.0						
1911			57.1					
1914	54.5			62.9	62.5	80.0	90.9	
1915		55.6						
1916			57.1					
1919	87.8			83.9	75.0	80.0	109.1	
1920		100.0						
1921			95.2					
1922	89.5							
1923	97.6	100.0						
1924	100.0	100.0	100.0	100.0	100.0	100.0	100.0	100.0

Source: Table A-4.

In Table A-6, the pre-1929 earnings data for engineering graduates (converted to monthly equivalents) are presented for the three experience groups with which we have been concerned in this appendix. The earnings experience of younger engineers has already been outlined. To summarize the data briefly, starting salaries of graduate engineers increased 146 per cent between 1894 and 1924. The largest increases were during the first World War and in the immediately following years; the smallest increases were in the decade prior to 1914. Thus, the increase in starting

TABLE A-6

Median and Quartile Base Monthly Salary Rates of Graduate Engineers, by Years of Experience, 1894–1924

	First Quartile	Median	Third Quartile	Ratio of Inter Quartile Difference to Median	Ratio of Third Quartile to First Quartile	Index of Median Salary (1924 = 100)
				Under 1 Year [a]		
1894		$ 50				40.7
1899		50				40.7
1904		60				48.8
1909		60				48.8
1914		67				54.5
1919		108				87.8
1922		110				89.5
1923		120				97.6
1924	$100	123	$130	0.24	1.30	100.0
				9–11 Years		
1904		200				60.1
1909		225				67.6
1914		208				62.5
1919		250				75.1
1924	259	333	425	0.50	1.68	100.0
				30–34 Years		
1924	385	667	1,354	1.45	3.52	100.0

[a] Starting salaries.

Source: Monthly equivalents of annual earnings given in *Report of the Investigation of Engineering Education, 1923–1929*, Society for the Promotion of Engineering Education, 1930, Vol. I, pp. 261–262. Data for 9–11 years interpolated and for 30–34 years extrapolated.

salaries in the decade 1894–1904 was 20 per cent; in the decade 1904–1914, 12 per cent; in the half-decade 1914–1919, 61 per cent; and in the half-decade 1919–1924, 14 per cent. Earnings for graduate engineers with 9–11 years' experience increased 66 per cent between 1904 and 1924, with the largest increases again coming after 1914. Between 1904 and 1914, the reported increase in earnings was 4 per cent; between 1904 and 1919, 20 per cent; and between 1919 and 1924, 33 per cent. For graduate engineers with 30–34 years' experience, an estimate of earnings for the pre-1929 period is available only for 1924.

Salary Rates, Classified by Years of Experience, 1946–1953

In the most recent period, comprehensive data are available only for privately employed graduate engineers, classified by years of experience (Table A-7). Much less information is available on

TABLE A-7

Base Monthly Salary Rates of Privately Employed Graduate Engineers, by Years of Experience, 1946–1953

	First Quartile	Median	Third Quartile	Ratio of Inter Quartile Difference to Median	Ratio of Third Quartile to First Quartile	Index of Median Salary (1946 = 100)
				Under 1 Year [a]		
1946	$209	$232	$262	0.23	1.25	100.0
1953	334	357	387	0.15	1.16	153.9
				9–11 Years [b]		
1946	340	401	472	0.33	1.39	100.0
1953	481	549	630	0.27	1.31	136.9
				30–34 Years		
1946	463	622	925	0.74	2.00	100.0
1953	630	771	1,008	0.49	1.60	124.0

[a] Data collected by a large private agency indicate that average starting salaries of research engineers and scientists with B.S. degrees were $281 per month in 1948; for those with one year's experience, average monthly salaries were $302.

[b] The agency referred to in the note above reported that average monthly salaries for research engineers and scientists with B.S. degrees and with nine years' experience were $434 in 1948; for those with ten years' experience, monthly salaries were $452; for those with eleven years' experience, $468.

Source: 1939–1946: Andrew Fraser, *The Engineering Profession in Transition*, Engineers Joint Council, 1947, pp. 46, 48. Restricted to members of the six principal engineering societies. 1953: *Professional Income of Engineers*, Engineers Joint Council, 1954, p. 14. Monthly equivalents of annual salaries. Excludes engineers on college faculties, estimated in the source to comprise about two per cent of all engineers, and all self-employed engineers. On p. 13, the average starting salary for privately-employed engineers is given as $341. Salaries for engineers with 9–11 years' and 30–34 years' experience interpolated.

publicly employed graduates but private employment heavily outweighs public employment.

For the younger and intermediate engineers, the movement of salary rates for privately employed graduates between 1939 and 1946 (for which period we do have data on both privately employed engineers and all engineers) conforms almost precisely to the movement for all engineers. For older engineers, somewhat smaller increases are recorded for the graduate group than for others.

All three groups of privately employed graduates show substantial increases in salary rates between 1946 and 1953. The increases (in relative terms) were larger, the lower the experience level, so that experience differentials were narrowed again during this seven-year period. Younger engineers' salaries increased 54 per cent between 1946 and 1953; intermediate engineers' salaries, 37 per cent; and older engineers' salaries, 24 per cent. The ratio of median salary rates for engineers with 9–11 years' experience to salary rates for engineers with less than one year's experience declined from 1.7 in 1946 to 1.5 in 1953; the corresponding ratio for older engineers declined from 2.4 to 2.2. A major decline in relative income variability also occurred within each of the three groups between 1946 and 1953.

Since the salary data for 1946 were based on reports from society members only, while the 1953 data include both society and non-society members, the actual increases in salary were probably slightly greater than those indicated in the table.

The validity of these estimates of salary rate increases depends on the accuracy of the 1953 survey. This survey was probably the least scientific of the four studies conducted since 1934. The sample appears to be mainly restricted to employees of larger companies, since the 295 companies which provided data had an average total employment of almost 10,000, and this limitation may impart some bias to the results. Similarly, no tests were made to check the age, industrial or geographical distribution of the reporting engineers against data from the 1950 census. Since the bulk of the data in the report relates to engineering salaries, classified by experience level, for individual industries, possible biases in industrial and age distributions were not too important for the EJC. But for the present analysis such biases may be serious. Accordingly, we have compared the salary data in the 1953 survey against other available data to see if at least the rough orders of magnitude seem reasonable.

The 1953 survey reported an average starting monthly salary for private employment of $341 and a median salary rate for engineers with less than a year's experience of $357. Surveys conducted by Frank S. Endicott, Director of Placement, Northwestern University, based on reports from business and industrial companies, show an average starting salary for graduate engineers of \$305 in 1952 and \$325 in 1953.[19] The National Industrial Conference Board reported average starting salaries for engineering graduates in private manufacturing employment as \$309 in 1952 and \$334 in 1953; for non-manufacturing private employment in 1953, average salaries were \$321.[20] A survey of starting salaries in 1953 by the Family Economics Bureau of the Northwestern National Life Insurance Company, based on data from universities, colleges and technical schools, indicated that the prevailing starting salary rate for graduate engineers was between \$325 and \$375 per month in 1953.[21]

All of these studies yield results quite close to the figures in the 1953 EJC survey. The Endicott and NICB estimates are between 2 and 6 per cent lower than those in the EJC report, while the latter are close to middle of the range indicated in the insurance company data. The difference could easily be accounted for by differences in timing, sampling variability and sample design.

Another study of engineering earnings was made by the National Society of Professional Engineers in 1952.[22] The members of this society are all registered under state registration laws and probably have somewhat higher salaries, at comparable experience levels, than all engineers or even all graduate engineers. Further, the data apparently refer to incomes, which of course are higher than base salaries. On both counts, then, one would expect the earnings of members of this society to exceed salary rates for graduate engineers. The data conform to this expectation.[23]

[19] *Journal of College Placement,* March 1953, p. 53.

[20] *Management Record,* January 1953, p. 2, as cited in "Shortage and Salaries of Scientists and Engineers," processed, Civil Service Commission, November 1953, pp. 7, 8.

[21] "Shortage and Salaries of Scientists and Engineers," p. 14.

[22] *Ibid.,* p. 23.

[23] In 1952 the median income of members of this society who had less than one year's experience and who were employed in private industry (excluding public utilities) was \$375 per month. This is about one-fifth higher than starting salaries for privately employed graduates with less than a year's experience in 1953 (Table A-7). However, the Endicott and NICB studies suggest that salaries for privately employed younger engineers increased from five to seven per cent between 1952 and 1953, so that median incomes for privately employed younger members of this society probably exceeded the 1953 estimate for all privately employed younger graduates by about 10 per cent.

For engineers with 9–11 years' experience, the median income of society members in 1952 was \$610 for employees of industry and \$517 for employees of public utilities. These figures bear a reasonable relationship to the EJC salary estimate of \$549 in 1953 for all privately employed graduates at the same experience level. At the 30–34 years' experience level, the median income of the

The scattered data gathered to test the reasonableness of the EJC 1953 salary estimates all appear to confirm the general levels of those estimates, particularly at the lower experience levels. There is thus considerable basis for accepting them as approximate measures of engineering earnings in that year.

TABLE A-8

Indexes of Median Salary for All Engineers and for Engineers at Stated Experience Levels, Selected Years, 1929–1953 (1929 = 100)

	All Engineers (1)	Engineers with Less than 1 Year's Experience (2)	Engineers with 9–11 Years' Experience (3)	Engineers with 30–34 Years' Experience (4)
1929	100.0	100.0	100.0	100.0
1932	81.3	74.5	78.6	81.4
1934	72.7	73.8	69.7	73.3
1939	95.8	85.9	82.2	103.6
1943 a	122.5	146.3	115.4	117.4
1946	135.6 b	155.0	129.9	131.2
1953	173.4 b	238.5	177.8	162.7

a Including overtime.

b Other data for 1946, restricted to members of professional engineering societies (as in cols. 2 through 4), would yield an index of 141.5 for 1946 and an extrapolated value for 1953 of 181.0

Column   Source

  1   *1929–1946:* Table A-1. *1939–1943:* Data restricted to members of professional engineering society. *1953:* 1946 value extrapolated by movement of median salary of graduate engineers, Table A-2.

2–4   *1929–1946:* Table A-3. *1939–1946:* Data restricted to members of professional engineering societies. *1953:* 1946 values extrapolated by movement of median salary of privately-employed graduate engineers, Table A-7.

Summary of Engineering Earnings, 1929–1953

Like the working population as a whole, the engineering profession has experienced a large increase in money income over the last decade and a half (Table A-8). The median salary of engineers declined about one-quarter between 1929 and 1934 but rose steadily thereafter until by 1953 it had reached a level three-quarters above that in 1929.

This movement of the median salary for all engineers is affected

---

society members who were employed by industry in 1952 was $846 and by public utilities, $763. These again are in reasonable agreement, in terms of expected differences, with the 1953 EJC salary estimate of $771 for all privately employed graduates at the comparable experience level.

by the changes in the relative salaries and the distribution of engineers in various experience levels. We can measure only the former influence, and the data show substantial divergences of movement of salary differentials over the period since 1929. Thus, although all three experience levels described in Table A-8 experienced the same decline in salaries between 1929 and 1934, salaries of older engineers (those with 30–34 years' experience) recovered more sharply by 1939 than did those of intermediate engineers (9–11 years' experience) and those of starting engineers.

Since 1939, however, the percentage increases in salary rates have been inversely related to years of experience. By 1953, starting engineers' salaries were 139 per cent above their 1929 level; intermediate engineers were earning 78 per cent more than their counterparts in 1929; and older engineers' earnings were only 63 per cent above their level in 1929.[24]

This has meant, of course, that the salary differential for experience has decreased appreciably. The ratio of intermediate engineers' salaries to those of starting engineers, which was 2.0 in 1929 and 1939, fell to 1.7 in 1946 and to 1.5 in 1953. The ratio of older engineers' salaries to those of new entrants into the profession rose from 2.8 in 1929 to 3.4 in 1939, but fell sharply to 2.4 in 1946 and to 2.2 in 1953. The decline in these differentials has important consequences for the engineering profession, including particularly the fact that expected life earnings of engineers have risen substantially less than is suggested by starting salaries alone.

Salary Rates, Classified by Major Field, 1929–1946

Earnings data for the five major engineering fields are available only for the period 1929–1946 (Table A-9 and Chart A-2). Median salaries in each field declined between 1929 and 1934 and rose continuously thereafter. Chemical engineers suffered the greatest relative loss in salaries during the thirties (falling more than one-third between 129 and 1934) and received the largest relative increase during 1939–1946. For the seventeen-year period as a whole, median salaries in electrical engineering rose about 43 per cent; median salaries in civil, mechanical and mining engineering, about 25 to 33 per cent; and salaries in chemical engineering, only 11 per cent.

[24] The EJC study of salaries in 1956, as reported in the *New York Times* (January 18, 1957), indicates that median monthly salaries in that year for engineers with 9–11 years' experience were about $688, and for engineers with 30–34 years' experience, about $883, or about 125 per cent and 115 per cent, respectively, of their 1953 level.

Chart A-2

Indexes of Base Monthly Salary Rates of All Engineers by Specialization, 1929–1946

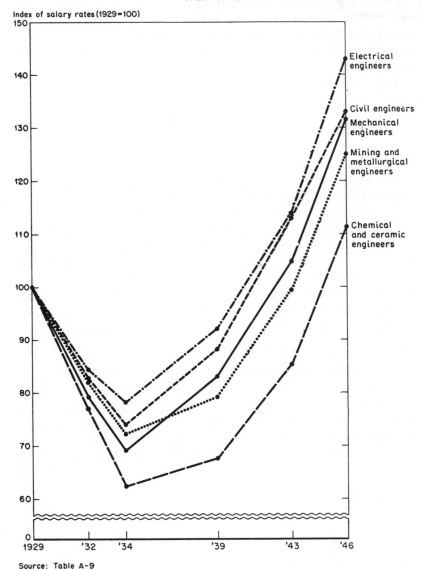

Index of salary rates (1929=100)

Electrical engineers

Civil engineers

Mechanical engineers

Mining and metallurgical engineers

Chemical and ceramic engineers

Source: Table A-9

Mining engineering commanded the highest base salary rates throughout the period.[25] Chemical engineers, whose median salary was second highest in 1929, fell to last place in 1946. In general, the salary differences among the several fields narrowed perceptibly between 1929 and 1946; the ratio of the highest to the lowest median salary falling from 1.21 to 1.15 (or from 1.19 to 1.13, if we exclude the relatively small field of mining engineering).

In every case, the variability of earnings increased between 1929 and 1934 and declined sharply to 1946. In 1929–1934, chemical engineering had the most variable earnings and civil engineering,

[25] This may be partly due to differences in age structure. Mining engineering grew less rapidly than other fields and its practitioners presumably had a higher average age.

TABLE A-9

Base Monthly Salary Rates of All Engineers by Specialization, 1929–1946

	First Quartile	Median	Third Quartile	Ratio of Inter Quartile Difference to Median	Ratio of Third Quartile to First Quartile	Index of Median Salary (1929 = 100)	Index of Median Salary (1939 = 100)
				Chemical and Ceramic			
1929	$221	$326	$490	0.83	2.22	100.0	
1932	157	251	400	0.91	2.55	77.0	
1934	131	203	339	1.02	2.59	62.3	
1939		220				67.5	100.0
1943		278				85.3	126.4
1943 a		303				92.9	137.7
1946	294	363	471	0.49	1.60	111.3	165.0
				Civil			
1929	213	277	372	0.57	1.75	100.0	
1932	169	229	311	0.62	1.84	82.7	
1934	150	205	279	0.62	1.86	74.0	
1939		244				88.1	100.0
1943		313				113.0	128.3
1943 a		328				118.4	134.4
1946	304	368	468	0.45	1.54	132.9	150.8
				Electrical			
1929	201	275	405	0.74	2.01	100.0	
1932	163	232	336	0.75	2.06	84.4	
1934	148	215	315	0.78	2.13	78.2	
1939		253				92.0	100.0
1943		313				113.8	123.7
1943 a		355				121.8	132.4
1946	311	393	503	0.49	1.61	142.9	155.3

TABLE A-9 (continued)

	First Quartile	Median	Third Quartile	Ratio of Inter Quartile Difference to Median	Ratio of Third Quartile to First Quartile	Index of Median Salary (1929 = 100)	Index of Median Salary (1939 = 100)
				Mechanical			
1929	225	311	455	0.74	2.02	100.0	
1932	155	246	356	0.77	2.14	79.1	
1934	145	215	313	0.78	2.16	69.1	
1939		258				83.0	100.0
1943		326				104.8	126.4
1943 a		356				114.5	138.0
1946	322	409	527	0.50	1.64	131.5	158.5
				Mining and Metallurgical			
1929	$241	$334	$503	0.79	2.09	100.0	
1932	183	274	409	0.82	2.23	82.0	
1934	154	241	371	0.90	2.41	72.2	
1939		267				79.1	100.0
1943		332				99.4	124.3
1943 a		348				104.2	130.3
1946	313	417	560	0.59	1.79	124.9	156.2

a Base salary plus overtime.

Source: *1929–1934: Employment and Earnings in the Engineering Profession, 1929 to 1934,* Bureau of Labor Statistics, Bull. 682, 1941, p. 165. *1939, 1943: Employment Outlook for Engineers,* Bureau of Labor Statistics, Bull. 968, 1949, p. 63. *1943 a: Ibid.,* p. 61. *1946:* Calculated from frequency distributions in *ibid.,* p. 107.

the least. By 1946, the range of income variability among the separate fields had narrowed considerably, with mining engineering having slightly higher and civil engineering slightly lower variability than the other fields.

Salary Rates in the Five Engineering Fields, Classified by Years of Experience, 1929–1946

The differences in salary increases for younger engineers in the five engineering fields in both 1929–1946 and 1939–1946 were quite small (Tables A-10 and A-11). For intermediate engineers, the differences among the engineering specialties were substantially larger in both the longer and shorter periods. For older engineers, the differences in salary increases among the several fields were substantial for 1929–1946 but quite small for 1939–1946 (almost as small, in fact, as among younger engineers).

There is almost no consistent order of engineering fields by degree of salary increase, either among the three age groups or between the 1929–1946 and 1939–1946 periods. The ranking of the five fields by percentage increase in salaries is shown in Table A-12 for all engineers and for each experience level in both periods.

TABLE A-10

Median Base Monthly Salary Rates and Indexes of Salary Rates of Graduate Engineers with Bachelor's Degree, by Professional Field and Years of Experience, 1929–1946

	Years of Experience	Chemical	Civil	Electrical	Mechanical	Mining and Metallurgical
				Salary Rates		
1929	Less than 1	$150	$155	$137	$141	$156
	9–11	383	299	329	331	359
	30–34	500	414	458	493	462
1932	Less than 1	116	103	106	97	143
	9–11	279	236	251	256	247
	30–34	n.a.	336	420	392	360
1934	Less than 1	107	116	106	106	113
	9–11	258	208	223	223	222
	30–34	426	294	373	342	341
1946	Less than 1	242	246	229	226	244
	9–11	393	348	365	403	385
	30–34	640	453	520	543	608
			Indexes of Salary Rates (1929 = 100)			
1929	Less than 1	100.0	100.0	100.0	100.0	100.0
	9–11	100.0	100.0	100.0	100.0	100.0
	30–34	100.0	100.0	100.0	100.0	100.0
1932	Less than 1	77.3	66.5	77.4	68.8	91.7
	9–11	72.8	78.9	76.3	77.3	68.8
	30–34	n.a.	81.2	91.7	79.5	77.9
1934	Less than 1	71.3	74.8	77.4	75.2	72.4
	9–11	67.4	69.6	67.8	67.4	61.8
	30–34	85.2	71.0	81.4	69.4	73.8
1946	Less than 1	161.3	158.7	167.2	160.3	156.4
	9–11	102.6	116.4	110.9	121.8	107.2
	30–34	128.0	109.4	113.5	110.1	131.6

n.a. = not available.

Source: *Employment Outlook for Engineers,* Bureau of Labor Statistics, Bull. 968, 1949, p. 109. Data for 9–11 years and 30–34 years interpolated for 1929, 1932 and 1934.

It can be seen there that electrical engineers, who ranked first in salary increases (without regard to experience levels) between 1929 and 1946, ranked first again among younger engineers, but third among intermediate and older engineers. Chemical engineers ranked first for the same period when no account is taken of ex-

---

perience levels, but ranked second among younger and older engineers and last among intermediate engineers. The same inconsistency holds for the 1939–1946 period, and holds also for both periods when attention is restricted to the three major engineering fields.

TABLE A-11

Median Base Monthly Salary Rates and Indexes of Salary Rates of All Engineers, by Professional Field and Years of Experience, 1939–1946

	Years of Experience	Chemical	Civil	Electrical	Mechanical	Mining and Metallurgical
		Salary Rates				
1939	Less than 1	$130	$144	$127	$129	$134
	9–11	299	218	240	261	284
	30–34	545	337	423	423	488
1943	Less than 1	177	183	186	179	203
	9–11	346	272	307	344	338
	30–34	595	372	482	456	526
1943 [a]	Less than 1	214	204	214	219	219
	9–11	361	302	332	369	358
	30–34	620	378	490	479	520
1946	Less than 1	242	247	228	226	247
	9–11	399	345	366	408	404
	30–34	655	427	513	514	608
		Indexes of Salary Rates (1939 = 100)				
1939	Less than 1	100.0	100.0	100.0	100.0	100.0
	9–11	100.0	100.0	100.0	100.0	100.0
	30–34	100.0	100.0	100.0	100.0	100.0
1943	Less than 1	136.2	127.1	146.5	138.8	151.5
	9–11	115.7	124.8	127.9	131.8	119.0
	30–34	109.2	110.4	113.9	107.8	107.8
1943 [a]	Less than 1	164.6	141.7	168.5	169.8	163.4
	9–11	120.7	138.5	138.3	141.4	126.1
	30–34	110.1	112.1	115.8	113.2	106.6
1946	Less than 1	186.2	171.5	179.5	175.2	184.3
	9–11	133.4	158.3	152.5	156.3	142.3
	30–34	120.2	126.7	121.3	121.5	124.6

[a] Base salary plus overtime.
Source: *1939–1943, 1946: Employment Outlook for Engineers,* Bureau of Labor Statistics, Bull. 968, 1949, p. 108. *1943* [a]: *Ibid.,* p. 109.

However, it was pointed out earlier that the dispersion of salary increases was small for the younger engineers for both 1929–1946 and 1939–1946 and for older engineers, for 1939–1946. Hence, any important effect of differential salary movements on the supply of engineers in the several specialties will stem from changes in salaries among intermediate engineers.

CENSUS DATA

The 1940 census presented data (in the form of frequency distributions) on wage and salary income of persons in various occupations who worked twelve months in 1939. The median annual salary income for engineers, derived from the full distribution, was $2,636, or $220 per month. However, the first class in the distribution comprised persons who received between zero and $99 in salary in

TABLE A-12

Ranking [a] of Engineering Fields by Percentage Increase in Salary Rates, 1929–1946 and 1939–1946

		YEARS OF EXPERIENCE		
	ALL ENGINEERS	*Less than 1*	*9–11*	*30–34*
1929–1946	Electrical	Electrical	Mechanical	Mining
	Civil	Chemical	Civil	Chemical
	Mechanical	Mechanical	Electrical	Electrical
	Mining	Civil	Mining	Mechanical
	Chemical	Mining	Chemical	Civil
1939–1946	Chemical	Chemical	Civil	Civil
	Mechanical	Mining	Mechanical	Mining
	Mining	Electrical	Electrical	Mechanical
	Electrical	Mechanical	Mining	Electrical
	Civil	Civil	Chemical	Chemical

[a] From high to low.
Source: Tables A-8 through A-10.

1939; about 9,600 engineers (or five per cent of the engineers who worked twelve months in 1939) fell into this class. Nearly all of these presumably were self-employed engineers and thus received no wages or salaries in 1939 even though they worked throughout the year.[26] Exclusion of this class from the distribution restricts the data chiefly to those engineers who were salaried employees. The median salary income for these engineers was $2,718, or $227 per month. Median salaries for the various engineering specialties, calculated in the same way, are presented in Table A-13 (column 1).

The 1950 census published distributions of total income of persons in various occupations in 1949. The median annual income

[26] Thus only 49 engineers were reported in the second income class ($100 to $199) and only 1,819 (or less than one per cent of the total) were reported in the second through the sixth classes ($100 to $999).

for engineers, derived from these data, was $4,688, or $391 per month. These data differ from those for 1939 in Table A-13 in two regards. First, they are not restricted to persons who worked throughout 1949; they therefore include some engineers who worked for only a portion of the year. Second, the data relate to total income, rather than wage or salary income; thus, self-employed engineers are included in the distributions and nonsalary income of employed engineers is included. The first difference lowers the median derived from the 1950 census volumes below what it would have been had definitions comparable to those used in the 1940 census been employed. The second difference raises the level of the median.

TABLE A-13

Median Monthly Incomes and Salaries of All Engineers, 1939 and 1949

	Salary, 1939 (1)	Income, 1949 (2)	Salary, 1949 (3)	Salary, Engineers who worked 50 weeks or more, 1949 (4)
All engineers	$227	$391		
Civil	215	377	$371	$391
Electrical	232	391	383	402
Mechanical	237	386	384	408
Aeronautical		404		
Other	221	403		

Column	Source
1	*Census of Population, 1940,* Volume III, Part 1, Table 72. Median salary income of all engineers who worked 12 months in 1939, excluding those who received less than $100 in salary for the year.
2	*Census of Population, 1950,* Volume II, Part 1, Table 129.
3, 4	Herman P. Miller, *Income of the American People,* John Wiley, 1955, Tables C-2, C-4.

Data based on unpublished 1950 census tabulations and comparable in definition to data presented in the 1940 census are available from another source.[27] Median salary or wage income is presented there for the three largest engineering specialties (comprising about three quarters of all engineers in 1950) but not for engineers as a whole (Table A-13, columns 3 and 4). In these tabulations, the data are restricted to engineers who received $1 or more in salary in 1949; thus, the problem of excluding self-employed engineers, encountered in the 1940 census data, is virtually eliminated here.

[27] Herman P. Miller, *Income of the American People,* John Wiley, 1955.

Median salaries for the three groups of employed engineers in 1949 were 1 to 2 per cent lower than median incomes for all engineers in the same specialties (column 3). But median salaries for those employed engineers who worked 50 or more weeks in 1949 (comparable to the 1940 restriction to engineers who worked 12 months in 1939) were about 1 to 4 per cent higher than median incomes (column 4). Presumably, then, median monthly salaries for all engineers who were employed for 50 or more weeks in 1949 were about 1 to 4 per cent higher than median monthly incomes of all engineers in 1949, or slightly above $400.

For the three engineering fields median monthly salaries increased 72 to 82 per cent between 1939 and 1949. For employed engineers as a whole, we may estimate that the increase was about 74 per cent.

The census definition of the engineering field was broader than that employed in the sample surveys; this is corroborated by the fact that census data on median engineering salaries are typically lower than estimates derived from such surveys. Thus, the Bureau of Labor Statistics study of engineering incomes, which attempted to cover all engineers, indicated median salaries in 1939 for the three largest engineering fields which were between 9 and 13 per cent higher than shown by the census for that year (Table A-13, column 1).[28] The EJC study, which was restricted to members of the six principal engineering societies, showed a median monthly salary in 1939 for all engineering fields combined of $277, or 22 per cent higher than that shown by the census.[29]

There are no survey data for 1949. Crude interpolations between the BLS survey data for 1946 and the 1953 EJC data, however, suggest that had a survey been taken covering 1949, with coverage equivalent to the BLS and EJC surveys, the resulting estimates of median engineering salaries would again have been somewhat higher than that obtained by the census.

ANNUAL SALARY DATA, 1947–1956

There are two sources of data on annual salaries of engineers during recent years. The first consists of the surveys of starting salaries and expected hirings of college graduates in various fields

[28] The BLS estimates of median monthly salaries were $244 for civil engineers, $253 for electrical engineers, and $258 for mechanical engineers (*Employment Outlook for Engineers*, p. 63).
[29] Fraser, *op. cit.*, p. 75. Base salary.

(including engineering), conducted annually since 1947 by Frank S. Endicott, Director of Placement at Northwestern University (Table A-14). These surveys, covering from 100 to 200 or more large and medium-sized business firms, are undertaken during the last months of the calendar year, i.e. during the middle of the academic year. The reported data apparently represent planned hiring and salary schedules for these companies with regard to the current graduating class. Thus, salary data gathered in November or December 1949 are shown by Endicott as applying to 1950. We follow this practice here.

TABLE A-14

Average Starting Monthly Salaries for College Graduates in
Various Specialties, 1947–1956

	In Engineering	In Accounting	In Sales	General Business Trainees	All Fields
1947	$244	$231	$225	$223	—
1948	250	215	226	221	$235
1949	261	240	240	236	245
1950	260	238	240	234	245
1951	270	246	247	241	251
1952	305	275	275	271	283
1953	325	297	301	292	304
1954	345	315	314	310	323
1955	361	332	336	327	341
1956	394	352	358	348	366

Source: Frank S. Endicott, "Trends in the Employment of College and University Graduates in Business and Industry," *Journal of College Placement,* May 1952, pp. 44, 45, March 1953, p. 56, March 1954, p. 60, March 1955, p. 41; National Industrial Conference Board, *Management Record,* January 1956.

Presumably, actual starting salaries for a given graduating class may vary somewhat from these salary scales, which are forecast six months before graduation, especially during periods of rapid salary change. But the relative changes in expected starting salaries should approximate quite closely changes in actual starting salaries over a several year period.

The second source of annual data on engineering salaries is the set of surveys of average salaries of research scientists and engineers, published annually since 1948 by the Los Alamos Scientific Laboratory. These surveys are conducted for the purpose of aiding the Laboratory in setting salaries for its scientific employees. While the 1948 survey gathered data on both scientists engaged in

APPENDIX A

research and engineers employed in nonresearch activities, the differences in salary at all experience levels were so small that, beginning with 1949, nonresearch engineers were excluded and the survey coverage was restricted to the combined group of scientists and engineers engaged in research. By 1954, the survey covered 221 organizations, including government laboratories, contractors of the Atomic Energy Commission, research institutions, private consulting firms, and manufacturing firms having research programs, which in total employed more than 50,000 research scientists and engineers.

Salary data are collected on engineers and scientists with bachelor's degrees and on those with doctorates.[30] Since relatively few engineers have acquired doctorates, we restrict our analysis to the salary experience of first degree holders.

TABLE A-15

Annual Percentage Changes in Average Monthly Salaries of
Research Engineers and Scientists with B.S. Degree,
by Years of Experience, 1948–1955

| | PERCENTAGE CHANGES | | | | |
	0	1	9	10	11
1948–1949	−3.2	−0.3	2.8	1.1	0.9
1949–1950	1.8	1.7	2.0	3.5	3.2
1950–1951	6.9	5.0	7.6	6.7	6.9
1951–1952	11.3	12.7	8.2	9.4	8.1
1952–1953	6.8	6.7	3.8	4.0	4.4
1953–1954	3.7	5.5	1.6	2.1	3.4
1954–1955	7.2	5.0	16.6	8.9	8.0

Source: *National Survey of Professional Scientific Salaries*, Los Alamos Scientific Laboratory of the University of California, 1949 through 1955. Each set of percentages derived from data collected in a single survey, to avoid the effects of changes in coverage.

In Table A-15 are shown annual percentage changes in average monthly salaries for starting engineers and scientists and for those with one year of experience, as well as in salaries for engineers and scientists with 9–11 years' experience, for each year 1948–1955.

A summary analysis of both the Endicott and Los Alamos data is given in Chapter II.

[30] Data on engineers and scientists with master's degrees are included in those for first degree recipients. The Laboratory data classify persons by the number of years since acquisition of the bachelor's degree. In Table A-15 we treat this classification as equivalent to number of years of experience.

CENSUS DATA ON NUMBER
OF ENGINEERS AND CHEMISTS,
1890–1950

WE HERE present the basic data on the number of engineers and chemists and the number of workers in the labor force that we use in Chapters I and III. Census definitions of occupations and industries have changed so greatly even within the last two decades that it proved impossible to utilize census data directly in our analyses. Rather we were forced to develop series with more consistent coverage. The details of our calculations are described in the notes to the following tables.

TABLE B-1

Growth of Labor Force and Engineering and Chemical Professions

Coverage	Labor Force	Engineers including Surveyors	Chemists including Metallurgists	Engineers and Chemists including Surveyors	Engineers excluding Surveyors	Engineers and Chemists excluding Surveyors
1. 1890 Gainful workers 10 years and over	23,318,183	28,239	4,503	32,742		
2. 1900 Gainful workers 10 years and over	29,073,233	43,239	8,847	52,086		
3. 1910 Gainful workers 10 years and over	37,370,794	88,755	16,273	105,028		
4. 1920 Gainful workers 10 years and over	42,433,535	136,121	32,941	169,062		
5. 1930 Gainful workers 10 years and over	48,829,920	226,249	47,068	273,317		
6. 1930 Labor force, 14 years and over	47,404,000	228,932	48,009	276,941	217,845	265,494
7. 1940 Labor force, 14 years and over	53,299,000	277,872	60,005	337,877	261,428	321,433
8. 1940 Civilian labor force	53,299,000	302,995	60,005	363,000	286,551	346,556
9. 1950 Civilian labor force	59,071,655	556,176	80,224	636,400	529,947	610,171
10. 1950 Civilian labor force	59,071,655	560,183	75,747	636,400	534,424	610,171
11. 1930 Total employment, gainful workers 10 years and over	45,642,273	218,215	45,703	263,918	208,178	253,881
12. 1940 Total employment, labor force, 14 years and over	45,166,083	258,632	57,025	315,657	245,288	302,313
13. 1940 Civilian employment, labor force, 14 years and over	44,888,083	285,489	57,025	342,514	272,145	329,170
14. 1940 Civilian employment, labor force, 14 years and over	44,888,083	288,669	53,845	342,514	275,325	329,170
15. 1950 Civilian employment, labor force, 14 years and over	56,225,340	546,177	78,833	625,010	520,856	599,689
16. 1950 Civilian employment, labor force, 14 years and over	56,225,340	550,577	74,433	625,010	525,256	599,689

144

APPENDIX B

NOTES TO TABLE B-1

Labor Force

Line   Source

1–5   Alba M. Edwards, *Comparative Occupation Statistics for the United States, 1870 to 1940,* Bureau of the Census, 1943, p. 104.

6–8   *Ibid.,* p. 12.
The figures for 1890–1940 (lines 1–8) include the following numbers in the armed forces in the United States.

1890	27,919
1900	43,195
1910	77,153
1920	225,503
1930	132,830
1940	222,485

1890–1930 from *ibid.,* p. 119; 1940, *ibid.,* p. 56.

9–10   *Census of Population, 1950,* Vol. II, Part 1, Table 124.
Since the number of persons in the armed forces in 1950 was very large, but the number of engineers and chemists in the armed forces is not available, we exclude the armed forces from the 1950 figures.

11   *Census of Population, 1930,* Vol. V, *General Report on Occupations,* Chapter 7, Table 1; and *Census of Unemployment, 1930,* Vol. I, Tables 21 and 22, and Vol. II, Table 3.

12   *Census of Population, 1940,* Vol. III, Part 1, Table 58.

13–16   *Census of Population, 1950,* Vol. II, Part 1, Table 125.
The figure for employment in 1940 as published in the 1950 census excludes the armed forces and public emergency workers. This estimate of civilian employment in 1940 is slightly smaller than the 1930 figure for total employment. Actually, total employment in 1940 was about 400,000 larger than in 1930 (see *Census of Population, 1940, Population, Estimates of the Labor Force, Employment, and Unemployment in the United States, 1940 and 1930,* prepared by John D. Durand and Edwin D. Goldfield). This discrepancy is due mainly to the fact that the 1930 employment figure is based on the gainful worker concept which includes persons 10–14 years of age. Partly it is due to the exclusion of about 300,000 armed forces from the 1940 census.

Engineers and Chemists including Surveyors

Line   Source

1–5   Edwards, *op. cit.,* p. 111.

6–7   *Ibid.,* p. 49.

Lines 1–7 include engineers and chemists in the armed forces in the United States.

8   Employed engineers in 1940 from *Census of Population, 1950*
(Vol. II, Part 1, Table 124),   275,325
plus unemployed engineers from 1940 census [a]   16,140
    Total engineers (including metallurgists)   291,465
    Total engineers (excluding metallurgists) [b]   286,551

145

Notes to Table B-1 (continued)

Employed chemists in 1940 from *Census of Population, 1950* (excluding metallurgists who are included in employed engineers) — 53,845

plus unemployed chemists from 1940 census [a] — 1,246

Total chemists — 55,091

Total chemists, including metallurgists [b] — 60,005

Employed surveyors in 1940 from *Census of Population, 1950* — 13,344

plus unemployed surveyors from 1940 census [a] — 3,100

Total surveyors — 16,444

Total engineers	286,551	
Total surveyors	16,444	302,995
Total chemists		60,005
Total engineers and chemists		363,000

[a] The numbers of unemployed engineers, chemists, and surveyors are the differences between the total number reported in each of these occupations by Edwards (*op. cit.*, p. 49) and the numbers of employed in each of these occupations as given in the 1940 census (see *Census of Population, 1940*, Vol. III, Part 1, Table 58).

[b] The total number of chemists was raised to 60,005 to correspond to the figure given in the 1940 Census, which includes metallurgists. The number of engineers was reduced accordingly to exclude metallurgists.

Line	Source
9–10	*Census of Population, 1950*, Vol. II, Part 1, Table 124.

Line 10 represents figures as given in the source. In line 9 the estimated number of metallurgists was shifted from engineers to chemists. Up to and including 1940, the census classified metallurgists as chemists. In the 1950 census metallurgists were shifted to engineers. The 1940 census reports 57,025 employed chemists, the 1950 census lists for 1940 only 53,845 employed chemists, a discrepancy of 5.91 per cent. The 1950 census figures for all and for employed chemists—75,747 and 74,433, respectively—were raised by 5.91 per cent to 80,224 and 78,833 respectively and the 1950 census figures for engineers were reduced accordingly.

11 — *Census of Population, 1930*, Vol. V, Chapter 7, Table 1 and *Census of Unemployment, 1930*, Vol. I, Tables 21 and 22, and Vol. II, Table 3.

12 — *Census of Population, 1940*, Vol. III, Part 1, Table 58.

Employed engineers	245,288	
Employed surveyors	13,344	258,632
Employed chemists		57,025
Total engineers and chemists (including surveyors)		315,657

13–16 *Census of Population, 1950*, Vol. II, Part 1, Table 125. Lines 14 and 16 are as given in source. In lines 13 and 15 metallurgists were shifted from engineers to chemists.

7, 12, 14 — The 1940 census reports 277,872 employed and unemployed engineers including surveyors, and 261,428 engineers excluding surveyors. The 1950 census reports for 1940 some 288,669 employed engineers including, and 275,325 employed engineers excluding, surveyors.

The 1940 census reports 16,140 unemployed engineers. If these had

Notes to Table B-1 (continued)

Line   Source

been added to the number of employed engineers in 1940, as shown in the 1950 census, the total for 1940 would be 291,465, instead of 261,428. This discrepancy of some 30,000 appears to be due to changes in classification.

The 1940 data on engineers in lines 13 and 14 are from the 1950 census and are comparable to the 1950 figures in lines 15 and 16. (The 1950 census does not give any data on the total number of engineers in 1940, including unemployed.)

Excluding Surveyors

Line   Source

6–16 For 1940 and 1950 the total numbers of surveyors and of employed surveyors are given in *Census of Population, 1950* (Vol. II, Part 1, Table 124), and in *Census of Population, 1940* (Vol. III, Part 1, Table 58). For 1930 the number of surveyors was estimated by reference to the ratio of surveyors to engineers in 1940 and 1950. The actual figures are:

	All Surveyors	Employed Surveyors
1950	26,229	25,321
1940	16,444	13,344
1930	11,447	10,037

TABLE B-2

Engineers and Chemists as a Percentage of the Labor Force

	Engineers including Surveyors	Chemists including Metallurgists	Engineers and Chemists including Surveyors	Engineers excluding Surveyors	Engineers and Chemists excluding Surveyors
1. 1890	0.121	0.019	0.140		
2. 1900	0.149	0.030	0.179		
3. 1910	0.237	0.044	0.281		
4. 1920	0.321	0.078	0.398		
5. 1930	0.463	0.096	0.560		
6. 1930	0.483	0.101	0.584	0.459	0.560
7. 1940	0.521	0.113	0.634	0.490	0.603
8. 1940	0.568	0.113	0.681	0.538	0.650
9. 1950	0.942	0.136	1.077	0.897	1.033
10. 1950	0.949	0.128	1.077	0.905	1.033
11. 1930	0.478	0.100	0.578	0.456	0.556
12. 1940	0.573	0.126	0.699	0.543	0.669
13. 1940	0.636	0.127	0.763	0.606	0.733
14. 1940	0.643	0.120	0.763	0.613	0.733
15. 1950	0.971	0.140	1.112	0.926	1.067
16. 1950	0.979	0.132	1.112	0.934	1.067

Source: Table B-1.

TABLE B-3

Total Employment and Employment of Chemists and Technical Engineers in Selected Industries, 1930, 1940, and 1950
(number of persons)

INDUSTRY	TOTAL EMPLOYMENT					EMPLOYMENT OF CHEMISTS AND TECHNICAL ENGINEERS				
						Including Surveyors		Excluding Surveyors		
	All Gainful Workers 1930	Estimated Total Employment 1930	Total Employment 1940 (comparable to 1930)	Total Employment 1940 (comparable to 1950)	Total Employment 1950	Gainful Workers 1930	Estimated Employed 1930	Employed 1940 (comparable to 1930)	Employed 1940 (comparable to 1950)	Employed 1950
I. Mining, total	1,156,377	966,885	907,520	907,520	928,260	9,137	8,391	10,940	10,080	13,860
1) Coal mining	691,288		523,680	523,680	510,180	2,485		2,020	1,700	2,610
2) Petroleum and natural gas	198,446		181,860	181,860	233,160	2,047		4,100	3,660	7,290
3) Metal mining	114,235		116,340	116,340	92,970	2,062		3,560	3,480	2,730
4) Other, including quarries	152,408		85,640	85,640	91,950	2,543		1,260	1,240	1,230
II. Construction	3,029,791	2,489,700	2,094,220	2,094,220	3,398,040	31,712	28,892	45,360	41,040	77,130
III. Manufacturing [a] (Durable goods [a])	5,472,037	4,972,946	5,626,440	5,626,440	8,182,290	73,543	70,496	114,700	114,560	253,580
	3,741,824	3,364,202	3,617,300	3,617,300	5,534,970	44,611	42,366	73,540	73,400	173,060
1. Iron and steel industries	1,931,857	n.a.	1,876,380	1,267,280	1,660,560	21,423	n.a.	34,200	18,940	33,840
a) Blast furnaces, steel works	620,894		545,300	545,300	661,380	7,126		9,500	9,500	13,860
b) Other primary iron and steel	1,310,963		1,331,080	721,980	285,180	14,297		24,700	9,440	4,050
c) Miscellaneous iron and steel products					714,000					15,930

148

	(1)	(2)	(3)	(4)	(5)	(6)	(7)	(8)	(9)	(10)
2. Non-ferrous metal industries	151,681	n.a.	202,880	202,880	320,040	2,176	n.a.	3,300	3,280	7,920
a) Primary nonferrous products	69,964		89,520	89,520	216,120	} 2,176		1,960	1,940	6,450
b) Miscellaneous nonferrous products	81,717		113,360	113,360	103,920	}		1,340	1,340	1,470
3. Not specified metal industries	168,899	n.a.	121,460	38,260	13,410	1,220	n.a.	3,120	500	300
4. Machinery	436,814	n.a.	464,080	1,073,180	2,054,610	13,639	n.a.	18,320	33,580	80,870
a) Electric machinery and equipment	383,570		372,940	372,940	770,970	13,311		16,980	16,980	38,070
b) Agricultural machinery	53,244		91,140	91,140	178,770	328		1,340	1,340	3,900
c) Office and store machinery	included in 5c		included in 5c	61,560	105,570	included in 5c		included in 5c	740	2,730
d) Miscellaneous machinery	}		}	547,540	999,300	}		}	14,520	36,170
5. Transportation equipment	968,693	n.a.	879,840	879,840	1,336,230	5,917	n.a.	14,140	14,020	42,240
a) Aircraft and parts	in 9d		in 9d	107,680	257,220	in 9d		in 9d	4,900	23,820
b) Motor vehicles and equipment	640,474		575,480	575,480	863,400	5,132		6,760	6,720	13,710
c) Ships and boats	93,437		151,420	151,420	153,780	444		1,820	1,740	3,030
d) Railroad and misc. transportation equipment	234,782		152,940	45,260	61,830	341		5,560	660	1,680
6. Professional equip. and instruments	83,880	n.a.	72,660	155,860	196,740	236	n.a.	460	3,080	7,890
a) Professional equipment	included in 7		included in 7	83,200	115,200	included in 7		included in 7	} 2,620	4,740
b) Photographic equipment	}		}		46,620	}		}	}	2,730
c) Watches, clocks, timepieces	83,880		72,660		34,920	236	28,130	460	460	420
(Nondurable goods [a])	1,730,259	1,608,744	2,009,140	2,009,140	2,647,320	28,932		41,320	41,320	80,520

TABLE B-3 (continued)

INDUSTRY	TOTAL EMPLOYMENT					EMPLOYMENT OF CHEMISTS AND TECHNICAL ENGINEERS				
						Including Surveyors		Excluding Surveyors		
	All Gainful Workers 1930	Estimated Total Employment 1930	Total Employment 1940 (comparable to 1930)	Total Employment 1940 (comparable to 1950)	Total Employment 1950	Gainful Workers 1930	Estimated Employed 1930	Employed 1940 (comparable to 1930)	Employed 1940 (comparable to 1950)	Employed 1950
7. Food, drink, tobacco	1,056,816	974,725	1,207,940	1,207,940	1,472,550	4,233	4,069	6,400	6,400	13,020
8. Chemicals and allied products	321,492	305,851	440,820	440,820	654,480	16,810	16,403	21,200	21,180	43,860
a) Synthetic fibres	33,982		52,480	52,480	53,370	723		1,160	1,160	2,220
b) Paints, varnishes, etc.	37,074		43,280	43,280	57,090	1,427		2,640	2,640	3,450
c) Drugs and medicines	250,436 }		345,060 }	345,060 }	57,030	14,660 }		17,400 }	17,380 }	3,570
d) Misc. chemicals					486,990					34,620
9. Petroleum and coal products	185,564	176,537	202,180	202,180	284,280	5,924	5,780	10,700	10,560	18,690
a) Petroleum refining	173,798		178,980	178,980	257,190	5,628		9,960	9,820	17,790
b) Misc. petroleum and coal products	11,766		23,200	23,200	27,090	296		740	740	900
10. Rubber products	166,391	151,631	158,200	158,200	236,010	1,965	1,878	3,020	3,020	4,950
Transportation, communications, and other public utilities	4,013,684	3,788,587	3,295,920	3,414,540	4,869,460	42,548	41,447	41,500	43,820	68,520
IV. Transportation	2,737,997	2,553,118	2,176,460	2,176,460	2,927,010	14,858	14,358	8,600	8,380	11,910
1) Air transportation	18,189		22,320	22,320	94,500	467		480	440	1,260
2) Railroads and express service	1,645,306		1,137,000	1,137,000	1,381,740	10,706		5,820	5,680	6,180

Table (rotated on page; categories III–IX continued). No column headers appear on this page.

Category	(1)	(2)	(3)	(4)	(5)	(6)	(7)	(8)	(9)	(10)
3) Streetcars and buses	195,408		202,320	202,320	325,200	1,549		900	900	1,320
4) Trucking and taxicabs	483,148		511,520	511,520	765,260	40		100	100	540
5) Warehousing and storage	59,394		62,060	62,060	97,350	429		240	240	840
6) Water transportation	299,804		180,240	180,240	203,250	1,325		400	320	480
7) Pipelines	25,001		17,420	17,420	20,220	217		460	440	990
8) Incidental transportation services	11,747		43,580	43,580	41,490	125		260	260	300
V. Communications	871,502	851,234	703,140	703,140	1,163,950	13,303	13,149	12,180	12,160	25,020
1) Postal service	283,936		309,240	309,240	460,510	0		80	80	150
2) Telephone	578,602		{370,300}	{370,300}	594,750	{12,760}		{9,820}	9,800	15,600
3) Telegraph					46,260				2,280	510
4) Radio and television	8,964		23,600	23,600	62,430	543		2,280	2,280	8,760
VI. Utilities and sanitary services	404,185	384,185	416,320	534,940	778,500	14,297	13,940	20,660	23,280	31,590
1) Electric light and power	289,255		329,880	329,880	448,890	12,633		18,640	18,280	22,860
2) Gas supply	114,930		86,440	86,440	114,720	1,664		2,020	1,980	2,760
3) Water supply	{n.a.}		{excl.}	{118,620}	73,700	{n.a.}		{excl.}	{3,020}	3,420
4) Sanitary services					105,820					1,170
5) Not specified utilities					35,370					1,380
VII. Professional and related services										
Including education	2,965,742	2,908,072	3,320,000	1,749,880	2,572,020	57,934	57,373	25,860	21,240	38,190
Excluding education										
VIII. Education	{included in 16}	{included in 16}	{included in 16}	1,570,120	2,076,630	{included in 16}	{included in 16}	{included in 16}	2,180	7,740
1) Government				n.a.	1,547,000				n.a.	4,980
2) Private				n.a.	529,620				n.a.	2,760
IX. Public administration										
Including armed forces	1,049,576	1,019,903	1,448,680			26,935		26,555	35,280	

{ } = value shown combined for the braced rows in the original table.

TABLE B-3 (continued)

INDUSTRY	TOTAL EMPLOYMENT					EMPLOYMENT OF CHEMISTS AND TECHNICAL ENGINEERS				
						Including Surveyors		Excluding Surveyors		
	All Gainful Workers 1930	Estimated Total Employment 1930	Total Employment 1940 (comparable to 1930)	Total Employment 1940 (comparable to 1950)	Total Employment 1950	Gainful Workers 1930	Estimated Employed 1930	Employed 1940 (comparable to 1930)	Employed 1940 (comparable to 1950)	Employed 1950
Excluding armed forces				1,147,180	2,030,160				28,100	54,480
1) Federal government	n.a.		excl.	299,280 }	1,006,260	n.a.		excl.	11,380 }	36,660
2) State government	n.a.		excl.	847,900 }	266,760	n.a.		excl.	16,720 }	5,400
3) Local government	n.a.		excl.		757,140	n.a.		excl.		12,420
Subtotal, above industries	17,687,257	16,146,093	16,692,780	16,509,900	24,103,480	241,719	233,154	273,800	261,020	513,500
All other industries b	31,142,663	29,496,180	28,688,580	28,569,960	31,700,040	31,598	30,764	39,000	34,980	79,000
Total, all industries										
Including armed forces	48,829,920	45,642,273	45,381,360	45,079,860	55,803,520	273,317	263,918	312,800		
Excluding armed forces									296,000	592,500

n.a. = not available.

a Includes industries listed under this heading; excludes manufacturing industries included in "All other industries," enumerated in footnote b.

b Includes agriculture, forestry, fisheries; the following manufacturing industries: lumber and wood products, glass products, stone and clay products, textiles and clothing, paper and printing, leather and leather products. Includes further: wholesale and retail trade, finance, insurance and real estate, business and repair service, entertainment and recreation, and personal services.

APPENDIX B

NOTES TO TABLE B-3 (continued)

Source: *Census of Population, 1930*, Vol. V, *General Report on Occupations*, Chap. 7, Table 2 (based on full count); *Census of Population, 1940, The Labor Force, Occupational Characteristics*, Table 19 (based on a 5 per cent sample); *Census of Population, 1950*, Special Report P. E., 1 C, *Occupation by Industry* (based on a 3⅓ per cent sample); *Census of Unemployment, 1930*, Vol. I, Tables 21 and 22; Vol. II, Table 3; Alba M. Edwards, *Comparative Occupation Statistics for the United States, 1870 to 1940*, Bureau of the Census, 1943.

Comparability and Adjustment of Data

a) *Gainful Workers and Employed Persons*

The 1930 census refers to "gainful workers, 10 years old and over"; the relevant tables of the 1940 and 1950 censuses to "employed persons (except on public emergency work), 14 years old and over." Partly because of these different concepts the total number of persons included in the occupation-by-industry cross-classification was 48.8 million in 1930 as compared to 45.4 million in 1940.

In the second column for 1930 the unemployed gainful workers have been excluded using the data given in the Census of Unemployment. Since this adjustment does not take account of the differences between the "labor force" and "gainful worker" concept, the resulting total for employed persons in 1930 (45.6 million) is still some 260,000 larger than the total employment figure for 1940. On a basis comparable to that of the 1940 census, total employment in 1930 would have been 45.0 million, that is, about 400,000 less than in 1940 (see *Census of Population, 1940, Population, Estimates of the Labor Force, Employment, and Unemployment in the United States, 1940 and 1930*, prepared by John D. Durand and Edwin D. Goldfield). These adjusted data, however, are available only for total labor force and employment, not for industries or occupations.

The 1930 Census of Unemployment gives data for broad industry groups, a few industrial subgroups, and for occupations. Unemployment data for occupation by industry and for most industrial subgroups are not available. For some other industry groups unemployment had to be estimated. The broad group "Chemicals and allied products" of the Unemployment Census was broken down into "Chemicals," "Petroleum and coal products," and "Gas works." Unemployment in these subgroups was assumed to be at the same rate as for the group as a whole. "Gas works" were shifted to "Utilities" and unemployment in "Electric light and power" (a group which is missing in the Unemployment Census) was estimated at the same rate as in "Gas works." For the remaining industry groups the Unemployment Census data were used.

The estimated numbers of unemployed chemists and engineers in the various industry groups were derived as follows: The rate of unemployment was calculated for each industry. These rates (which varied from 1.9 to 16.4 per cent) were applied to the total number of chemists and engineers attached to each industry group. Since unemployment in these professions was far below the average rate, the resulting figures added up to a total almost twice as large as the number of unemployed chemists and engineers given in the Unemployment Census. These figures for the various industry groups were then reduced using the ratio of the given total to the above-mentioned calculated total.

b) *Occupational Classification*

In 1930, "Surveyors" are included in "Civil Engineers" and could not be separated. In the attached tables they are included in the 1940 column comparable to 1930; excluded from the 1940 figures comparable to 1950.

In 1930 and 1940 "Chemists" include also "Assayers and Metallurgists" and

153

possibly also some metallurgical engineers. In 1950, metallurgists are allocated to "Technical Engineers." This shift in classification is largely responsible for the apparent decline in the employment of chemists in the metal industries, and especially in "Primary metals" between 1940 and 1950.

At the 1940 census persons under 35 years were not classified as technical engineers unless they had had at least four years of college education. In 1930 this rule did not apply (see Edwards, *op. cit.*, p. 24), nor did it in 1950.

The 1930 and 1950 data for chemists and engineers attached to the various industries refer to males and females, the 1940 data to males only. But in this year the number of employed females in these professions was negligible. The final census count (not the sample statistics used for the attached tables) reports 2,384 employed female chemists and engineers, that is, 0.78 per cent of the total employment in these professions.

c) *Industrial Classification*

The 1930 data and the data for 1940 comparable to 1930 refer to all industries, including the armed forces, but excluding public emergency work. The 1950 data and the 1940 totals comparable to 1950 exclude the armed forces.

The 1940 and 1950 censuses use basically the same industrial classification. The 1950 Census lists a number of additional subgroups which for comparison with earlier years had to be combined into larger units, e.g. "Professional equipment" and "Photographic equipment" are one subgroup in 1940. A few subgroups had to be shifted, as for instance, "Broadcasting and television" from "Entertainment and recreation" to "Communications." The 1940 subgroup "National defense" was removed from "Public administration" which in 1950 is limited to civilians. For a few subgroups comparability could not be established: in 1950 there is a separate category "Watches, clocks, and timepieces," while "Jewelry and silverware" are included in "Miscellaneous manufacturing industries." In 1940, watches and clocks are combined with jewelry and silverware and could not be separated. In the nonferrous industries, the subgroups "primary products" and "miscellaneous products" are not identical in 1940 and 1950, but the group as a whole appears to be comparable for these years.

Generally, large relative changes in small subgroups should be interpreted with caution. Thus the large increase in professional employment in "Warehousing" or "Trucking" appears to be due partly to changes in classification or errors resulting from the small size of the sample. (Since in the 1950 occupation-by-industry-tables the number of persons in the sample was multiplied by 30, these tables include small industrial subgroups which show 30 females, but no males as employed chemists.)

The industrial classification system used in the 1930 census was markedly different from the later systems. First of all, the group "Professional service, including education, excluding amusement and recreation" includes a considerable number of engineers and chemists who were not allocated to specific industries although most likely they were not working as independent professionals but were employed by different industries. The 1930 census reports 57,934 chemists and engineers in "Professional service" as compared to 25,860 in 1940. That is, comparability with later years is impaired by the fact that some 30,000 to 35,000 were not distributed among the various industries. It appears that the construction industry is especially affected and that a much larger number of engineers was attached to this group in 1930 than shown by the census data.

For two of the most important industry groups—chemicals and iron and steel industries—the 1930 classification is so different from the later systems that Edwards and also Daniel Carson in his "Changes in the Industrial Composi-

APPENDIX B

tion of Manpower since the Civil War" (in *Studies in Income and Wealth, Volume Eleven,* National Bureau of Economic Research, 1949) declare these 1930 and 1940 industries are not comparable. In the attached tables the attempt has been made to establish more or less comparable groups, mainly by shifting and combining of subgroups. Thus the 1940 category "Miscellaneous machinery" was combined with "Miscellaneous iron and steel products" for comparison with 1930. But certain inconsistencies could not be eliminated. The subgroup "Agricultural machinery" includes tractors in 1940 but not in 1930; the 1930 group "Blast furnaces and steel rolling mills" includes some workers in manufacturing establishments, etc.

The 1930 group "Utilities" consists of "Gas works" (shifted from Chemicals and allied products) and "Electric light and power" from the census group "Miscellaneous manufacturing industries." Other utilities, for which 1930 data are not available, were excluded from the 1940 column comparable to 1930 and shifted to "All other industries."

Except for the different treatment of "Other utilities" and "Jewelry and silverware" (see above—1950), the broad group "All other industries" includes in 1930 the same categories as in 1940 and 1950. It combines all those industries in which employment of engineers was negligible and has not been computed for this survey. The groups included are: agriculture, forestry and fishing; textiles and clothing; leather and leather products; lumber and wooden goods; paper and printing; stone, clay and glass products; wholesale and retail trade; finance, insurance and real estate; business and repair services; personal services; amusement and recreation; and industry not specified.

In conclusion it should be pointed out that the comparability of the 1930 figures with later data is affected more strongly by the difference between the "gainful worker" and "employed persons" concept and the incomplete industrial distribution of professional personnel than by inconsistencies in the composition of specific industries or subgroups.

APPENDIX C

TABLES ON ENGINEERING
ENROLLMENTS AND DEGREES

IN THIS appendix we present various tables on the number and the distribution among the several specialties of enrollments and degrees in engineering. There is no single comprehensive source of such information for the period in which we are interested. We are forced, therefore, to use a number of different sources for varying overlapping periods. The data are here presented together to provide the reader with as complete a view of historic trends in engineering education as the scattered information permits.

TABLE C-1

Enrollments in Engineering Courses in Universities, Colleges, and Technological Schools, 1904–1915

Academic Year Ending June	Civil	Chemical	Electrical	Mechanical	Mining	Other	Total [a]
1904	4,431	499	2,662	3,778	1,465	17	12,852
1905	7,356	759	5,204	6,654	2,547	2,065	24,585
1906	7,962	1,234	5,696	7,426	2,826	4,231	29,375
1909	9,649	1,117	7,154	6,142	3,150	n.a.	27,212
1910	7,889	869	5,450	6,377	2,656	n.a.	23,241
1911	8,939	1,452	6,128	7,052	2,337	n.a.	25,908
1915	7,182	2,383	6,637	7,751	1,922	7,185	33,060
Percentage Distribution							
1904	34.5	3.9	20.7	29.4	11.4	0.1	100.0
1905	29.9	3.1	21.2	27.0	10.4	8.4	100.0
1906	27.1	4.2	19.4	25.3	9.6	14.4	100.0
1909	35.5	4.1	26.3	22.5	11.6	n.a.	100.0
1910	34.0	3.7	23.5	27.4	11.4	n.a.	100.0
1911	34.5	5.6	23.7	27.2	9.0	n.a.	100.0
1915	21.7	7.2	20.2	23.4	5.8	21.7	100.0

[a] The total number enrolled in engineering was not given in the source; it was obtained for each year by adding the numbers reported in the specified fields.
Source: *Annual Report of the Commissioner of Education, 1903–1904,* and *1915–1916,* Office of Education.

TABLE C-2

Total Enrollments of Students in Engineering in the United States, 1920–1953

Academic Year Ending June	TOTAL ENROLLMENTS		UNDERGRADUATE ENROLLMENTS		GRADUATE ENROLLMENTS	
	Office of Education (1)	Journal of Engineering Education (2)	Office of Education (3)	Journal of Engineering Education (4)	Office of Education (5)	Journal of Engineering Education (6)
1920	51,908	57,017	51,908	. . .	. . .	. . .
1922	56,649	. . .	56,649	56,649	. . .	368
1924	57,690	. . .	57,690	. . .	. . .	. . .
1926	59,315	57,313	59,315	56,299	. . .	1,014
1927	. . .	60,899	. . .	59,133	. . .	1,766
1928	66,637	64,692	66,637	63,023	. . .	1,669
1930	74,000	. . .	74,000	. . .	. . .	. . .
1931	. . .	76,325	. . .	73,386	. . .	2,939
1932	77,041	. . .	73,766	. . .	3,275	. . .
1933	. . .	67,046	. . .	63,119	. . .	3,927
1934	65,406	. . .	62,600	. . .	2,805	2,756
1936	74,752	66,541	71,827	64,137	2,933 [a]	2,404
1937	. . .	69,976	. . .	67,515	. . .	2,461
1938	92,724	87,943	89,440	84,547	3,284	3,396
1939	. . .	87,760	. . .	82,585	. . .	5,175
1940	107,918	108,426	103,270	102,879	4,648	5,547
1941	. . .	114,116	. . .	108,911	. . .	5,205
1942	119,339	112,709	115,018	108,091	4,321	4,618
1943	. . .	124,647	. . .	121,541	. . .	3,106
1944	112,749	48,061	109,138	45,404	3,611	2,657
1945	. . .	38,017	. . .	34,892	. . .	3,126
1946	. . .	67,045	. . .	63,064	. . .	4,010 [a]
1947	. . .	211,782	. . .	197,797	. . .	13,985
1948	250,009	244,390	236,370	230,180	13,639	14,210
1949	. . .	241,549	. . .	225,655	. . .	15,432 [a]
1950	228,914	219,712	210,806	201,927	18,108	17,785
1951	. . .	180,262	. . .	161,592	. . .	18,670
1952	176,549	165,637	156,080	145,997	20,469	19,640
1953	. . .	176,549	. . .	156,080	. . .	20,469

. . . = not available.

[a] The figures for undergraduate and graduate enrollments in the sources do not total to the figures for total enrollments.

Column	Source

1, 3, 5 *Biennial Surveys of Education,* Office of Education, 1920–1950; "Engineering Enrollments and Degrees," processed, Office of Education, Circular 364, January 21, 1953.

Total enrollment figures for the years 1920–1936 were derived by summing the numbers enrolled in specified fields, as reported in the Biennial Surveys. For the years

Column	Source

1938–1952 the source gives total enrollment data and it is this total which is shown in the table for each of these years.

The classification of schools for which engineering enrollments were reported by the Office of Education has varied over the years as follows:

1920–1930: Students in engineering courses in universities, colleges, and professional schools.

1932–1938: Students enrolled in professional schools, both independent and university schools.

1940–1944: Resident student enrollment in professional schools.

1948: Students in professional school of engineering.

1952: Engineering students enrolled in U.S. schools.

2, 4, 6 *Journal of Engineering Education,* annual statistics on engineering enrollments and graduates, November 1932 to February 1954.

For the years 1942 through 1953 enrollments were reported as of October or November of the preceding year.

Beginning with the year 1950, the *Journal of Engineering Education* presented separate data on enrollments in ECPD accredited schools as follows:

Total Enrollments: 1950, 198,266; 1951, 161,324; 1952, 147,694; 1953, 158,518.

Undergraduate Enrollments: 1950, 180,646; 1951, 142,954; 1952, 128,367; 1953, 138,170.

TABLE C-3

Undergraduate Enrollments in Engineering Schools, in the
United States, by Class, 1926–1953

Academic Year Ending June	Number of Institutions	Freshmen	Sophomores	Juniors	Seniors	5 year Course
1926	143	20,063	14,493	10,695	9,063	. . .
1927	148	22,765	16,123	11,562	9,403	. . .
1928	148	23,360	16,905	12,685	10,073	. . .
1931	145	25,332	19,631	16,262	12,161	. . .
1933	143	17,441	17,028	15,542	13,108	. . .
1935	68	13,275	9,452	8,868	7,923	. . .
1936	124	20,128	14,821	12,031	10,436	363
1937	115	23,058	15,842	12,528	9,671	379
1938	126	27,532	20,326	15,536	11,824	625
1939	122	25,444	19,988	16,701	12,420	508
1940	146	30,787	23,378	18,936	16,235	845
1941	149	33,175	29,242	20,120	16,310	985
1942	. . .	34,993	24,349	19,009	16,291	1,311
1943	166	50,263	27,912	21,164	17,341	1,105
1944	143	16,609	7,985	6,334	7,737	329
1945	. . .	17,823	5,203	3,213	2,373	143
1946	. . .	32,455	11,248	6,648	4,081	106
1947	130	80,703	50,406	30,615	20,740	705
1948	143	57,507	71,615	48,227	32,369	1,846
1949	145	47,672	52,949	59,945	45,695	1,924

TABLE C-3 (continued)

Academic Year Ending June	Number of Institutions	Freshmen	Sophomores	Juniors	Seniors	5 year Course
1950	. . .	41,077	39,558	46,077	55,698	2,664
1951	. . .	34,299	30,915	34,423	41,702	3,514
1952	. . .	39,571	26,741	27,545	30,722	3,214
1953	. . .	51,631	30,219	25,011	25,964	3,065

. . . = not available.

Source: *Journal of Engineering Education,* annual statistics on engineering enrollments, various issues November 1932 to February 1954. For the years 1942 through 1953 enrollments are as of October or November of the preceding year.

TABLE C-4

Male Enrollments in Engineering as Per Cent of Total Enrollments, 1934–1952

Academic Year Ending June	Office of Education (1)	Journal of Engineering Education (2)
1934	99.98	. . .
1936	99.73	. . .
1938	99.51	. . .
1940	99.61	. . .
1942	99.59	. . .
1944	98.46	. . .
1945	. .	96.35
1946	. . .	97.31
1947	. . .	99.87
1948	99.41	. . .
1949	. . .	99.47
1950	99.60	99.65
1951	. . .	99.62
1952	99.61	99.79

. . . = not available.
Source: Same as in Table C-2.

TABLE C-5

Total U.S. Enrollments in Engineering, by Field, 1920–1953, Percentage Distribution

Academic Year Ending June	OFFICE OF EDUCATION [a]							JOURNAL OF ENGINEERING EDUCATION [b]						
	Civil	Mechanical	Electrical	Chemical	Mining	Other	Total	Civil	Mechanical	Electrical	Chemical	Mining	Other	Total
1920	17.1	22.7	18.2	11.1	5.9	25.0	100.0	22.7	25.4	23.5	12.5	5.1	10.8	100.0
1922	17.1	21.5	21.8	9.5	5.7	24.4	100.0							
1924	17.4	18.4	24.3	7.2	4.8	27.9	100.0							
1926	18.3	16.4	26.4	7.1	2.8	29.0	100.0	21.5	18.3	31.4	8.4	3.5	16.8	100.0
1927								22.2	16.6	33.0	9.4	3.2	15.6	100.0
1928	17.3	15.7	23.7	7.4	2.3	33.6	100.0	21.6	17.3	31.0	9.2	3.2	17.7	100.0
1930	15.6	15.7	21.1	6.0	1.9	39.7	100.0							
1931								18.5	20.2	25.4	12.5	3.8	19.6	100.0
1932	14.8	18.1	20.2	12.0	3.3	31.6	100.0							
1933								21.1	23.4	22.9	14.7	3.7	14.2	100.0
1934	13.3	18.2	18.2	11.5	2.6	36.2	100.0							
1936	11.7	18.7	15.8	14.4	3.3	36.1	100.0	13.3	19.4	17.6	15.0	2.3	32.4	100.0
1937														
1938														
1939														
1940								10.2	25.5	14.3	15.0	2.0	33.0	100.0
1941								9.9	24.8	13.3	15.4	1.3	35.3	100.0
1942								9.9	25.6	13.9	15.2	1.2	34.2	100.0
1943								9.9	22.4	15.6	17.0	0.9	34.2	100.0
1944														
1945														
1946								9.9	18.5	16.5	10.6	0.7	43.8	100.0

TABLE C-5 (continued)

Academic Year Ending June	OFFICE OF EDUCATION [a]							JOURNAL OF ENGINEERING EDUCATION [b]						
	Civil	Mechanical	Electrical	Chemical	Mining	Other	Total	Civil	Mechanical	Electrical	Chemical	Mining	Other	Total
1947								14.2	21.0	18.4	8.4	0.9	37.1	100.0
1948								12.6	22.4	22.4	10.8	1.0	30.8	100.0
1949								13.9	22.1	22.2	9.7	0.9	31.2	100.0
1950								14.7	23.0	23.1	10.1	1.0	28.1	100.0
1951								15.2	21.9	21.2	10.1	1.0	30.6	100.0
1952	13.9	20.6	20.2	8.8	C.7	35.8	100.0	14.8	20.6	20.3	9.5	0.9	33.9	100.0
1953								14.1	20.7	20.7	9.5	0.7	34.3	100.0

[a] *Biennial Survey of Education*, Office of Education, 1920–1936; "Engineering Enrollments and Degrees, 1952," processed, Office of Education, Circular 364, January 21, 1953. The Office of Education did not publish data on engineering enrollments by field for the years 1938–1950.

[b] *Journal of Engineering*, annual statistics on enrollment, November 1932 to February 1954.

Note: For the years 1942 through 1953 enrollments were reported as of October or November of the preceding year. The figure for the year 1945 does not include graduate enrollments. The figures for the years 1939 through 1949, with the exception of 1943, and undergraduate enrollments in 1947, include enrollments in Canadian schools. For the years 1950–1954 enrollments are reported for ECPD accredited schools only.

TABLE C-6

Total Degrees Awarded in Engineering in the United States, 1920–1953

Academic Year Ending June	FIRST DEGREES (Baccalaureate and First Professional Degrees)			GRADUATE DEGREES						
				Total Graduate Degrees		Master's Degree		Doctor's Degree		
	Office of Education (1)	Bureau of Labor Statistics (2)	Journal of Engineering Education (3)	Office of Education (4)	Journal of Engineering Education (5)	Office of Education (6)	Journal of Engineering Education (7)	Office of Education (8)	Journal of Engineering Education (9)	National Science Foundation (10)
1920	4,400	5,000	...	207	...	206	...	1	...	5
1921	...	6,100	...	...	...	...	...	...	...	1
1922	6,823	7,500	...	350	...	348	...	2	...	4
1923	...	7,700	...	...	...	...	...	...	...	5
1924	7,470	8,000	...	315	...	315	...	...	...	5
1925	...	7,800	...	...	...	...	...	...	...	2
1926	7,389	7,600	...	632	...	631	...	1	...	11
1927	...	7,800	...	...	...	...	...	...	...	10
1928	7,633	7,900	...	785	...	771	...	14	...	28
1929	...	7,800	...	...	...	...	...	...	...	34
1930	7,395	7,700	...	813	...	811	...	2	...	49
1931	...	9,200	...	...	...	...	...	...	...	25
1932	10,374	10,700	...	1,630	...	1,514	...	116	...	47
1933	...	11,300	...	...	...	...	...	...	...	75
1934	11,419	12,000	...	1,394	...	1,259	...	135	...	97
1935	...	11,600	...	...	...	...	...	...	...	63
1936	10,629	11,200	8,847	1,280	817	1,169	735	111	82	48
1937	...	11,400	7,881	...	1,184	...	1,058	...	126	70
1938	11,039	11,600	8,245	1,261	1,248	1,117	1,156	144	92	59
1939	...	13,300	8,697	...	1,316	...	1,219	...	97	44

TABLE C-6 (continued)

	(1)	(2)	(3)	(4)	(5)	(6)	(7)	(8)	(9)	(10)
1940	14,348	15,100	12,408	1,460	1,426	1,336	1,318	124	108	77
1941	....	15,200	11,358	....	1,532	....	1,358	....	174	76
1942	15,519	16,000	12,709	1,172	....	1,043	....	129	....	47
1943	....	15,300	....	....	721	....	637	....	84	22
1944	12,785	13,500	14,145	762	623	681	529	81	94	30
1945	....	8,500	4,190	....	519	....	450	....	69	37
1946	....	11,500	7,381	....	1,072	....	988	....	84	89
1947	....	21,000	18,592	....	3,217	....	3,090	....	127	94
1948	31,096	32,000	27,391	....	4,555	....	4,303	....	252	257
1949	....	44,000	41,793	5,007	5,200	4,647	4,783	360	417	360
1950	52,246	47,000	48,160	4,913	5,357	4,496	4,865	417	492	417
1951	....	36,000	37,887	....	5,720	....	5,134	....	586	520
1952	30,286	29,000	27,051	4,727	4,718	4,141	4,132	586	586	529
1953	....	....	21,556	....	4,318	....	3,726	....	592	518

Source

Column

1, 4, 6,   *Biennial Surveys of Education*, Office of Education, 1920–1942, "Earned Degrees Conferred by Higher Educational Institutions,
8   1949–1950," processed, Office of Education, Circular 282, December 1950.
    "Engineering Enrollments and Degrees, 1952," processed, Office of Education, Circular 364, January 21, 1953.
    For the years 1920–1936 figures on degrees awarded were obtained by totalling the number of degrees reported by spe-
    cified fields for each of these years in the biennial surveys.
    The classification of schools for the period covered changed as indicated in note to Table C-2.
    Separate data for engineering degrees conferred by arts and science schools were reported in the biennial surveys of 1934–
    1944. However, the surveys of 1940 and 1942 did not include the number of such degrees in their total figures of engineering
    degrees awarded for those years. They are included in this table.

2   *Employment Outlook for Engineers*, Bureau of Labor Statistics, Bull. 968, 1949, Appendix D, Table D-3.
    Estimates for years 1920–1949 are based on an adjustment for schools not reporting each year. Figures for years 1950–1952
    are forecasts of BLS based on enrollments for the academic year 1948–1949 published in the *Journal of Engineering Education*,
    February 1949.

3, 5, 7,   *Journal of Engineering Education*, annual statistics on engineering enrollments and graduates, December 1935 to February 1954.
9   For the years 1949–1954 the number of engineering degrees were reported for ECPD accredited schools only.

10   "Scientific Personnel Resources," processed, National Science Foundation, May 1954, Table No. IV-76.

163

TABLE C-7

First Degrees in Engineering, by Field, 1920–1952, Percentage Distribution

Academic Year Ending June	Civil	Mechanical	Electrical	Chemical	Mining	General	Other	Total
				Office of Education [a]				
1920	24.8	28.1	21.2	16.6	6.2	3.1	...	100.0
1922	23.7	24.5	21.8	14.8	6.8	8.4	...	100.0
1924	23.4	27.5	27.4	11.2	6.7	3.8	...	100.0
1926	25.3	24.5	30.4	10.0	5.5	4.3	...	100.0
1928	24.6	21.2	33.6	9.2	3.7	7.7	...	100.0
1930	26.7	22.6	32.8	11.1	3.2	3.6	...	100.0
1932	20.2	20.1	23.9	11.1	4.4	...	20.3	100.0
1934	19.0	22.9	23.9	12.7	2.8	...	18.7	100.0
1936	18.2	22.9	20.5	16.1	3.5	...	18.8	100.0
1950	14.9	27.6	25.4	8.6	...	...	23.5	100.0
1952	17.7	25.1	21.0	9.4	1.4	...	25.4	100.0
				Journal of Engineering Education [b]				
1935	18.0	22.2	23.6	14.6	3.4	...	18.2	100.0
1938	17.5	21.4	19.6	17.6	2.5	...	21.4	100.0
1941 1942	10.9	27.5	18.8	18.2	2.4	...	22.2	100.0
1943	12.0	29.6	16.4	18.4	1.9	...	21.7	100.0
1944	13.3	30.2	18.4	20.3	1.4	...	16.4	100.0
1945	13.6	29.0	18.1	16.3	1.3	...	21.7	100.0
1946	15.2	24.6	18.4	17.4	0.8	...	23.6	100.0
1947	13.4	30.3	19.0	13.3	1.2	...	22.8	100.0
1948	11.1	27.8	22.0	11.3	1.0	...	26.8	100.0
1949	14.6	27.8	24.7	9.9	0.9	...	22.1	100.0
1950	15.2	27.1	27.7	9.2	0.9	...	19.9	100.0
1951	17.1	25.4	22.7	9.5	1.2	...	24.1	100.0
1952	18.1	25.1	21.6	10.1	1.4	...	23.7	100.0

[a] *Biennial Surveys of Education,* Office of Education, 1920–1936; "Earned Degrees Conferred by Higher Educational Institutions, 1949–1950," processed, Office of Education, Circular 282, December 1950, "Engineering Enrollments and Degrees, 1952," processed, Office of Education, Circular 364, January 21, 1953.

[b] *Journal of Engineering Education,* annual statistics on engineering enrollments and graduates, December 1935 to February 1953. The years 1941, 1942, and 1944–1947 include schools in Canada; the data for years 1949–1953 are limited to ECPD accredited schools only.

APPENDIX C

TABLE C-8

Graduate Degrees in Engineering by Field, 1920–1952,
Percentage Distribution

Academic Year Ending June	Civil	Mechanical	Electrical	Chemical	Mining	Other	Total
			Office of Education				
1920	32.9	18.8	15.9	6.3	2.9	23.2	100.0
1922	23.1	19.7	16.3	9.2	5.7	26.0	100.0
1924	17.1	19.1	15.2	5.4	8.3	34.9	100.0
1926	17.8	10.0	13.0	2.4	1.6	55.2	100.0
1928	13.6	9.7	8.7	3.1	2.5	62.4	100.0
1930	12.7	8.7	9.1	2.3	2.7	64.5	100.0
1932	20.3	14.8	21.5	14.8	5.0	23.6	100.0
1934	14.7	17.5	20.2	13.8	3.1	30.7	100.0
1936	17.5	14.6	17.8	18.4	3.2	28.5	100.0
1950	14.6	16.9	23.1	17.8	n.a.	27.6	100.0
			Journal of Engineering Education				
1940	21.5	12.3	16.3	25.0	2.2	22.7	100.0
1941	17.1	12.1	15.0	29.6	1.5	24.7	100.0
1942							
1943	15.6	16.4	10.5	25.8	1.8	29.9	100.0
1944							
1945	11.1	16.5	14.1	24.0	1.5	32.8	100.0
1946	13.0	16.1	17.4	21.1	2.9	29.5	100.0
1947	20.8	15.9	17.7	21.7	1.4	22.5	100.0
1948	20.6	14.9	19.6	19.6	0.9	24.4	100.0
1950	14.0	16.3	23.3	16.6	0.7	29.1	100.0
1951	12.7	18.2	22.6	16.0	0.8	29.7	100.0
1952	13.3	15.1	24.1	14.8	0.7	31.9	100.0

Source: Same as in Table C-7.

165

PROJECTIONS OF THE NUMBER
OF ENGINEERING DEGREES TO 1970

IN THIS appendix we develop several projections of the number of engineering graduates for the period to 1970. Our purpose is not to provide precise quantitative estimates of the numbers of such graduates that we expect in the next decade and a half. To obtain such estimates would require a close study of the factors determining the number of students specializing in engineering and the future strength of these factors. Rather we merely wish to indicate the rough orders of magnitude of graduates if past trends persist.

The number of engineering graduates is a function of the number of persons of college age, the proportion of this number who are graduated from college, and the proportion of the latter who obtain engineering degrees. The number of persons reaching college graduation age through 1970 can be forecast with reasonable accuracy on the basis of past birth data and current age-specific death rates. The proportion of those who will attend college can be projected with somewhat less accuracy, although the historic rising trend in this proportion is quite clear and rather well defined. Projection of the proportion of college students specializing in engineering is subject to much uncertainty, however, because the trend in this proportion is less clearly defined and has fluctuated markedly.

In Table D-1 we use data on population aged 22,[1] number of bachelor's and first professional degrees granted, and number of engineering degrees granted, 1910–1950, to provide one set of estimates of engineering degrees through 1970.

The population data and the number of first degrees for the next fifteen years are taken from data prepared by the staff of the Commission on Human Resources. The population data are based on corrected birth registrations and age-specific death rates. The number of first degrees is derived by the Commission staff by

[1] Throughout, we use changes in the population aged 22 as an index of the movement of the population group from which new college graduates derive. This is the age group employed by the staff of the Commission on Human Resources, whose forecasts on first degrees are used in Table D-1. A more refined measure in which we would employ the movement of, say, the age classes 20–24, weighting each age class by the proportion of persons in that class who are new graduates in some current year, might yield slightly lower estimates in the next decade (see Chapter V).

TABLE D-1

An Estimate of the Future Number of Engineering Graduates

	Total Population Age 22 (1)	Total First Degrees (2)	Total First Degrees as Percentage of Population Aged 22 (3)	Total Engineering Degrees (4)		Engineering Degrees as Percentage of Total First Degrees (5)	
1910	n.a.	37,200	n.a.	1,709		4.6	
1920	1,887,000	48,500	2.6	4,716		9.7	
1930	2,203,000	122,500	5.6	7,395		6.0	
1940	2,292,000	186,500	8.1	13,808		7.4	
1950 a	2,399,000	272,340	11.4	26,893		9.9	
				A	B	A	B
1960	2,309,000	326,000	14.1	32,600	38,800	10.0	11.9
1965	2,909,000	454,000	15.6	45,900	58,600	10.1	12.9
1970	3,455,000	591,000	17.1	60,300	81,600	10.2	13.8

n.a. = not available.

a The degree data exclude veterans on the assumption that few veterans were as young as 22 in 1950 and therefore that the population aged 22 against which the recipients of degrees are measured was essentially a nonveteran universe. To the extent that any veterans receiving degrees in 1950 were 22 years old, the percentage in column 3 is understated.

Column	Source
1	Toby Oxtoby, Robert Mugge, and Dael Wolfle, "Enrollment and Graduation Trends: From Grade School to Ph.D.," *School and Society,* October 1952. *1920–1940,* taken from census data. *1950–1970,* projected on the basis of corrected birth data.
2	*1910, Biennial Survey of Education,* Office of Education, Chapter 1, 1950, p. 39. *1920–1940,* Oxtoby, Mugge, and Wolfle, *op. cit. 1950,* derived by subtracting the estimated number of first degrees awarded to veterans in 1950 from the total number of first degrees in that year. *1960–1970, ibid.* Derived by applying the percentages in col. 3 to the population estimates in col. 1.
3	*1920–1950,* col. 2 divided by col. 1. *1960–1970, ibid.* Derived by projecting the 1920–1940 trend in the ratio of first degrees to population aged 22.
4	*1910, Annual Report of the Commissioner of Education,* 1909–1910. *1920–1940, Biennial Surveys of Education,* Office of Education. *1950,* estimated total of degrees awarded to nonveterans. Derived by assuming that nonveterans accounted for 51 per cent of all engineering degrees in 1950, or a slightly higher proportion than in 1947 and 1948 (see *Journal of Engineering Education,* January 1948 and February 1949). This percentage was applied to the total number of first degrees awarded in engineering in 1950 (from *Biennial Survey of Education,* Chapter 1, 1950, p. 36). *1960–1970,* percentages A and B in col. 5 applied to total projected degrees in col. 2.
5	*1910–1950,* col. 4 divided by col. 2. *1960–1970,* two projections of the ratio of engineering degrees to total degrees. The first assumes a slight rise from 1950 levels; the second, a continuance of the 1930–1950 trend.

167

projecting forward the 1940 ratio of new graduates to population aged 22 at the average annual rate by which this ratio rose between 1920 and 1930. The population projections show a decline from 2.4 million persons aged 22 in 1950 to 2.3 million in 1960 (when the children born in 1938 reach 22 years of age) and then a sharp rise to 2.9 million in 1965 and 3.5 million in 1970. The magnitude of this twenty-year rise of 1.1 million (or 44 per cent) in graduation-age population between 1950 and 1970 is even more striking when we compare it with that experienced during the preceding 30 years. From 1920 to 1950 the population aged 22 rose only 0.5 million or 27 per cent.

The number of degrees may be expected to rise from the 270,000 received by nonveterans in 1950 to 330,000 in 1960, 450,000 in 1965 and 590,000 in 1970. The last figure is more than double the number of nonveteran degree recipients in 1950. The rise between 1950 and 1960 is a function of the expected increase in the propensity to attend college, while the rise between 1960 and 1970 is a result of both this increasing propensity and the roughly 50 per cent rise in graduation-age population.

This forecast may be a conservative one, even though it is based on a growth rate experienced during the prosperous 1920's and disregards the depressing effect of the depression on college attendance.[2] According to this projection, 266,000 first degrees would have been granted in 1950 under "normal" trend conditions. This estimate was presented by the Commission staff in the original table, and is 6,000 less than the actual number of degrees granted to nonveterans in 1950 (see Table D-1).[3] That is, the projection implies that 11.1 per cent of the population aged 22 would have received first degrees in 1950, while the actual proportion was 11.4 per cent. And even this latter percentage makes no allowance for the difficulties nonveterans encountered in entering college during the flood of veteran students. The predicted number of college graduates was slightly too low.

We accept these forecasts, however, for the present analysis and apply to them alternative estimates of the proportion of all first degrees accounted for by degrees in engineering.[4] The first set of

[2] Between 1920 and 1930 the proportion of the population aged 22 who received first degrees rose at an average annual rate of 0.3 per cent; the corresponding rate for 1930–1940 was 0.25.

[3] We exclude veterans from the 1950 degree data in Tables D-1 and D-2 not only because they had special inducements to attend college but also because nearly all were older than 22.

[4] For a discussion of past trends in this ratio, see Chapter IV.

estimates (A) in Table D-1 assumes merely a slight growth over 1950 levels in the ratio of engineering first degrees to total first degrees. The second (B) and more liberal set presupposes a continuation after 1950 of the 1930–1950 growth rate in the engineering ratio. According to these projections the number of engineering graduates should rise to between 33,000 and 39,000 in 1960, as compared to 27,000 nonveterans in 1950.

By 1970, the projections indicate a volume of graduates of between 60,000 and 82,000. The low figures in each case are based essentially on post-1950 ratios of engineering to total degrees, while the high figures imply a growth in the attractiveness of the engineering profession in the minds of college students at about the same rate as in the last several decades.

We can refine these projections somewhat by employing a related technique. This technique is based on the fact that almost all engineering graduates are men.[5] By restricting our attention to the changing proportion of males who graduate from college and the changing proportion of male graduates who have been trained in engineering, we are able to focus more precisely on the group from which engineers are obtained and to make more explicit the behavior of the male population with respect to college training and specialization in engineering. In the first set of projections, assumptions about this behavior are concealed within more general assumptions about the trends in total population size and propensity to attend college and specialize in engineering.

In Table D-2 we present data on total male population aged 22 and on bachelor's and first professional degrees received by males at decennial dates between 1910 and 1950,[6] and two projections of these data to 1970. The population data are forecast on the basis of corrected male birth registrations and rates of survival through age 22 as indicated in the footnotes to the table. The degree estimates are projected on the basis of alternative assumptions as to the rate of growth in the ratio of male first degree recipients to total male population aged 22. The first set of forecasts (A) assumes a rate of growth in this ratio after 1950 equal to that experienced in 1920–1930. The second (B) assumes that the 1930–1950 rate of

---

[5] The percentage of students enrolled in engineering schools who were women did not rise above 0.6 per cent between 1934 and 1952, except for the war years 1944–1946. *Biennial Survey of Education,* Office of Education, 1934 to 1950, and *Engineering Enrollments and Degrees, 1952,* Office of Education, Circular 364, January 21, 1953. See Appendix C.

[6] We again exclude veterans from the degree data for 1950 for reasons described earlier.

TABLE D-2

A Second Estimate of the Future Number of Engineering Graduates

Year	Total Male Population Age 22 (1)	Total First Degrees Received by Males (2)		Total Male First Degrees as Percentage of Male Population Age 22 (3)		Total Engineering Degrees (4)		Engineering Degrees as Percentage of Total Male First Degrees (5)	
1900	730,104	22,173		3.0		840		3.8	
1910	925,234	28,762		3.1		1,709		5.9	
1920	918,849	31,980		3.5		4,716		14.8	
1930	1,078,834	73,615		6.8		7,395		10.1	
1940	1,123,714	109,546		9.7		13,808		12.6	
1950 [a]	1,114,265	169,123		15.2		26,893		15.9	
		A	B	A	B	A	B	A	B
1960	1,206,000	223,000	234,000	18.5	19.4	35,700	44,000	16.0	18.8
1965	1,501,000	303,000	323,000	20.2	21.5	48,800	65,600	16.1	20.3
1970	1,758,000	383,000	415,000	21.8	23.6	62,000	90,100	16.2	21.7

[a] The degree data for 1950 again exclude veterans.

Column	Source
1	*1910–1950, Census of Population,* Bureau of the Census. *1960–1970,* derived by applying a survival rate through age 22 to corrected male birth registrations. Birth registrations from *Statistical Abstract of the United States,* Dept. of Commerce, 1953, p. 64 and *Statistical Abstract,* 1954, p. 66. Survival rate through age 22 derived by successively applying male age-specific death rates to survivors of initial cohort and obtaining ratio of final survivors to initial cohort. Male age-specific death rates obtained by deriving weighted average of male white and nonwhite age-specific death rates for 1950. The latter from *Statistical Abstract,* 1954, p. 72. Weights were 86 for white death rates and 14 for nonwhite death rates, computed on basis of per cent of total white male births and nonwhite male births in recent years. The latter fluctuated between 13.6 per cent and 14.4 per cent of total male births for benchmark dates between 1935 and 1953, *Statistical Abstract,* 1954, p. 65.
2	*1900–1940, Biennial Survey of Education, in the United States, 1949–50,* Office of Education, 1953, Chap. 4, sec. 1, p. 40. *1950,* estimate of nonveteran degrees derived by applying to total male degrees the percentage of nonveteran enrollments in prior years. *1960–1970,* derived by applying percentages A and B in col. 3 to male population in col. 1.
3	*1900–1950,* col. 2 divided by col. 1. *1960–1970,* two projections of the ratio of male first degree recipients to total male population aged 22. The first assumes a growth in the ratio after 1950 at the rate experienced in 1920–1930; the second, a continuance after 1950 of the 1930–1950 growth rate.
4	*1900–1950,* see Table D-1. *1960–1970,* figures in col. 2 multiplied by percentages A and B in col. 5.
5	*1900–1950,* figures in col. 4 divided by those in col. 2. *1960–1970,* two projections of the ratio of first degrees in engineering to total male first degrees. The first assumes a ratio in 1960 about equal to the ratio of new engineering students to total male freshmen in the fall of 1952 and a slight growth thereafter. The second implies a growth rate after 1950 equivalent to that experienced in 1930–1950.

170

growth in the ratio will continue. The projections for the ratio of male first degrees to male population aged 22 rise from 19 per cent for 1960 to 22–24 per cent for 1970, as contrasted with a rise from 7 to 15 per cent between 1930 and 1950.

Total male population aged 22 rose only about 200,000 between 1910 and 1950 (or 23 per cent). The effects of the recent rise in births can be seen in the fact that this male age class will increase almost 650,000 (or 58 per cent) in only two decades after 1950. The bulk of this increase will take place between 1960 and 1970 when the full impact of the war and early postwar baby boom will be felt.

Total first degrees received by men are expected to rise from the 169,000 received by nonveterans in 1950 to around 220,000 to 230,000 in 1960. By 1970, male first degree recipients are expected to reach levels between 380,000 to 415,000. Thus, the number of such recipients in 1970 will be almost two and a half times as large as the number of male nonveterans receiving first degrees in 1950.

From these data we develop a second set of projections of the future volume of engineering degrees. The ratio of engineering degrees to total male first degrees has risen over time (Table D-2) from slightly less than 4 per cent in 1900 to almost 16 per cent (for nonveterans) in 1950, with the ratios for the years before World War II running around 12 to 13 per cent. The highest ratios were experienced after each World War, with some decline thereafter. Wolfle reports that the ratio of all engineering first degrees (including those received by veterans) to all first degrees received by males (including veterans) declined continuously between 1947 and 1953—from 18.0 per cent to 12.0 per cent.[7] A portion of this decline was due to the decrease in this period in the proportion of male college students who were veterans; male veterans concentrated slightly more heavily in engineering than did nonveterans. Another portion of the decline in the later years was due to the general concern in 1948 and 1949 about the possibility of a surplus of engineers after the graduation of the large classes of 1949 and 1950.

There has been a shift back toward engineering since the low degree ratio of 1953. In the fall of 1952, engineering enrollments accounted for 12.7 per cent of all male college enrollments and

[7] The annual ratios are: 1947, 18.0 per cent; 1948, 17.7; 1949, 16.5; 1950, 15.9; 1951, 14.9; 1952, 13.5; 1953, 12.0 (Dael Wolfle, *America's Resources of Specialized Talent*, Harper, 1954, p. 97).

new engineering students represented almost 16 per cent of all male students entering college for the first time.[8]

In Table D-2, the two projections of the proportion of male graduates specializing in engineering are derived in the same manner as in Table D-1. The first (A) assumes a level in this proportion in 1960 only slightly higher than in 1950 and a very small increase to 1970. The second (B) assumes a continuance after 1950 of the 1930–1950 growth in this ratio. We apply the low projection of the ratio of engineering degrees to male degrees to the low projection of the ratio of male degrees to male population aged 22, and the high engineering degree projection to the high total male degree projection. The resulting projections of the number of engineering degrees range from 36,000 to 44,000 in 1960 and from 62,000 to 90,000 in 1970. These projections run slightly higher than those derived earlier on the basis of total population aged 22 and of graduation trends (both total and engineering) in relation to this population group.

In summary, then, if there is only a moderate rate of increase in the proportion of persons aged 22 graduating from college and main-. tenance of approximately the current degree of concentration on engineering among such graduates, engineering schools will graduate roughly 33,000 to 36,000 engineers in 1960 and 60,000 or more engineers in 1970. If the proportion of men aged 22 graduating from college rises in the next decade and a half as it has since 1930, and if the degree of specialization in engineering increases as it has since 1930, the number of engineering graduates in 1960 will be over 40,000 and the number in 1970 will reach the staggering total of 90,000. In all likelihood, with a rising level of demand for engineering services, the lower estimates will be exceeded. But it is at least doubtful whether the higher estimates will be realized in view of the increasing difficulty which is likely to be encountered in diverting students from other academic programs.

The most conservative estimates yield an indicated total of college-trained engineers in 1965 of about 720,000, contrasted with a 1950 total of about 300,000. The high estimates lead to an indicated 1965 total of about 820,000 college-trained engineers. These projections allow for deaths and retirements but take no account of prospective losses to the profession and prospective inflows of new college graduates from other disciplines. If we make allowance for these changes at rates experienced in the early fifties, we obtain

[8] *Engineering Enrollments and Degrees, 1952,* p. 1.

172

totals about 50,000 lower, the net result of anticipated losses of both new engineering graduates and of older graduates of over 100,000 during the fifteen year period and anticipated accessions of graduates of other disciplines of over 50,000.

APPENDIX E

RECONCILIATION OF 1940 AND 1950
CENSUS COUNTS OF ENGINEERS

THERE has been considerable disagreement about the accuracy of the 1950 census total count of 534,000 technical engineers. This figure is substantially higher than was anticipated for 1950 by investigators in the late 1940's and, indeed, is still considered too high by some.[1] Fraser, writing in 1947 on the basis of data from a 1946 survey, estimated that there were 317,000 members of the engineering profession in 1946 and forecast that this number would rise to 337,000 by 1950.[2] The Bureau of Labor Statistics in 1949 estimated that the number of engineers in 1948 was about 350,-000.[3] And in 1951 it estimated the number in 1950 at "over 400,000." [4]

This question, of course, is partly a matter of determining the boundary between engineers and nonengineers. For the objection to the 1950 census count is usually on the grounds that many persons who were not engineers so classified themselves in the 1950 census.

Wolfle, in discussing this issue, states: "It is quite possible that a considerable fraction of the 543,000 [5] [engineers] included in the 1950 Census were not engineers by anybody's definition but their own. The Bureau of the Census did, however, make special efforts to limit the engineering category to persons who were clearly qualified. Another probable explanation lies in the assumption that the high demand during the past decade led to the promotion of a considerable number of subprofessional engineering aides. On-the-job training, upgrading of employees, and even sometimes changing job titles could all have had the effect of increasing the number

[1] See Dael Wolfle, *America's Resources of Specialized Talent,* Harper, 1954, pp. 95–96.
[2] Andrew Fraser, *The Engineering Profession in Transition,* Engineers Joint Council, 1947, p. 59.
[3] *Employment Outlook for Engineers,* Bureau of Labor Statistics, Bull. 968, 1949, p. 98.
[4] *Effect of Defense Program on Employment Outlook in Engineering,* Bureau of Labor Statistics, Supplement to Bull. 968, 1951, p. 2.
[5] The 534,400 engineers, indicated as such in the 1950 census, plus about 8,300 professors and instructors in engineering who were not so classified in the published census materials (see Table 1).

174

of people who had legitimate reasons to call themselves engineers in reporting to census enumerators." [6]

But it is not our goal here to determine whether a narrower definition of the engineering profession than that used by the Census Bureau would yield lower totals; of course it would. Nor is it our goal to produce a new and supposedly more desirable definition. Rather, our purpose is to determine whether the 1950 census data are comparable in scope to the 1940 census data and thus can be used in conjunction with the 1940 (and earlier) data to describe the growth of the engineering profession, for none of those who have questioned the 1950 count have raised objections against earlier census data.

In Table E-1 we derive an estimate of the gross flow of persons into the engineering profession. The difference between the 1940 and 1950 census counts (the former adjusted for comparability) is the net increase in the profession, to which we add estimates of losses during the decade to obtain an estimate of the gross increase in engineers of 320,000. The bulk of the components of this gross inflow can be directly estimated: 179,000 new engineering graduates, 18,000 new nonengineering graduates and 20,000 former engineers [7] returning to the profession. This leaves a residual of 103,-000 other persons, primarily nongraduates, who entered the profession during the decade.

Some of these estimates are, of course, very crude and the actual figures may be somewhat higher or lower. Thus, it is entirely possible that fewer than 20,000 former engineers returned to the profession and it is equally possible that more than 18,000 new nonengineering graduates entered the profession during the decade. But the estimates probably represent correct orders of magnitude and provide reasonably adequate basis for judging the validity of the 1950 census results.

The test of this validity, then, essentially centers on whether the magnitude of the residual category seems reasonable. This category consists primarily of persons who were not college graduates but who entered the engineering profession during the 1940–1950 decade. It also may include some older nonengineering graduates who entered the profession during the decade and some members

---

[6] Wolfle, op. cit., p. 95. Wolfle chose to accept the 1950 census count.

[7] Who were in public emergency work or seeking work in 1940 (and classified themselves as engineers at that time) or for whom engineering was their usual but not current occupation in 1940.

APPENDIX E

TABLE E-1

Reconciliation of 1940 and 1950 Census Data on Engineers

1. Engineers employed in 1950		525,000
2. Engineers employed in 1940 (1940 census data)	245,000	
3. Reclassification in 1950 of 1940 census data to make latter comparable with 1950 census data	30,000	
4. Engineers employed in 1940		275,000
5. Net increase, 1940–1950		250,000
6. Estimated deaths and retirements, 1940–1950, of engineers under 55 in 1940	28,000	
7. Engineers 55 or over in 1940, assumed to have died or retired by 1950, less engineers over 65, employed in 1950	17,000	
8. Estimated transfers out of profession, 1940–1950	25,000	
9. Losses to profession, 1940–1950		70,000
10. Gross increase in engineering profession, 1940–1950		320,000
11. New engineering graduates, 1940–1949, less those who never entered the profession	179,000	
12. Other new college graduates who entered the profession, 1940–1950	18,000	
13. Reentry during decade of engineers who, in 1940, were in public emergency work or seeking work, or for whom engineering was their usual but not current occupation in 1940	20,000	
14. Accessions of graduates and reaccessions of experienced engineers		217,000
15. Accessions of nongraduates and of older nonengineering graduates		103,000

Line   Source

1, 2   Table B-1, Appendix B.

3   Letter from David I. Kaplan, Chief, Occupation and Industry Statistics Section, Population and Housing Division, Bureau of the Census, December 30, 1954.

4   Line 2 plus row 3.

5   Line 1 minus row 4.

6   Deaths and retirements estimated on basis of 1940 age distribution and tables of working life.

7   1940 and 1950 census data.

8   Rough estimate based on transfer rates in Chapter 3 and average size of profession during 1940–1950 decade.

9   Sum of lines 6, 7, and 8.

10   Line 5 plus line 9.

11   Appendix Table C-6, col. 2, less 7 per cent (see Chap. III for derivation of loss estimate).

12   Rough estimate based on accession rates for new nonengineering graduates, described in Chapter IV.

13   It is assumed that 20,000 out of the 23,000 engineers in public emergency work or seeking work in 1940 or for whom engineering was their usual but not current occupation in 1940, reentered the profession after 1940.

14   Sum of lines 11, 12 and 13.

15   Line 10 minus line 14.

of the very large engineering graduating class of 1950 who may have already begun engineering work by April 1, 1950 (the date the census was taken).

The Bureau of Labor Statistics has estimated that at least 26,000 persons (largely nongraduates) between the age of 35 and 60 entered the engineering profession during the depression decade of the thirties, a period during which "many engineers lost their jobs and had to seek other employment, and when many graduates were unable to find engineering jobs." [8] To these must be added the 20,500 engineers under 35 years of age (in 1940) with less than four years of college training, who were excluded from the engineering category by the 1940 census definitions. Presumably nearly all of these entered the profession during the thirties.

BLS also has estimated that a minimum of 35,000 nongraduates entered the profession during the twenties; however, this estimate, it is pointed out, makes no allowance for losses to the profession other than through death and retirement.[9] If transfers out of the profession and losses of new graduates occurred at the same rate during that decade as they have in more recent years, they amounted to about 17,000 over the ten years. Thus at least 50,000 nongraduates probably entered engineering work during the twenties.

Conditions were more favorable to the entry of nongraduates during the forties than during the twenties, and substantially more favorable than during the thirties. Not only was the demand for engineers at extremely high levels during and shortly after the war, but also at least 60,000 engineers were inducted into the armed forces. "Steps were taken to secure the services of men who had dropped out of school before completing the engineering course, persons holding degrees in related fields, and experienced semi-professional technical personnel who could be upgraded with intensive training. Many were prepared for some phase of engineering work in connection with war production by the Engineering, Science and Management War Training Program . . . , which gave instruction at college level, but by shorter and more intensive courses. . . . Information gathered from employers in 1946 indicates that considerable numbers of men holding engineering jobs were upgraded during the war from semiprofessional positions. Also, for appointments to some Federal Government positions, completion of ESMWT courses was accepted for at least partial satisfaction of the requirements." [10]

[8] *Employment Outlook for Engineers,* p. 41.
[9] *Loc. cit.*
[10] *Ibid.,* pp. 41–42.

Others were given technical training while in the armed forces. And still others participated after the war in engineering training programs conducted by large corporations.

In view of the numbers of nongraduates entering the profession during the twenties and thirties, and the extremely favorable conditions during the forties, an inflow of nongraduates between 1940 and 1950 of the order of magnitude of 100,000 seems quite reasonable, and surely exceeded 50,000 (the number entering in the twenties).[11] In other words, there is no clear evidence that the 1950 census substantially overstated the number of engineers (measured by historic census definitions); but if it did, the overstatement was less than 50,000.[12]

[11] The ratio of nongraduate accessions to new engineering graduates was about two-thirds in the twenties and about four-tenths in the thirties. If the relative rate of accessions of nongraduates during the forties had been equal to that in the twenties, about 130,000 nongraduates would have entered the profession between 1940 and 1950; had it been equal to that in the thirties, about 75,000 would have entered between 1940 and 1950.

[12] The estimates in Table E-1 are not fully consistent with the 1940 census data on the number of graduate and nongraduate engineers and unpublished tabulations of 1950 census data on the education of engineers (see Appendix F). After making some rough adjustments for changes in definition and for incomplete coverage in the education data, as well as a crude estimate of losses among nongraduate engineers, one obtains an estimate of the inflow of nongraduates during the decade that is about 25,000 higher than indicated in Table E-1. But the data in Table E-1 agree quite closely with Wolfle's estimate of 316,000 graduates (and, therefore, 227,000 nongraduates) employed in engineering in 1950 (Wolfle, *op. cit.*, pp. 95–96).

APPENDIX F

TABLES ON YEARS OF SCHOOL COMPLETED FOR ENGINEERS, 1940, AND AGE AND YEARS OF SCHOOL COMPLETED FOR ENGINEERS AND SCIENTISTS, 1950

APPENDIX F

TABLE F-1

Years of School Completed by Employed Engineers and Experienced Engineers Seeking Work, by Field of Specialization, 1940

FIELD OF SPE-CIALIZATION	TOTAL	HIGH SCHOOL		COLLEGE		
		1–3 Years	4 Years	1–3 Years	4 or more Years	NOT RE-PORTED
Civil	86,140	9,540	11,180	14,200	51,000	220
Electrical	55,440	8,380	6,760	6,320	33,540	440
Mechanical	82,920	12,400	10,720	10,320	49,120	360
Other [a]	30,980	2,540	2,640	3,680	22,100	20
All engineers	255,480	32,860	31,300	34,520	155,760	1,040

[a] Chemical, industrial, and mining and metallurgical.
Source: *Census of Population, 1940, The Labor Force, Occupational Characteristics*, pp. 59–61.

TABLE F-2

Age and Years of Schooling for All Employed Engineers, 1950

YEARS OF SCHOOL COMPLETED	TOTAL EMPLOYED	AGE				
		14–19	20–24	25–34	35–44	45 and Over
High School						
1–3 years	62,680	350	2,165	9,485	16,685	33,995
4 years	80,455	645	4,805	23,665	24,280	27,060
College						
1–3 years	90,130	240	5,460	28,925	27,455	28,050
4 years	206,055	40	14,580	84,475	50,775	56,185
5 or more years	73,010	25	3,660	29,525	20,905	18,895
Not reported	11,125	195	625	3,265	2,920	4,120
Total	523,455	1,495	31,295	179,340	143,020	168,305

Source: Special unpublished tabulations of the Bureau of the Census manpower occupations card file for the Bureau of Labor Statistics and sponsored by the National Science Foundation.

APPENDIX F

TABLE F-3

Age and Years of Schooling for Employed Aeronautical Engineers, 1950

YEARS OF SCHOOL COMPLETED	TOTAL EMPLOYED	AGE				
		14–19	*20–24*	*25–34*	*35–44*	*45 and Over*
High School						
1–3 years	1,020	. . .	50	295	365	310
4 years	2,245	10	90	1,220	615	310
College						
1–3 years	3,635	. . .	185	2,005	1,040	405
4 years	7,425	. . .	560	4,480	1,865	520
5 or more years	3,315	. . .	260	1,770	995	290
Not reported	210	5	10	110	60	25
Total	17,850	15	1,155	9,880	4,940	1,860

Source: Same as in Table F-2.

TABLE F-4

Age and Years of Schooling for Employed Chemical Engineers, 1950

YEARS OF SCHOOL COMPLETED	TOTAL EMPLOYED	AGE				
		14–19	*20–24*	*25–34*	*35–44*	*45 and Over*
High School						
1–3 years	1,360	25	95	360	410	470
4 years	1,520	45	115	585	430	345
College						
1–3 years	2,160	25	190	890	605	450
4 years	17,015	. . .	1,340	9,565	3,775	2,335
5 or more years	8,880	. . .	415	4,780	2,385	1,300
Not reported	760	5	35	400	195	125
Total	31,695	100	2,190	16,580	7,800 ·	5,025

Source: Same as in Table F-2.

TABLE F-5

Age and Years of Schooling for Employed Civil Engineers, 1950

YEARS OF SCHOOL COMPLETED	TOTAL EMPLOYED	AGE				
		14–19	*20–24*	*25–34*	*35–44*	*45 and Over*
High School						
1–3 years	15,160	145	840	2,415	3,895	7,865
4 years	18,090	215	1,510	3,875	5,225	7,265
College						
1–3 years	23,710	70	1,605	5,325	7,155	9,555
4 years	48,380	25	3,115	14,085	12,485	18,670
5 or more years	15,410	10	690	4,550	4,365	5,795
Not reported	1,455	25	110	305	350	665
Total	122,205	490	7,870	30,555	33,475	49,815

Source: Same as in Table F-2.

TABLE F-6

Age and Years of Schooling for Employed Electrical Engineers, 1950

YEARS OF SCHOOL COMPLETED	TOTAL EMPLOYED	AGE				
		14–19	*20–24*	*25–34*	*35–44*	*45 and Over*
High School						
1–3 years	11,340	40	430	1,790	2,895	6,185
4 years	17,145	120	1,310	5,695	5,005	5,015
College						
1–3 years	17,345	25	1,495	6,265	4,930	4,630
4 years	41,660	5	3,350	16,565	10,390	11,350
5 or more years	14,330	5	945	5,615	4,365	3,400
Not reported	5,330	5	290	1,555	1,600	1,880
Total	107,150	200	7,820	37,485	29,185	32,460

Source: Same as in Table F-2.

182

TABLE F-7

Age and Years of Schooling for Employed Industrial Engineers, 1950

YEARS OF SCHOOL COMPLETED	TOTAL EMPLOYED	AGE				
		14–19	*20–24*	*25–34*	*35–44*	*45 and Over*
High School						
1–3 years	4,855	35	70	610	1,650	2,490
4 years	8,590	35	250	2,990	3,045	2,270
College						
1–3 years	8,530	20	245	2,780	3,390	2,095
4 years	12,415	. . .	940	5,560	3,510	2,405
5 or more years	4,555	10	160	2,000	1,420	965
Not reported	665	30	55	210	120	250
Total	39,610	130	1,720	14,150	13,135	10,475

Source: Same as in Table F-2.

TABLE F-8

Age and Years of Schooling for Employed Mechanical Engineers, 1950

YEARS OF SCHOOL COMPLETED	TOTAL EMPLOYED	AGE				
		14–19	*20–24*	*25–34*	*35–44*	*45 and Over*
High School						
1–3 years	17,675	55	415	2,385	4,500	10,320
4 years	17,510	130	735	4,780	5,155	6,710
College						
1–3 years	17,475	50	895	5,840	5,005	5,685
4 years	43,300	5	3,235	19,900	9,145	11,015
5 or more years	12,905	. . .	710	5,615	3,335	3,245
Not reported	1,395	85	75	370	295	570
Total	110,260	325	6,065	38,890	27,435	37,545

Source: Same as in Table F-2.

TABLE F-9

Age and Years of Schooling for Employed Metallurgical Engineers
and Metallurgists, 1950

YEARS OF SCHOOL COMPLETED	TOTAL EMPLOYED	AGE				
		14–19	20–24	25–34	35–44	45 and Over
High School						
1–3 years	1,110	20	40	255	350	445
4 years	1,675	20	200	630	505	320
College						
1–3 years	1,630	20	115	605	520	370
4 years	4,530	. . .	175	2,150	1,300	905
5 or more years	2,455	. . .	70	1,010	840	535
Not reported	245	25	10	55	55	100
Total	11,645	85	610	4,705	3,570	2,675

Source: Same as in Table F-2.

TABLE F-10

Age and Years of Schooling for Employed Mining Engineers, 1950

YEARS OF SCHOOL COMPLETED	TOTAL EMPLOYED	AGE				
		14–19	20–24	25–34	35–44	45 and Over
High School						
1–3 years	1,395	5	55	200	2,525	760
4 years	1,125	5	85	315	375	460
College						
1–3 years	1,090	5	55	325	260	385
4 years	4,805	. . .	360	2,175	320	1,210
5 or more years	1,800	. . .	100	755	1,060	480
Not reported	165	5	. . .	50	465	65
Total	10,380	20	655	3,820	45	3,360

Source: Same as in Table F-2.

TABLE F-11

Age and Years of Schooling for Employed Engineers Not Elsewhere
Classified, 1950

YEARS OF SCHOOL COMPLETED	TOTAL EMPLOYED	AGE				
		14–19	20–24	25–34	35–44	45 and Over
High School						
1–3 years	8,765	25	170	1,175	2,245	5,150
4 years	12,555	65	510	3,575	4,040	4,365
College						
1–3 years	14,555	25	675	4,890	4,490	4,475
4 years	26,525	5	1,505	9,995	7,245	7,775
5 or more years	9,360	. . .	310	3,430	2,735	2,885
Not reported	900	10	40	210	200	440
Total	72,660	130	3,210	23,275	20,955	25,090

Source: Same as in Table F-2.

TABLE F-12

Age and Years of Schooling for Employed Agricultural Scientists, 1950

YEARS OF SCHOOL COMPLETED	TOTAL EMPLOYED	AGE				
		14–19	20–24	25–34	35–44	45 and Over
High School						
1–3 years	1,270	65	60	265	260	620
4 years	720	25	115	215	185	180
College						
1–3 years	670	15	155	220	75	205
4 years	1,555	. . .	105	685	385	380
5 or more years	1,705	. . .	70	660	480	495
Not reported	65	. . .	. . .	30	15	20
Total	5,985	105	505	2,075	1,400	1,900

Source: Same as in Table F-2.

TABLE F-13

Age and Years of Schooling for Employed Biological Scientists, 1950

YEARS OF SCHOOL COMPLETED	TOTAL EMPLOYED	AGE				
		14–19	*20–24*	*25–34*	*35–44*	*45 and Over*
High School						
1–3 years	360	15	25	105	120	95
4 years	365	15	35	110	105	100
College						
1–3 years	730	5	105	285	175	160
4 years	3,090	. . .	575	1,375	620	520
5 or more years	4,420	. . .	245	1,930	1,310	935
Not reported	110	. . .	30	45	10	25
Total	9,075	35	1,015	3,850	2,340	1,835

Source: Same as in Table F-2.

TABLE F-14

Age and Years of Schooling for Employed Chemists, 1950

YEARS OF SCHOOL COMPLETED	TOTAL EMPLOYED	AGE				
		14–19	*20–24*	*25–34*	*35–44*	*45 and Over*
High School						
1–3 years	6,830	75	650	1,680	1,810	2,615
4 years	9,340	395	1,555	3,540	2,240	1,610
College						
1–3 years	9,930	80	1,690	3,890	2,390	1,880
4 years	26,915	5	3,315	12,055	6,400	5,140
5 or more years	20,035	20	1,060	8,760	6,255	3,940
Not reported	1,905	95	160	705	425	520
Total	74,955	670	8,430	30,630	19,520	15,705

Source: Same as in Table F-2.

TABLE F-15

Age and Years of Schooling for Employed Geologists and Geophysicists, 1950

YEARS OF SCHOOL COMPLETED	TOTAL EMPLOYED	AGE				
		14–19	*20–24*	*25–34*	*35–44*	*45 and Over*
High School						
1–3 years	440	25	55	105	110	145
4 years	575	25	105	195	150	100
College						
1–3 years	920	15	135	270	240	260
4 years	4,380	...	420	1,955	1,125	880
5 or more years	3,505	...	165	1,420	1,145	775
Not reported	105	...	5	60	35	5
Total	9,925	65	885	4,005	2,805	2,165

Source: Same as in Table F-2.

TABLE F-16

Age and Years of Schooling for Employed Mathematicians, 1950

YEARS OF SCHOOL COMPLETED	TOTAL EMPLOYED	AGE				
		14–19	*20–24*	*25–34*	*35–44*	*45 and Over*
High School						
1–3 years	70	10	5	15	10	30
4 years	140	5	30	65	15	25
College						
1–3 years	215	...	45	110	30	30
4 years	490	5	95	270	70	50
5 or more years	560	...	100	255	120	85
Not reported	35	...	...	10	...	25
Total	1,510	20	275	725	245	245

Source: Same as in Table F-2.

TABLE F-17

Age and Years of Schooling for Employed Physicists, 1950

YEARS OF SCHOOL COMPLETED	TOTAL EMPLOYED	AGE				
		14–19	*20–24*	*25–34*	*35–44*	*45 and Over*
High School						
1–3 years	355	. . .	25	130	100	100
4 years	560	15	75	280	135	55
College						
1–3 years	515	10	55	280	110	60
4 years	1,710	. . .	225	965	355	165
5 or more years	3,675	5	235	1,915	1,040	480
Not reported	115	5	5	65	30	10
Total	6,930	35	620	3,635	1,770	870

Source: Same as in Table F-2.

TABLE F-18

Age and Years of Schooling for Employed Miscellaneous Natural Scientists, 1950

YEARS OF SCHOOL COMPLETED	TOTAL EMPLOYED	AGE				
		14–19	*20–24*	*25–34*	*35–44*	*45 and Over*
High School						
1–3 years	315	10	40	75	80	110
4 years	440	10	65	180	65	120
College						
1–3 years	670	. . .	25	320	210	115
4 years	805	. . .	35	400	235	135
5 or more years	835	. . .	20	425	275	115
Not reported	80	. . .	25	15	15	25
Total	3,145	20	210	1,415	880	620

Source: Same as in Table F-2.

APPENDIX G

ANALYSIS OF RATES OF TRANSFER OUT OF
THE ENGINEERING PROFESSION FOR
ENGINEERS WITH VARYING YEARS
OF EXPERIENCE

In 1954 a survey was made of the alumni of Stevens Institute of Technology for the purpose of gathering information for a revised Alumni Directory. In this connection, a questionnaire was sent to all alumni whose addresses were known. About three-quarters of the questionnaires were returned. Because of budget limitations, only the questionnaires for each fifth class, starting with 1952 and going back to 1902, were tabulated.

TABLE G-1

Percentage of Stevens Alumni Who Are Currently Engaged in Engineering Work, Classified by Years of Graduation

Class	Total Number of Respondents	Per Cent in Engineering Work
1902	16	75
1907	23	65
1912	27	78
1917	32	75
1922	81	75
1927	73	78
1932	90	76
1937	75	96
1942	90	86
1947	73	84
1952	160	86
Total	740	82

Source: "A Report on Engineering Careers," a reprint from *Stevens Indicator*, Stevens Institute of Technology, October 1954, Table IA, p. 8.

One of the questions related to whether the respondent was currently engaged in engineering work. The data collected on this question are shown in Table G-1. We have attempted to use these data to determine whether there is any pronounced tendency for rates of transfer out of the profession to be greater during the

189

earlier or later portions of an engineer's working life. The results are instructive even though the sample is small and restricted to one institution of higher learning.

One problem involved in analyzing the data relates to the fact that a significant proportion of engineering graduates do not enter the profession upon graduation. Indeed, if we treat all members of graduating classes of engineering schools as part of the supply of engineers (as is commonly done), it appears that the year of greatest loss to the profession is precisely the year of graduation. In Chapter III, we estimate that 5 to 7 per cent of the graduating engineers of the class of 1951 in all colleges did not enter the engineering profession. Apparently, this proportion is higher at Stevens, for 14 per cent of the class of 1952 said they were not engaged in engineering work at the time of the survey.

We are interested here in determining whether the annual rate of transfer out of the profession differs with varying years of experience for those engineers who did enter the profession. Accordingly we have assumed in column 2 of Table G-2 that 10 per cent of the Stevens graduates in each class did not enter the profession upon graduation, and alternatively, in column 3 that 14 per cent did not engage in engineering work upon graduation. The first assumption involves an initial loss to the profession of somewhat greater magnitude than we found for all engineering graduates in 1951 but somewhat smaller than the loss suggested by the data for the Stevens class of 1952. The second assumption is based directly upon the proportion of the Stevens class of 1952 found not working in engineering at the time of the survey. In column 1 we simply disregard the question of initial loss and treat all graduates as if they entered the profession upon graduation.

The data in Table G-2 show the annual average rates of transfer out of the profession for each listed Stevens class, computed successively on the basis of each of the three assumptions as to initial loss. The rates were so derived as to measure the average ratio of each year's loss to the number still remaining in the engineering profession at the beginning of the year. If the true annual rate of loss among older engineers was greater than the rate among younger engineers, we would expect that the average rate for older graduates over their entire working life to date (shown in Table G-2) would be higher than that for recent graduates. The reverse would be expected if transfers were more common among younger engineers.

When no account is taken of the initial loss to the profession (column 1), the average rates rise for the more recent classes. But when we roughly take account of initial losses (columns 2 and 3), we find no discernible trend in average rates of transfer when classified by years of experience. Since the sample is small, there is considerable irregularity in the figures. But, except for the most recent classes, there does not seem to be any striking difference among the several classes. And the conclusions for the recent classes are ambiguous since one assumption suggests a higher rate of transfer and the other, a lower.

TABLE G-2

Annual Rates of Transfer Out of the Engineering Profession, Estimated on Basis of Alternative Assumptions as to Proportion of Graduates Never Entering the Profession

YEARS SINCE GRADUATION	AVERAGE ANNUAL RATE OF TRANSFER		
	Assumption A [a] (1)	Assumption B [b] (2)	Assumption C [c] (3)
52	0.55%	0.36%	0.27%
47	0.92	0.70	0.58
42	0.59	0.31	0.22
37	0.78	0.54	0.38
32	0.90	0.62	0.43
27	0.91	0.52	0.35
22	1.24	0.79	0.58
17	0.24	d	d
12	1.25	0.33	0.00
7	2.46	1.03	0.29
2	7.26	2.02	0.00

[a] It is here assumed that all graduates enter the profession upon graduation.

[b] It is here assumed that 10 per cent of each graduating class never enters the profession.

[c] It is here assumed that 14 per cent of each graduating class never enters the profession.

[d] Under the given assumptions, this class would have a negative rate of transfer.

Source: Table G-1.

THE ENGINEERS JOINT COUNCIL SURVEYS

AT THE end of this appendix we partially reproduce the 1953 questionnaire on demand for engineers, prepared by the Engineers Joint Council, and here discuss several important questions relating to the interpretation of the survey results.

The first major question involves the definition of the engineering universe. The EJC questionnaires are clearly intended to be restricted to forecast and realized employment, losses, and accessions of degree-holding engineers. Yet the EJC estimates of engineering employment in the United States, total and by industry, with which the engineering employment of the reporting firms and agencies is compared in order to indicate the degree of coverage of the reporting sample, clearly include nongraduate engineers. The summary of the 1952 survey estimates total engineering employment at 450,-000, and the 1953 summary estimates employment at 440,000. Although these estimates are somewhat inconsistent (more engineers were probably employed in 1953 than in 1952), they are substantially above estimates of employed college-trained engineers. Wolfle, for example, estimates the number of college graduates employed as engineers in 1953 at 361,000, 30,000 below the EJC engineering employment estimate for 1953 and 90,000 below the estimate for 1952.[1]

This uncertainty about the limits of the universe of engineers is related to the feeling on the part of the engineering societies and BLS that current estimates of the number of engineers based on 1950 census data are overstated by virtue of the inclusion of a large number of persons without engineering degrees who incorrectly claim to be engineers. An even more restricted view of the bounds of the engineering profession is implicit in the apparent assumption on the part of the EJC that new entrants to the profession are recruited solely from among new graduates. For the standard procedure in trying to assess the degree of "shortage" of engineers is to set the expected net increase in demand, derived from the EJC surveys (whose data are explicitly or implicitly expanded to cover all engineering employment), against the current number

---

[1] Dael Wolfle, *America's Resources of Specialized Talent*, Harper, 1954, p. 96.

of new graduates. Yet there is much evidence that even now substantial numbers enter the profession without acquiring engineering degrees (see Chapter IV). If this is true, then one clearly underestimates the current inflow of engineers by restricting the comparison to new graduates alone and overestimates any prospective "shortage" that the calculation may suggest.[2]

Another serious problem is the representativeness of the sample. The EJC summaries are concerned with this question and suggest that the respondents to the questionnaire "may have somewhat greater need for engineers than is typical in their respective industries." Any evaluation of the results of the survey is clearly dependent on this question of representativeness. It is not clear whether the Council's worries are concerned with the dominance of large companies in the sample or with the possibility that those firms which are rapidly expanding their employment of engineers are more likely to respond than firms with smaller increases in engineering staff. In any case, if the surveys are to be continued, and the substantial accuracy of the 1953 survey argues in favor of this decision, it would seem advisable to test directly the degree of representativeness of the kind of small sample the EJC typically obtains. Perhaps this could be accomplished by obtaining data on the previous year's experience alone for a larger sample of firms and government agencies and comparing growth in engineering

[2] In its report on its most recent demand study (conducted in late 1955 and early 1956) the EJC comments on this question as follows:

"In undertaking its survey of engineering demand shortly after World War II, the Special Surveys Committee of EJC decided that the most practicable basis for measuring such demand was the needs of the responding companies for engineering graduates rather than for individuals to fill engineering positions. This decision stems from the difficulty of defining engineering positions in a wide variety of organizations and the fact that in recent years individuals sought from outside an organization for work requiring engineering knowledge or skill had been very largely graduates, although comparable positions frequently are filled from within the organization by those developing such skills through experience.

"On this same basis, the responding organizations had been asked to indicate their . . . need for engineering graduates, regardless of expected assignment, recognizing that some may enter upon training for technical supervision or similar fields rather than strictly engineering work.

"The total population from which the survey sample is drawn, therefore, is the number of engineering graduates in the country, excluding those who are retired, which at the end of 1955 has been estimated as approximately 560,000 from data of the Commission on Human Resources and Advanced Training— as of 1953 and brought up to date. This compares with the total of about 675,000 individuals classified as engineers in industry, government and other activities as of the same date estimated from the 1950 census and subsequent additions and losses."

staffs for this larger group with the experience of the firms making up the EJC sample.

Finally, the meaning of the estimates of "required" increases in engineering staff is open to considerable question. It is not at all clear how the respondents interpreted the questions on "required" net accessions in the 1953 and 1954 surveys, despite the explanation in the questionnaires themselves. In view of the data shown in Table H-1, however, it appears that one of two things was happening during these years to companies' views of the "shortage" of engineers which the difference between "expected" and "required" net accessions was designed to measure. Either the deficits in required hirings were being made up rapidly, in which case the

TABLE H-1

Comparison of Expected, Required, and Realized Net Accessions of Engineers, 1952–1954

	1952		1953			1954	
	Expected	Realized	Expected	Required	Realized	Expected	Required
Constant group sample	8,118	3,416	3,085	—	3,137		
Larger sample used in detailed analysis			4,643	8,422	4,767	3,372	5,891

Source: Company and government agency reports, Engineers Joint Council surveys, 1952, 1953, and 1954.

current increase in demand for engineers was considerably smaller than was generally realized, or companies were taking a harder look at their needs for engineers and finding them substantially smaller than had been thought. The latter could have been due to more efficient use of engineers, or to conversion of nonengineering personnel to engineering work, or simply to decreasing uncertainty or concern about the "shortage" situation.[3]

Thus, the deficit in realized net hirings of engineers as compared with expected net hirings in 1952 for our constant group sample was 4,700, or about 7,000 when expanded to the size of our larger sample used in the detailed analysis of the 1953 returns. Yet the forecast deficiency in net hiring in 1953—i.e., the difference between required and expected net accessions—was only 3,800. And the difference between required net hirings and actual net hirings was only 3,600. In the next year (1954) the predicted deficiency,

[3] Ginzberg points out a similar phenomenon in 1951 and 1952 (A Policy for Scientific and Professional Manpower, National Manpower Council, 1953, p. 171).

i.e. the difference between expected and required net hirings, was again reduced, this time to 2,500.

In other words, either the original 1952 backlog was being reduced in 1953 and 1954 by a portion of actual hirings, in which case the current net increases in demand in these two years were smaller than would at first appear, or companies were continually revising downward their estimates of the degree of engineering shortage. Both developments probably took place.[4]

---

[4] In its most recent demand study, the EJC comments:

"There is little indication . . . that engineering demand is accumulative over the years. Quite obviously, organizations have learned somehow to perform satisfactorily with undercomplements of engineering personnel. Nevertheless, and considering all factors, the data would seem to warrant the assertion that the situation would be considerably eased if the total number of engineering graduates this year were of an order of magnitude between 35,000 and 40,000.

"It should be emphasized that this situation does not necessarily have implications for the intermediate future. Looking ahead to the next three years when the size of the graduating class in engineering will average about 35,000 per year, it is pertinent to note that this increase in the size of graduating classes combined with a somewhat reduced technological momentum may have the effect of easing the present situation of extreme shortage. On the other hand, it is clear that given continuing technological activity with a growth factor similar to that of the recent past, there is very little to promise merely numerical relief during the next four years."

Please return one completed copy to: March 25, 1955
T. A. Marshall, Jr., Executive Secretary
Engineering Manpower Commission of EJC   *CONFIDENTIAL*

1953 SURVEY OF DEMAND FOR ENGINEERS

In order to obtain authoritative information concerning the needs of industry and government for engineering graduates, we would appreciate your help to the extent of furnishing the data requested below. Where exact data are not available please furnish us with your most reliable estimate. All replies will be kept strictly confidential.

QUESTIONNAIRE

I. *Requirements for Engineering Graduates*

                             1952   1953

1. a. Total Number of engineering
graduates in your company's
employ on January 1st   _____   _____

   b. Total Number of engineering
graduates on military leave.
(not included above)   XXXXX   _____

195

1953

	(Actual)	(Expected)	(Required)
2. Total losses during the year through death, retirement, resignation, entry to military service, etc.	___	___	___
3. Employment during the year: (See note 1)	___	___	XXXXX
a. From current classes:			
a. Bachelors	___	___	___
b. Masters	___	___	___
c. Ph. D.'s	___	___	___
Total	___	___	___
b. From earlier classes:	___	___	___
4. Number returning from Military Leave	___	___	XXXXX
5. Total net accessions (See Note 2)	___	___	___
6. Total engineering graduates in company's employ on December 31st	XXXXX	___	XXXXX

Note 1: The "Expected" and "Required" columns regarding employment are used in recognition of the apparent arbitrary downward adjustment some companies have made in recruiting goals—based on the anticipated shortage of engineering graduates. "Expected" refers to the number the company anticipates actually hiring. "Required" refers to the company needs to hire based on firm plans and commitments.

Note 2: If total net accessions for 1953 are expected to differ substantially from those of 1952, please explain briefly.

196

APPENDIX I

ADVERTISEMENTS FOR ENGINEERS

MANY people have commented upon the great growth in the use of newspaper advertisements to recruit engineers, and often interpret this growth as evidence of shortages. We have not investigated this phenomenon in detail, but a few remarks can be made.

The growth of display advertisements for engineers has been truly enormous; it is illustrated by a few measurements of Sunday issues of the New York Times in the past decade (see Table I-1). The square inches of display space rose from 30.6 in the spring of 1950 to 2248.1 (or 15.6 square feet) in the fall of 1955.

TABLE I-1

Advertisements for Engineers, New York Times

	May 5, 1946	May 7, 1950	Nov. 5, 1950	May 1, 1955	Nov. 1, 1955
Classified (entries)	18	31	74	174	164
Display					
Space (sq. in.)		30.6	163.0	1216.8	2248.1
Defense industries		12.8	114.4	1173.6	1926.8
Other		17.8	48.6	43.2	321.3
Per cent defense		41.8	70.1	96.4	85.7
Insertions		6	25	76	143
Defense		2	17	70	111
Other		4	8	6	32
Per cent defense		33.3	68.0	92.1	77.6
Companies		6	22	56	101
Defense		2	14	50	69
Other		4	8	6	32
Per cent defense		33.3	63.6	89.3	68.3

Source: Sunday issues of the *New York Times*.

We have classified the advertisements according to whether the company was engaged in defense work or normal civilian work; where we were in doubt, the company was put in the latter class. Even with this conservative bias, something like nine-tenths of the space, seven-eighths of the insertions, and four-fifths of the companies are working on defense contracts. It may well be that this type of employment is relatively less attractive to engineers, because of security provisions, uncertain tenure, etc., so recruit-

197

ment is more difficult. Moreover, recruitment costs are fully reimbursed by the government.

In the nondefense industries, hardly any expansion of this method of recruitment took place up through May 1955. Increased use of this method of recruitment appears to have taken place by November of 1955. This increase may be temporary, or strongly influenced by sampling fluctuations.

The volume of advertisements cannot be assumed to vary with the unsatisfied demand for engineers at going salary rates. The newspapers are a relatively new source of recruitment for a trained profession. One may assume that the advertisements have been growing as this method of recruitment has become more widely imitated, and that there has been growth in periods when the unsatisfied demand for engineers fell. Thus the growth of advertisements between May 1946 and May 1950 (which of course precedes the Korean emergency) took place while relative earnings of engineers were not rising but falling.

INDEX

Advertisements for engineers, 197-198
Air Force, 30
American Council on Education, 7 n., 95 n.
American Society of Electrical Engineers, 41 n.
Armsby, Henry H., 77 n.
Atomic Energy Commission, 17

Bureau of the Census, *see* Census data
Bureau of Labor Statistics, 7, 9 n., 33 ff., 58, 64 n., 67, 68 n., 70, 106 n., 108-139 *passim*, 177

Carson, Daniel, 55 n., 154 n.
Cavanaugh, W. T., 37 n.
Census data: on earnings of engineers, 24 n., 137 ff.; on educational background of engineers and scientists, 11, 88-90, 180-188; on numbers of engineers and chemists, 4 f., 8-12, 48-51, 143-155, 174-178; on numbers of natural scientists, 8, 93
Commission on Human Resources, 6, 69, 71, 83, 84, 166 ff.
Conrad, Herbert S., 77 n.

Defense, Department of, 16 f.
Degrees awarded: in engineering, 7, 75, 78-82, 162-165; in natural sciences, 6-7; projections of, in engineering, 76-77, 166-173; *see also* Educational background . . .
Demand for engineers and chemists: concepts and definitions, 19-24; factors influencing, 15-18, 35-36, 47-72; government support for research and, 15-18, 57-62; gross vs. net, 68-72; and industrial structure, 35-36, 48-56; short-run changes in business activity and, 66-68; research and, 15-18, 57-62, 65-66; technological change and, 63-66; *see also* Predictions of requirements for engineers
Demand for mathematicians and physicists: college enrollments and, 98-103; factors influencing, 93-103; faculty-student ratios and, 94-98
Durand, John D., 145 n.

Earnings of engineers: (1894-1924) 121-127; (1929-1956) 24-28, 114-121, 127-141; census data on, 24 n., 137-139; and choice of field, 79-83; compared with other occupations, 24-29, 63, 140; controls over, 23, 30-31, 33; as criterion for defining shortage, 23-24, 28-29, 31-33; data from sample surveys, 114-137, 139-141; experience and, 27, 116-131, 134-137, 141; by field, 26, 79-83, 131-138; sources of sample survey data on, 107-114; variability of, 115-116, 120-121
Education, American Council on, 7 n., 95 n.
Education, Office of, 7 n., 17 n., 94 n., 99 n., 100 n., 103 n., 156-165
Educational background of engineers and scientists, 10-12, 88-90, 180-188
Edwards, Alba M., 5 n., 154 n.
Endicott, Frank J., 25 n., 26 n., 27 n., 76, 128 f.
Engineering Education, Society for the Promotion of, 69 n., 107 n.
Engineers: definition of, 4, 8-9, 10-12, 87, 192; distribution by field, 79-83; leaving profession, 10, 69-72, 189-191; unemployment among, 82, 118 n.; *see also* Demand for engineers and chemists, Earnings of engineers, Prediction of requirements for engineers, *and* Supply of engineers
Engineers Council for Professional Development, 11 n.
Engineers Joint Council, 37-46, 52 n., 91, 110-139 *passim*, 192-196
Engineers, Professional, National Society of, 129
Enrollments: in engineering, 156-161; trends in total, 98-100
Ewell, Raymond H., 16 n., 17 n.

Faculty-student ratios in mathematics and physics: enrollment characteristics of institutions and, 95-96; financial characteristics of institutions and, 97-98

199